D0906572

How Literature Changes the Way We Think

Also by Michael Mack:

Spinoza and the Specters of Modernity: The Hidden Enlightenment of Diversity from Spinoza to Freud

How Literature Changes the Way We Think

Michael Mack

continuum

Continuum International Publishing Group
The Tower Building   80 Maiden Lane
11 York Road   Suite 704
London SE1 7NX   New York NY 10038

www.continuumbooks.com

Library of Congress Cataloging-in-Publication Data
Mack, Michael, 1969-
How literature changes the way we think / Michael Mack.
    p. cm.
Includes bibliographical references and index.
ISBN-13: 978-1-4411-0320-8 (hardcover : alk. paper)
ISBN-10: 1-4411-0320-1 (hardcover : alk. paper)
ISBN-13: 978-1-4411-1914-8 (pbk. : alk. paper)
ISBN-10: 1-4411-1914-0 (pbk. : alk. paper) 1. Literature–Philosophy. I. Title.
PN45.M319 2011
801'.3--dc23   2011019845

Typeset by Deanta Global Publishing Services, Chennai, India
Printed and bound in India

Contents

Acknowledgements

I am most grateful to Haaris Naqvi of Continuum for his valuable help, advice and encouragement. It was a pleasure to work with him. I am also grateful to the readers for their enthusiastic reports and for their astute recommendations as to how the book manuscript could be best improved.

I am also very grateful for the continued support of Sander L. Gilman, Eric Santner, Françoise Meltzer, Gillian Beer, Alaida and Jan Assmann, Berel Lang, David Jasper, Paul Mendes-Flohr, Richard Rosengarten, Joel Kraemer, Jacqueline Rose, Lars Fischer and Hugh Goddard. It was a pleasure meeting Mikhail Epstein who is working in a related but different area of the new 'Trans-Humanities'. I am most grateful to Mark Sandy who carefully read an earlier draft of this manuscript. His criticism and his comments were helpful, inspiring and illuminating, thank you Mark. I also want to thank the Wellcome Trust whose funding of the new field of Medical Humanities has made the work on this book possible. Thanks too are due to my mother, Nonica Datta, Stephen Regan and Richard Smith, Alastair Blanshard, Andrew Benjamin, Paul Crawford and Dimitris Vardoulakis for their encouragement and support over the years.

Think Again: An Introduction

> And then a red bear arrived/who did not know of this world/
> and he did not need to know of this world/because he was a
> red bear. "Red Bear" Bertolt Brecht

This book challenges the common paradigm underlying much of our current approach towards arts and humanities. It shifts the emphasis from representation to performance and delineates how arts and humanities help us change accustomed forms of action and perception. This study maintains that arts do not merely describe our world and do not necessarily prescribe how we should conduct ourselves in conformity with established representations and rules. Instead arts and humanities have the unique and underappreciated capacity to make us aware of how we can change accustomed forms of perception and action.

In this way *How Literature Changes the Way we Think* marks a departure from a separation between life and literature. A conflict between rhetoric and action has characterized much of the preceding literary theory and criticism. Rhetoric thus understood obstructs an understanding of our world. This view of rhetoric is characteristic of Paul de Man's literary theory, which has shaped the approach towards literature of the last couple of decades: 'Rhetoric, in this conception, is thus nothing other than that very structure of aporia which, actively *crosses* every reading effort, systematically undoing understanding'.[1] *How Literature Changes the Way we Think*, by contrast, focuses not on the undoing of understanding but on ways in which we are able to understand our increasingly complex and ever changing world. What is proposed here, however, is not a return to traditional approaches towards arts and humanities that see them as a representation of the world. Instead this book interprets arts in terms of performance that helps us change harmful practices within politics, religion, medicine and society at large. In contrast to traditional approaches towards literature and arts, *How Literature Changes the Way we think* emphasizes discovery rather than simple knowledge. Via the readings of philosophy, literature

---

1 Shoshana Felman, *Writing and Madness (Literature/Philosophy/Psychoanalysis)*, (Palo Alto, California: Stanford University Press, 2003), p. 25.

and contemporary media we discover ways of changing our lives, as well as ways in which we could come to terms with the often disturbing changes that we are facing now. The traditional approach from Aristotle to Heidegger and de Man to Žižek has conceptualized literature and arts as compendiums of knowledge (moral, historical, legal, economic or philosophical knowledge). Here arts serve to represent or illustrate a more detached and abstract form of perception. *How Literature Changes the Way we Think* departs from this tradition, by showing how literature and arts not only represent what we know but how they enable us to discover new forms of politics, medicine, religion and ethics.

Aesthetics here meets ethics. Much of the discussion focuses on literature's interaction with both people and political as well as biomedical issues of the real world. Art's ethics is one of resilience. On account of its distance from the real world—its virtuality, in other words—the aesthetic has the unique capacity to help us explore different and so far unthinkable forms of action and interaction. Resilience here denotes more than strategies for coping with change. Art performs an ethics of resilience which resists the repetition and thus perpetuation of harmful practices. These harmful biomedical as well as political practices pervade human history in such forms as stereotype, stigma, exclusion, exertion of violence and so forth.[2] Walter Benjamin has called the persistence of catastrophe a perpetual state of exception—thus undermining Carl Schmitt's plea for the implementation of sovereignty's non-legality and violence in states of crisis. According to Benjamin, the violence of sovereign power does not distinguish crises but rather shapes our sense of normality.[3] (Benjamin's famous notion of messianic break or interruption brings theology and communism together).

The messianic disrupts the perpetuity of the sovereign state of exception. I therefore argue throughout this book that art enacts such a break from

---

2　Issues associated with social isolation (i.e. stereotyping and stigma) are not only economic, cultural, religious and political problems. As researches in social neuroscience—John Cacioppo amongst others—have recently shown, social isolation is a grave medical problem, with health risks comparable to those involved in smoking. See Greg Miller's 'Why Loneliness Is Hazardous to Your Health' in *Science*, 14 January 2011: *Vol.* 331, no. 6014, pp. 138–140.

3　For detailed discussion of Benjamin's political philosophy, see Mack's *German Idealism and the Jew: The Inner Anti-Semitism of Philosophy and German Jewish Responses*, (Chicago: University of Chicago Press, 2003), pp. 155–167 as well as Mack's 'Transzendentaler Messianismus und die Katastrophe der Entscheidung. Anmerkungen zu Carl Schmitts und Walter Benjamins Eschatologie,' Stephan Loos and Holger Zaborowski *Leben, Tod und Entscheidung. Studien zur Geistesgeschichte der Weimarer Republik*, (Berlin: Duncker & Humbolt, 2003), pp. 155–166.

harmful practices to which we have become habituated. According to this view, the aesthetic is closely related to ethics—to an ethics of resilience—by virtue of its disruptive force. More importantly, art is disruptive to the degree of interrupting itself. Thanks to this interruption it goes beyond what has traditionally been called representation or mimesis. As Paul Ricoeur has shown, from antiquity onwards, representation has been closely bound up with the memory of the past. The work of memory is that of the imagination. The imagination attempts to make present what is past. Memory engages in a quasi-magical undertaking: it tries to produce a faithful copy of bygone people and things.

Plato thus distinguishes between false copies and those that are faithful resemblances: 'On the other side we have the simulacrum or appearance, for which Plato reserves the term *phantasma*. So here we have *eikon* opposed to *phantasma*, "eikastic art" to "fantastic" art, the making of likeness to the making of appearance.'[4] The question between falsehood and faithfulness in representation thus concerns the accuracy of the copying process: whether the artistic copy is indeed an accurate image of a past event. In this way, the imagination has traditionally executed the task of memory. This book does not refute the validity of mimesis in terms of the remembrance of things past. As we will see in Chapter 3, the remembrance of the past potentially participates in an interruption and disruption of the status quo. The argument developed in this book focuses, however, on a so far underappreciated dimension of art and literature: forms of intervention in the real world of the present and the future—rather than merely the representation of current and past events.

Contemporary media and the internet highlight art's interaction with the real world. In the twenty first century, we live in a world where the distinction between the virtual and the real, between representation and the present, between simulation and embodied reality becomes increasingly blurred. As Wendy Steiner has recently put it, 'the problem is not that art will be treated as a threat to the body politic', but that the body politic has become hard to distinguish from art'.[5] This blurring of the distinction between the political and the aesthetic has both disturbing and liberating repercussions for the wider societal role and the relevance of art. The increasing indetermination of the boundaries dividing the virtual from the real instantiates a radical break within the history of aesthetics: 'For millennia, images and representations have been

---

4 Ricoeur, *Memory, History, Forgetting*, translated by Kathleen Blamey and David Pellauer, (Chicago: University of Chicago Press, 2004), p. 11.

5 Steiner, *The Real, Real Thing: The Model in the Mirror of Art*, (Chicago: University of Chicago Press, 2004), p. 7.

understood as the opposite of the real. Art is a realm of the 'as if', framed, demarcated from the rest of experience, and imitation or 'thought experience' that call for the suspension of disbelief.'[6] In the twenty first century, the traditional 'as if' factor of art encroaches upon the 'is' of reality. This book argues that in this current hybrid state the work of art has the potential to bring about social change that has not been witnessed before.

The fusion of aesthetics with ethics depends, however, on art's sense of interdependence. In order to change the world, arts and humanities have to accentuate their autarky from the status quo of the real. If they want to make a difference in society, they have to remain different from what we have become used to as accepted social practice. This book therefore does not attempt to invalidate traditional literature and art. On the contrary, it argues that the tradition of humanities and arts partake of a disruptive element that can interrupt harmful practices of our as well as past societies—Chapters 5 and 6 discuss romanticism to emphasize this point.

The scholarly focus on mimesis has to some extent obscured this innovative potential. Innovation within arts is of course not something new. What has, however, not been sufficiently appreciated is how artistic transformation interacts with politics and the larger fabric of society (and not only with the 'creative' advertisement industry as will be discussed in the following chapter). By dint of its non-mimetic distinctness literature intervenes in and interferes with the status quo: it interrupts harmful practices that have shaped past as well as current politics.

In a society where the aesthetic keeps losing its virtuality—its distinctness from the real—Plato's banning of the poets from his city is worth bearing in mind (as we will do in the concluding chapter): 'For Plato, virtuality was art's undoing, since even a painting that faithfully rendered some aspects of the physical world was, as he saw it, twice removed from the Real: the physical chair is only a shadow of the idea, Chair, and the painting of the physical chair is a shadow of that.'[7] Plato's concern is thoroughly mimetic and he faults art and poetry for not being accurate enough, for misleading its audience. Why, however, does he banish the poets from his ideal city? If art is a pathetic and rather misleading copy of both physical and ideational reality, banishment does not seem to be warranted. Art's inadequacy should be obvious to anyone. As we shall see in a discussion of Philip Roth's Zuckerman novels, Plato may have been all too aware of literature's disruptive and transformative powers—

6   Steiner, *The Real, Real Thing*, p. 68.
7   Steiner, *The Real, Real Thing*, pp. 66–67.

hence the sense of danger that it provokes and hence the exclusion of poets from Plato's republic.

Plato demonizes art for its failure to produce accurate copies or *eikons* (and he blames poetry for the construction of the appearance of different worlds—*phantasmas*—instead). According to Plato art has failed the test of mimesis and for this reason his dismissal of art may actually assist us, in an appreciation of its disruptive and transformative power (as will be done in Chapter 7). Subscribing to a similar standard of representation, Aristotle, by contrast, extols literature's civic and moral virtues: 'In contrast, Aristotle considered tragedy's value to lie specifically in its mimetic possibilities. At once like and unlike the real, by holding a human action up to view as a knowable, shaped structure, a tragedy provokes cleansing and uplifting of emotions in its audience.'[8] Aristotle thus develops a didactive notion of the aesthetic. In an equivocal way romanticism as well as modernism returns to Plato's sense of art's uselessness for—and worse still corruption of—the republic's moral and political life. Modernism, in particular, celebrates literature in terms of a mental experiment: 'It held up autonomy, self-enclosure, and self-reflexivity as unquestioned, indeed axiomatic values, and aggressively defended the virtual nature of art against "vulgar" realists who chose to treat works of art as political or sociological documents.'[9] Today, however, the virtual has morphed into the real.

According to Wendy Steiner, in the twenty first century our sense of reality is almost indistinguishable from that of Aristotle's mimesis. We seem to live in and through various forms of representation:

> Two millennia ago, the term *mimesis* defined art as an imitation of the real, but today the word is more likely to be used of reality itself. Genetics has taught us to understand life as a copying technology, and cloning is making that copying literal as never before. The aesthetic issues of replication, expression and proliferation are core notions in bioengineering and information technology. The *Wikipedia* Website, for example, calls the internet 'the ultimate meme vector,' employing the evolutionary Richard Dawkin's coinage, *memes*: 'infectious ideas or any other things that spread by imitation from person to person...Memes propagate from brain to brain, much as genes spread from body to body.' Here genetics and information theory cross in ideas of mimesis.[10]

8   Steiner, *The Real, Real Thing*, p. 67.
9   Ibid.
10 Steiner, *The Real, Real Thing*, p. 68.

The traditional notion of mimesis as an imitation (as a copy) here leaps from the aesthetic into the real world of biomedicine, genetics and politics. Contemporary science, such as genetics, assumes the mantle of traditional literary studies, yet again focusing on mimesis. This book takes issue with this uncritical espousal of copies—be they medical or artistic or humanistic. In a sense, medicine has become a rival of art, claiming to turn our health and appearance into copies of standardized versions of beauty and normative perfection. In Chapter 3, we develop a critique of memes and in Chapter 1 we see how much the advertisement industry relies on meme-like copying processes.

In our century, we thus witness a reversal of mimetic roles. While previously art attempted to copy reality, now reality tries to copy art: 'With art a model for life, the distinction between representation and reality becomes—forgive the inevitable pun—a Cat-and-mouse game.'[11] It becomes thus increasingly difficult to distinguish between referent and reference, between representation and the represented. Wendy Steiner argues that the internet driven breakdown of the distinction between the virtual and the real brings to the fore the representational character of our sense of reality: 'Without collapsing representation and reality, we must acknowledge that representation is our only access to much that counts as real.'[12] The arguments developed in the following chapters question the primacy of this representational paradigm that has shaped traditional and contemporary approaches to arts and humanities.

A rather traditional paradigm of representation seems to have been adopted—if not copied—by biomedicine (or bioengineering) and our internet/media grounded twenty-first century form of politics. Art as disruptive and interruptive force is more than a model for genetic, sociological and political copying processes. This book insists on literature's distinction from mere representational devices and realities. Literature is capable of changing the way we think via a double pronged strategy. It help us resist forms of exclusion and stereotyping, which have been passed on to us in various forms of representations—various up-dated translations of these representations, thus rendering these contemporary. At the same time, literature alerts us to and helps us cope with demographic transformations in an ever more complex world where biomedical advances and ecological upheavals overtake our capacity to keep up with their social and political consequences (increased life expectancy; the explosive force of climate change driven forms of social deprivation and so forth). This disruptive and interruptive work of resistance and change distinguishes literature's ethics of resilience.

---

11 Steiner, *The Real, Real Thing*, p. 75.
12 Steiner, *The Real, Real Thing*, pp. 81–82.

Art's ethics of resilience does not so much replicate representations but works as a critique of those representations that have become our reality—a reality that needs change as well as resistance to some forms of change (climate change is a striking example) and is actually undergoing ever-increasing processes of biomedical, financial and ecological alternations. In this context, this book analyzes the way in which literature critiques various fictions that have come to shape our world. Our contemporary familiarity with the representational character of our sense of reality holds out the promise of morphing art's critique into social, medical and political actions. The mental space of a distance between the aesthetic and the status quo preconditions, however, this kind of change that would mark literature's social difference. How can art and literature disrupt forms of exclusion if it has already been absorbed—as Wendy Steiner argues—by the body politic whose practices are often harmful to marginalized or excluded groups of people?

Addressing this question requires three major tasks that lie ahead: first a rethinking of the social role of the humanities beyond the limitations of the mimetic; second an analysis of the ways in which some forms of mimesis or representation do not yield knowledge of truth—as the traditional account from Aristotle to Heidegger and beyond has maintained—but instead perpetuate and reinforce fictions that have a deleterious effect on social life; and third, a novel discussion of how literature plays a unique role in the critique of such destructive fictions that harm social inclusion through stereotyping both certain groups of people and certain intergenerational formations.

The problematic of stereotyping is implicitly related to a rigidly representational mindset that shapes various biopolitical scenarios. Whoever is seen not to live up to a certain image of either beauty or morality or youthfulness falls prey to representations that are stereotypical. The representation of stereotypes identifies what society stigmatizes and excludes as either inferior or, in the genocidal form of biopolitics, as life that had better not been born and thus has to be annihilated.

Preparing for an analysis of biopolitics and creativity in Chapter 3, the book first discusses what I call a culture of 'flat mimesis' in the contemporary TV series *Mad Men*. 'Flat mimesis' betrays the attraction of the repetitive, the non-complex and the static or fixed. The first chapter opens with a background discussion of our current longing for change, which grows out of a sense of being stuck within an aged age. There is a general sense of living in the end times. More than a decade after the collapse of communism, capitalism—at least in its current form—seems to approach its end too. As Slavoj Žižek has recently put it, 'the global capitalist system is approaching its apocalyptic zero-point'.[13] He names four apocalyptic riders who traverse the fields of the biomedical, of climate change, of capitalism's financial instability and the ever increasing global growth of the stigmatized and excluded social groups and subgroups: 'Its 'four riders of the apocalypse' are comprised by the ecological crisis, the consequences of the biogenetic revolution, imbalances within the system itself (problems with intellectual property; forthcoming struggles over raw materials, food and water) and the explosive growth of social divisions and exclusion.'[14] In a similar way Cormac McCarthy's recent novel *The Road* evokes 'the ashes of the late world' which 'are carried on the bleak and temporal winds to and fro in the void'.[15] There is a sense that we live in a 'late world'. In this void, where things come to an end, thoughts circle around the not- to-be-thought: death. The narrator of *The Road* tells of 'hundred nights they'd sat up arguing the pros and cons of self destruction with the earnestness of philosophers chained to a madhouse wall'.[16] Why are we so engrossed, on both a philosophical and literary level, by the prospect of destruction, self destruction and apocalypse?

In order to address this question the last section of Chapter 1 focuses on a sense of decay and weariness in the current TV series *Mad Men*. An analysis of *Mad Men* illuminates the psychological allure of the death drive. The death drive does not manifest itself so much in acts of destruction and self destruction but in more ordinary habits and longings: those of smoking and a refusal to engage with complex and non-repetitive forms of life and thought. It seeks to avoid the forever changing nature of our environment. The advertisement industry of the *Mad Men* thrives on the death drive, hence the smoke filled screen that pervades the series. The death drive lies at the core of what Freud has analyzed as the pleasure principle and the pleasure principle is at loggerheads with the reality principle. Where reality undergoes change—and is thus potentially hurtful or traumatic—pleasure sees as well as seeks rest in copies of what has been given, of what has been pre-established. The pre-established copy insinuates the illusion of a non-complex and static world.

In Chapter 2, we turn to Spinoza's critique of mimesis for a better philosophical understanding of the demographic and literary, cultural and theoretical issues on which this book focuses. Taking forward Spinoza's philosophical critique of mimesis, Chapter 3 analyzes the ways

---

13 Žižek, *Living in the End Times*, (London: Verso, 2010), p. x.
14 Ibid.
15 McCarthy, *The Road*, (London: Picador, 2007), p. 10.
16 McCarthy, *The Road*, p. 60.

in which contemporary biopolitics operates via representations that are like advertisements: they spread like memes throughout a given population and attempt to predetermine both what is beauty and what is truth. Via a discussion of Ishiguro's *Never Let Me Go* we will see how the representation of modernity's knowledge (especially that of biomedicine and bioengineering) has been increasingly linked to free market choices.

From the eighteenth century onwards there has been a shift in the meaning of truth, knowledge and mimesis. From now on the verification as well as representation of truth is no longer significantly informed by traditional religion and metaphysical philosophy. Instead global markets decide what is worthy of knowledge for an expanding population. In the last section of Chapter 3, we discuss Arendt's work on totalitarianism within this biopolitical context of populations and memes. We will attend to ways in which Arendt critiques various totalitarian representations of substantive truth as fictions. We shall see how she turns to arts to mediate between the substantive and the subjective. In her work, literature forms the basis for her idiosyncratic notion of politics that is grounded in the Kantian idea of judgment. The term judgment belongs to Immanuel Kant's aesthetics rather than his politics. It is his term for aesthetic experience and Arendt makes it the foundation for her notion of politics. She does so to establish a participatory public realm which does not impose a subjective or ideological version of the world as if it were an accurate representation of our substance. Aesthetic judgment performs such mediation between the fluid realms of the subjective and the substantial: according to Kant 'judgment finds itself referred to something that is both in the subject himself and outside him'.[17] The sphere outside the subject is that of substance. The question of representation concerns precisely the relationship between subject and substance.

In Chapter 4, we examine the ways in which literature critiques representations of substance that promulgate fictions while posing as truths. Here a critique of Žižek's notion of 'a substance less subject' prepares for an analysis of Ishiguro's *The Remains of the Day*. This novel takes issues with the fictive or subjective representation of substance that has a deleterious impact on social and political life. The main protagonist of *The Remains of the Day* is a butler, Stevens, who accepts such subjective representations of socio-political substance. The servant Stevens conceptualizes dignity as a copying of roles. In Chapters 5 and 6 we discuss romanticism as literature's as well as philosophy's interference with various copying processes. In Chapter 5, we develop a nascent theory of

---

17 Kant, *Critique of Judgment*, translated by Werner S. Pluhar and Mary J. Gregor, (Indianapolis: Hackett Publishing, 1987), p. 229.

literature that differs from the mimetic one in that here arts cease to be mirrors or representational copies of knowledge's status quo. In contrast to the prevailing mimetic one, my nascent theory does not subordinate literature to the historical or economic or the political but rather makes it the ground for a radical re-conceptualization of other disciplines (i.e. history, politics, economics and medicine). In Chapter 6, I show how Benjamin develops his idiosyncratic notion of communism on the basis of his reading of literature. Benjamin's break with a mimetic tradition contrasts with Heidegger's subordination of poetry to the forces of history. According to Benjamin, art disrupts historical continuity, whereas for Heidegger arts represent and interpret political events. In the latter, literature is subordinated to politics while in the former literature constitutes politics' interaction with reality by changing the way we think. By turning the poem into a function of history, politics and national identity, Heidegger, aligns humanities and arts with the biopolitical. Here mimesis meets biopolitics: the work of art represents the character of species existence.

Chapter 7 concludes this book's discussion about aging and birth by rendering the two terms complementary to each other (rather than exclusive of each other). The arguments developed throughout this book moves literature, art, religion, philosophy and film studies into an ambience beyond what has commonly been understood as representation. Representation here is seen not merely as a mirroring of what is already given. In a similar way, the term mimesis undergoes a subtle change in meaning: it is not primarily concerned with copying what exists, but with making neglected or marginalized realities present to us and opening up a space, a place, within which the uncertainties that belong to those realities—and so the possibilities that reside within them—become available to us. Representation here moves beyond what I call 'flat mimesis'. It does not only represent to us our world, but also places us within the world in new ways that allows us to see alternative modes of adaptation. Literature's cognitive, religious and ethical dimensions are bound up with the difference it can make in society if its imaginative coping strategies with change and its social consequences are more fully realized. The book is concerned with demographic, social, cultural, economic and political aspects of philosophical ethics. Literature has the potential to change our attitude to the current and future demographic challenges by changing the way we think.

The arguments developed here focus on both a re-evaluation and re-conceptualization of literature as promoting our social capacity to adapt to change. I argue that literature (and the arts more generally) has not been appreciated sufficiently for its potential impact on individual as well as societal coping strategies. These coping strategies are crucial for meeting major challenges that require change in our behaviour. The book makes a case for literature's role in providing ethical and cognitive resources through which we can become more resilient for future adaptations to demographic, social, religious, theological, economic and political changes. The arguments and ideas revolve around what could be called an ethics of resilience out of a novel reading of literature's social relevance.

How Literature Changes the Way we Think attempts to illuminate literature's ethics of resilience by re-conceptualizing our understanding of representation. Literature not only represents to us our world but it also shows us ways in which we can change the world or adapt to changes which have already taken place without our realization. Literature's cognitive dimension helps us cope with the current as well as future challenges by changing the way we think about ourselves, our society and those who are excluded from or marginalized within our society. In a way humanities and arts act and react like the red bear of Brecht's poem cited above: they do not know or care about how the world has worked so far and are thus rich and never ending sources of, as well as resources for innovation and renewal. Indeed one wager of this book is to argue that the aesthetic is the hidden heart that enlivens—as well as the blood that pulses through—much political and revolutionary thought from Walter Benjamin's idiosyncratic understanding of communism to Hannah Arendt's redefinition of the term politics.

The literary discussion of the book attends to the ways in which contemporary novels (by Philip Roth and Kazuo Ishiguro amongst others) question the traditional opposition between birth (youth) and aging. By rendering these seemingly oppositional terms, complimentary literature changes the way we think about the demographic challenges our society increasingly faces. These cognitive changes prepare for the strengthening of our adaptive human behaviour that makes us more resilient confronted as we are by new biomedical, economic, cultural-religious and political realities of aging: an aging population, a sense of an aged age—disillusioned as it may sometimes feel with various aged ideologies of communism and capitalism—a fear of aged religions, and an apprehension of our aged economic system.

1   Death Again: Reimagining the End

1.1 The Humanities, the Demography of Aging, and the Philosophy of Birth

> But people change, don't they? One minute we're one thing, and then another. Paul Auster, *The New York Trilogy*

It is the inclination of our age to await change. Barack Obama in the US and David Cameron in the UK have capitalized on this inclination. In different but related ways they have both won elections with rather vague, hazy and not fully substantiated slogans that promote a rather ill-defined desire for change. At the beginning of the century, we are less driven by the hopes inspired by various traditions of political thought, or modes of artistic representation, than by the desire to establish something that marks a clear break with what has preceded us, our society and the kind of politics with which we are familiar. No doubt this desire for change emerges from a profound disillusionment, disappointment and dissatisfaction with the various utopias, ideologies and social experiments that have marked scarred and scared modernity, from the European via the industrial revolutions to left and right-wing forms of totalitarianism of the past centuries. It is with deceptive promises of what we took to be authentic claims of ideologies that we have become livid.

Socialism and capitalism's respective pledge to provide for emotional and material fulfilment have turned out to be rather hallow and of course quite shallow in its intellectual and spiritual implications. This sense of disappointment with secular ideologies is apparent in some aspects of popular culture, in 'popular modes of horror and science fiction'.[1] Our disappointment with these conflicting promises that seemed to offer valid alternatives to various roads to a better and more flourishing future for humanity might also have given rise to a wide-spread sense of futility, cynicism, anger and depression. Despite all the glamour of late capitalism with its spectacular display of advertisements, pop art and culture we seem to live in a decrepit

---

1   Victoria Nelson, *The Secret Life of Puppets*, (Cambridge, Mass.: Harvard University Press, 2001), p. 22.

and evermore deteriorating world. The various deficits in commercial, private and public finances may appear as the tip of the iceberg that crowns our current cultures of dissatisfaction. Whether it is broken Britain, the broken economy or the entropy of both energy use and ecological sustainability, we seem to be faced with an almost infinite variety of decline and catastrophe.

There is an overwhelming sense that we live at the edge of an aged age, of an age that has become almost synonymous with aging. Discussing age in such a metaphorical way (as aged age) may partake of a metaphysical approach. As Helen Small has recently pointed out, 'for Adorno, metaphysics has a recurrent connection to old age [2]'. Aging itself is, however, a pressing physical demographic issue. Due to the medical advances and the consider-able increase in living standards, our life expectancy tends to move on an upward tangent. How can we account for this discrepancy between the medical or clinical fact of increased longevity and our rather dreary pros-pects for life? The clear gulf that opens between the tremendous technical expertise offered by medical services and the often depressing and debilitat-ing experience of life that shapes much of our outlook on a social as well as on an individual scale warrants a cultural analysis, which is the domain of humanities. Yet it would be unhelpful to focus only on this discrepancy between biomedical as well as other forms of techno-scientific enhancement of life and the cultural, politico-social dissatisfaction with the world we actu-ally share and live in. Rather than circumscribing this inquiry to the current state of affairs, this book attempts to uncover ways out of our present mal-aise. It does so by propounding what I call a philosophy of birth that has a literary blueprint in the so far neglected impetus that propels works of art beyond the sphere of mimetic replication into the regions of the new, which break with established forms of living, interacting and thinking.

Works of art have a mimetic element: they represent something or some-one, the state of society, a historical epoch or psychological conditions (the list could go on and could of course include animals, landscapes and so forth). Every representation changes, however, what it represents. A satirical depiction does not proffer an exact copy of its subject matter and yet never-theless purports to bring some truth to the fore which we tend to neglect when we look at the world in a one-dimensional way (and one meaning of the word satire denotes precisely the multi-layered and polyphonic).[3] We

---

2 Small, *The Long Life*, (Oxford: Oxford University Press, 2007), p. 179.

3 For a detailed discussion of polyphony in literature see Mikhail M Bakhtin's *The Dialogic Imagination: Four Essays. Edited by Michael Holquist*, (Austin: University of Texas Press, 1981). For an analysis of satire and the polyphonic in modernism see Mack's *Anthropology as Memory: Elias Canetti's and Franz Baermann Steiner's Responses to the Shoah*, (Tübingen: Niemeyer, 2001).

could say that this is the domain of art we are familiar with: art as being primarily engaged in representing conditions of society and humanity, albeit in a way that is critical and can enable us to see what may be wrong with us or with some forms of our acting, interacting and thinking.

There is another dimension to literature (and by extension to music and the visual arts); one that creates a space not only for representation but also for experimentation. Victoria Nelson has analyzed the transformative potential of arts in her discussion of the grotesque:

> The grotesque is a mode that is first and foremost about crossing into a different and transformative order of reality, and second about the unexpected recombination events, objects, species we encounter once we are inside. And for centuries it has been a secular society's only path back to the transcendent. We crawl into the hole—the grotto, the Symmes Hole, the black hole of the cosmos, the hole in our own heads—in the unspoken and often unconscious hope of undergoing change.[4]

This book focuses on how such transformation is not peculiar to one genre, period, or artistic style—the grotesque which is the exclusive focus of Nelson's more specialist discussion—and how a natal or transformative energy informs literature and arts in all their diverse forms.

Artistic transformation is also complementary to scientific and medical discoveries and revolutions. Innovation, testing and experimentation are frequently associated with the sciences. They are, however, also part of the humanities. Indeed they are a substantial element of what is called thinking. Thought is a form of experimenting. As we shall see in the following chapter, there are, however, rather dreary and mind-occluding aspects to pre-ordained and pre-formulated tests and there are rather wearying ways in which we test something. In theses cases the outcome of the test has already been established before it has begun. Here the test serves to confirm an established belief or truth: it does not promote free inquiry but reassurance of the validity of what we already take to be true. The test could, however, also be conceptualized as an open exploration where we can investigate the cogency of what has so far not been contemplated. Here testing is indeed conducive to innovation and creativity; and this not only in the sciences but also in humanities and arts.

The creativity and innovation that lie at the heart of arts and humanities are capable of scooping out the mental space in which we can rethink what it means to be aged and/or born. As social science research has

---

4   Victoria Nelson, *The Secret Life of Puppets*, p. 22.

recently shown, demographic changes and the current economic crisis are driving a shift in the perception and socio-political categorization of age. The recent economic upheavals in housing and the stock market have resulted in drastic decrease in the value of retirement accounts: in the US alone, they have been devalued by 1.6 trillion dollars or 18.3 per cent.[5] Increased longevity brings about a radically changing demography in the developed as well as in the developing world. The increase in longevity is due to huge advances in biomedicine. The biomedical changes have profound effects on our society and culture because they not only facilitate the absence of early death but also prolong the period of mentally alert and physically stable lives.

These biomedical changes have, however, not been matched by social and cultural innovations. As Small has recently argued, 'one of the questions that the philosophy and literature of old age therefore requires us to ask is how far conventional attitudes are rooted in reality, how far in prejudice and fear'.[6] The prejudices and fears apropos old age are, however, not isolated phenomena: 'Rather than isolate the old as the difficulty, we need to think in terms of (for example) the deeper causes of a gross disparity in national life expectancy around the world; rather than thinking about the 'burden of retirees,' we should think more broadly about the wider nature and purpose of work.'[7] What role do self-perpetuating representations of old age and other marginal groups play in the persistence of social exclusion? In order to address this question, I discuss economic, medical and political issues as part of a larger discussion that concerns mimesis. The topic of old age instigates investigations into how harmful social practices are abetted and promoted by certain forms of representation. As regards the economics and politics of disparity, the authors of the recent medical-social scientific study *The Spirit Level: Why Equality is Better for Everyone* pose the following crucial question: 'How is it that we have created so much mental and emotional suffering despite levels of wealth and comfort unprecedented in human history?'[8] One important proposition of this book is to argue that a novel approach

---

5   These figures and the information about new demographic and economic realities that force us to change both our perception of age and concomitantly exiting retirement policies are derived from Terry Hokenstad's lecture 'Older persons in an ageing world: Redefining retirement,' delivered at Durham University/ Department of Geography on 24 May 2010.

6   Small, *The Long Life*, p. 3.

7   Small, *The Long Life*, p. viii.

8   Richard Wilkinson and Kate Pickering, *The Spirit Level: Why Equality is Better for Everyone*, (London: Penguin, 2010), p. 3.

towards representation can assist us in adequately addressing questions like these.

Humanities and arts have a crucial role to play here. Martha C. Nussbaum's recent book 'Not For Profit: Why Democracy Needs the Humanities' makes a powerful and persuasive plea for their social and political relevance. Nussbaum argues, however, to some degree within a certain mimetic paradigm of the arts, which (as will be shown in Chapter 3) has shaped much of the traditional and contemporary discussion. Nussbaum discusses in what ways the humanities further abilities that are central to democracy and global citizenship. The education that nourishes such abilities is lost in the single-minded public endorsement of nothing else but economic growth and career advancement, which governs the current mind-set of parents and policy makers.

In a discussion of the TV series 'Mad Men', we shall see how such a single-minded society dedicated exclusively to economic growth operates along the lines of what I call 'flat mimesis'. Nussbaum appraises artistic and humanistic ways of representation that are not flat but complex, multilayered and thus train us to think as well as act within an increasingly interdependent global society. Nussbaum lists the following abilities that she maintains 'are associated with humanities and arts: the ability to think critically; the ability to transcend local loyalties and to approach world problems as a 'citizen of the world'; and, finally, the ability to imagine sympathetically the predicament of another person'.[9] The abilities listed here combine a certain capacity for nuanced representation with one that furthers innovation.

Nussbaum does not neglect the innovative aspect of arts and humanities, which makes them compatible with the sciences (another major topic of the present book); and she advances a strong case for their economic importance in this context arguing that: 'Although it is difficult to construct a controlled experiment on such an issue, it does seem that one of the distinctive features of American strength is the fact that we have relied on a general liberal arts education and, in the sciences, on basic scientific education and research, rather than focusing more narrowly on applied skills.'[10] Education that narrowly focuses on applied skills operates within the logic of the copy, because it is exclusively concerned with the mechanistic replication of the already existing forms of thinking and acting. The ability to think critically, by contrast, is premised on an analysis of the current state of affairs as well as on reflection upon alternatives

---

9   Nussbaum, *Not For Profit: Why Democracy Needs the Humanities*, (Princeton: Princeton University Press, 2010), p. 7.
10 Nussbaum, *Not For Profit*, p. 53.

that might transform the *status quo*. In a similar way we need to combine mimesis with both the imagination and the creation of the new, if we attempt to see the world from someone else's point of view—be that as a 'citizen of the world' or as a friend, parent or partner.

Arts and humanities are thus dependent on mimesis and they also go beyond what they, in various and complex forms, represent. The innovations they provide are to do with changes in perception. The creation of novel ways of seeing our society and the world are therefore not simply a question of mimesis. They go beyond the mimetic, while of course not abandoning issues of representation. Representation here transcends itself; it is capable of representing not only a copy of what we already know—however complex rather than flat such a copy may be—but also an image of what is new and what makes us stare and startle as if we have been witnessing a scientific experiment that brought to the fore the so far unthinkable.

A strong case could be made for giving humanities and arts the furlough and the social recognition of facilitating changes of cognition and perception. These cognitive changes may help us discover human potentials which could be beneficial for a coming to terms with new realities of what it means to be born and what it means to be of age. Our traditional identities of age and growth have become subject to change. The binary opposition between age and birth may well be subjected to experimental questioning. As we will see throughout this book, literature offers the free space for such mental experiments. Literature not so much as representational but as an experiential mode of scientific inquiry into our transforming life and our ever more transmogrifying world, could help enable legal-socio-political as well as cultural changes. The cognitive upheavals, which literature initiates and impels, could match the changes in age and longevity that are due to advances in biomedicine.[11]

Aging thus requires change. This means that we cannot discuss aging outside the context of what is a new beginning; and perhaps the most powerful metaphor for new beginnings is that of birth. By coupling age with birth, the two seemingly opposed terms become unstable so that they are capable of referring to each rather than opposing each other. Such cross-referencing is already at work in the term aging, because it denotes a process of change and change is of course the force at work in the new beginning manifested in birth. In a way similar to which birth

11 For the line of argument that prepares for a view of literature as a form of experimentation see Paul H Fry's *A Defense of Poetry: Reflections on the Occasion of Writing*, (Stanford, Calif.: Stanford University Press, 1995).

changes the world by enriching it with new life, we and our society undergo changes. These changes may appear lugubrious in terms of getting older and ill. Age and aging is frequently represented in terms of illness and debilitation but it does not need to be so. As we shall see in the discussion of Philip Roth's novels (in the concluding chapter to this book), literature questions rather than copies an apparent causal link between aging and danger. This causality turns out to be fictitious but is nevertheless a powerful one that governs much of our current discourse.

We live in an aged and aging world. Age and aging are here synonymous with illness and debilitation. This perception might be technically or biomedically wrong (various forms of technology and biomedicine are of course capable of prolonging our life as well as of mitigating the effect of aging) but it is nevertheless a perspective that shapes our attitudes to politics, science and the economy. It is as though our societal dissatisfaction with broken promises, broken politics, the disturbing sight (oil spills and other images of ecological crisis) and side of technology were in fact the unarticulated presence of the humanities within the everyday life of our society. Arts shed light on what we would otherwise not see, because it does not belong to our accustomed ways of thinking. They alert us to the risk that we are used to classify as 'risk-free'—the destructive weapons of technically refined high finance (credit default swaps, and hugely complex to the point of incomprehensibly packed mortgage packages that have been touted as being 'risk-free').

The humanities bring to the fore what has been brushed under the carpet; they uncover what lurks behind or within the closet. They illuminate the unsavoury sub-trends and subterfuges of the world we live in. So once what has been ignored rises to public attention, the public dismay about that which has been thought to be unthinkable (the collapse of our economic and ecological order) may appear to be an echo of some of the concerns and revelations that have already come to the fore within literary and philosophical inquiry.[12] While critique does its work via mimesis, it also operates via experimentation because it plays through different vistas of possibility which might become real or might already hold to be true but in ways that have so far not been uncovered. The humanities do not only shed light on

---

12 The late Derrida's application of the medical term auto-immunity for an analysis of current economic, social and political/military practices or Žižek's work on the death drive in contemporary society: for a discussion of this see Mack's *Spinoza and the Specters of Modernity: The Hidden Enlightenment of Diversity from Spinoza to Freud*, (New York: Continuum, 2010).

the various risks that lie at the heart of our desire for security[13]—as has become clear in the emergence of the destructive nature of financial instruments whose purpose it has been to guarantee the absence of any exposure to loss—but they also resume what has been lost, excluded or marginalized. They are capable of granting us a new lease on life; a birth or rebirth of sorts. Within this context the humanities are understood to be not only scholarly disciplines dedicated to the study of arts but also and more importantly free spaces where we can perform the creativity and innovation that goes with artistic creation—be it literary, visual, tactile or acoustic.

From this perspective, humanities and arts perform what I call a philosophy of birth. Through their natal or innovative force, arts disrupt homogeneity, flat mimesis or the reproduction of what we are used to. In this way literature and arts thus counteract various forms of managerial control. This is part of their remaining appeal. There is certainly an overwhelming apprehension of supervisory monitoring or testing whether we all confirm to the role we are expected to perform in the work place and, more broadly speaking, as subjects who are expected to assume preordained roles.

This is not to downplay or to deny the crucial role the state can and sometimes needs to perform in various endeavours to improve our lives. As Kwame Anthony Appiah has shown 'the state can make our lives go better without imposing a conception of the good upon us, without imposing its will upon us at all.'[14] The absence of such imposition guarantees the validity and valence of humanity's diverse individuality. If, however, we are asked to subject ourselves to tests not of open inquiry but rather to tests that should confirm to already established outcomes, we are likely to impoverish our creative and innovative potential.

As we shall see in the following chapter, there is some historical ground for being suspicious of tests and testing. As Avital Ronell has recently shown, testing is closely related to torture. 'What is the provenance of this need to torture, to test', she asks and continues to trace a historical itinerary: 'A link between torture and experiment has been asserted ever since Francis Bacon; yet, what has allowed acts and idioms of testing to top out as an essential and widening interest, a nearly

---

13 For a detailed discussion of this desire for security see Mack's "Between Elias Canetti and Jacques Derrida: Satire and the Role of Fortifications in the Work of W. G. Sebald," in Gerhard Fischer (ed.) *W. G. Sebald: Schreiben ex patria/ Epatriate Writing*, (Amsterdam: Radopi, 2009), pp. 234–256.

14 Appiah, *The Ethics of Identity*, (Princeton: Princeton University Press, 2005), p. 170.

unavoidable *drive*?'[15] The term drive implies a quasi-biological and yet psychic force (comparable to Freud's death drive).

As drive, however, testing and experimenting seem to belong to what constitutes our particular constitution, our common humanity. So Ronell does not take issue with science, the biomedical and testing as such. What she attempts to alert us to are, the rather violent and catastrophic consequences of a split between the literary and scientific: '*Mary Shelley has already inscribed the disaster of such a split—in the creation of the unforgettable, unnameable, the monster that came to be known as Frankenstein.*'[16] In her *Telephone Book,* Ronell argues that the technological is not only premised on such splitting and cutting but is also concerned with remedying various cuts and splits within nature and culture: 'Technology, perhaps more so than any other thing except for a certain illumination of a god, is inseparable from catastrophe in a radically explicit way. Cutting lines and catastrophizing, the telephone has been associated with the maternal voice.'[17] The maternal voice of the telephone attempts to heal the splitting and cutting that goes with birth.

Reading science and technology from the perspective of the telephone, we are in a world of connections that bridge various separations and most importantly that between the humanities and the sciences. The hoped for correlation between the two fields would have a transformative effect on society at large so that the 'Other, suffocating within, begins a correspondence with the persecuted historical subject Aimed at breaking out of caricaturing structures, the telephone blasts through prison walls, racial barriers, or the desolation of home.'[18] There is some hope that the disconnection between the sciences and the humanities can be remedied, and Ronell's telephone can do its work, connecting various strands of our cosmopolitan society via such fusion of the humanistic and the scientific. The emerging fields of trans-disciplinary studies may prove to be a major step in the direction of bridging the gap between scientific and humanities based research. Testing and experimentation are indeed common to both the humanities and the sciences. How could it be absent from the life of the mind? It is after all not only a mental activity but also a drive that runs through our constitution.

---

15 Ronell, *The Test Drive. With Photographs by Suzanne Doppelt,* (Urbana: University of Illinois Press, 2005), p. 5
16 Ronell, *The Test Drive,* p. 17.
17 Ronell, *Telephone Book: Technology, Schizophrenia, Electric Speech,* (Lincoln: University of Nebraska Press, 1989), p. 341.
18 Ronell, *The Test Drive,* p. 402.

1.2 The Test and the Copy of the *Mad Men*

There is, however, a growing unease with our test driven culture and society. The unease is rather disturbing because experimentation or, in other words, playfulness is part of our flourishing. The problem is that science testing and the experimental have increasingly become bound up not with the flourishing but with the dreariness and the aching that seems to go with aging. Our distrust and dissatisfaction with science and the biomedical seems to be a symptom of our aging age. This is so because the scientific on its own can only provide some but not all the answers to the questions our existence raises. As writers and thinkers, from Tolstoy, through Nietzsche to Max Weber and Heidegger have pointed out and as Ronell has recently summarized 'Science cannot tell whether something is worth being known just as medicine does not presume to ask whether life—the life that it finds obligated to save—is worth living. Nor, for that matter, do we find aesthetics, which takes as given the fact that there are works of art, asking whether there *should* be works of art.'[19] Here Ronell includes the humanities (i.e. aesthetics as part of the humanities) into the sphere of the sciences: both are experimental and both keep experimenting because they cannot find conclusive replies to the questions their respective experiments set out to address. Could it be that we have become rather tired of the process of testing because it seems to be inexhaustible and thus quite exhausting? In this case, it is not the experiential nature of the test but instead the promise of a firm outcome as the endpoint that keeps disappointing us. Here the test turns bio political; it tests our conformity to a pre-given norm which we are supposed to copy.

The issue of an already formed, formulated and to be copied norm, of a preconceived endpoint brings us to the topic of the certainty of the end or what has become known in philosophy as *teleology*. On a psychological level Freud has called 'death drive' the pleasure associated with the restfulness of such certainty. By "death drive" Freud does not understand the state of being dead but the wish to be so. According to Žižek's recent interpretation, Freud's term denotes the uncanny persistence not of death but of life: 'The paradox of the Freudian death drive is therefore that it is Freud's name for its very opposite, for the way immortality appears within psychoanalysis, for an uncanny *excess* of life, for an "undead" urge that persists beyond the (biological) cycle of life and death, of generation and corruption.'[20] Emotions are highly ambivalent and the

---

19 Ronell, *The Test Drive*, p. 199.
20 Žižek, 'A Plea for a Return to *Différance* (with a minor *Pro Domo Sua*),' *Critical Inquiry* 32 (Winter 2006): pp. 226–249 (245).

desire to be dead is no exception, for what drives such desire is the fearful wish not ever to reach the object of desire: death.

This is why the suggestion of the psychologist Dr. Guttmann in the first episode of the highly intriguing TV series *Mad Men* to employ the death drive in order to make attractive the health risks of smoking is not as mad as it might seem at first sight. Don Draper, the mad man or advertising agent to whom she makes this suggestion, dismisses her and her advice. We do not encounter her again in the series but what seems to drive the action through-out is precisely what she has stipulated: the death drive. How? For one thing, as has been noticed, *Mad Men* is filled with smoke and smokers. Smoke and smokers seem to constitute the cinematic technique of the series. Then there is the prominence of the cigarette brand *Lucky Strike* that permeates the series almost like a narrative thread. Third, on a material level, at the close of series three, the advertisement agency survives in new form (after a destructive take over) and independently largely thanks to the million dollar account it holds (and can extract from the clutches of the company it would otherwise be vanquished by) with the makers of *Lucky Strike*.

Smoking is almost a metonymy for the death drive: in small format it represents the addiction to death within life. Above and beyond the deadly matter of smoking *Mad Men* depicts capitalism's love affair with death. The object of the libido here is of course fashion: *Mad Men* is a very stylistic, styl-ized, fashion conscious and fashion driven series. Indeed the selling of ever different styles and fashions is the very subject matter of advertisement—the profession around which *Mad Men* revolves (the very term mad men has been used by Madison Square- based advertisement agents to describe themselves in the early sixties of the last century). Fashion, as Walter Benjamin has shown, could be called the sex appeal of death, because it thrives on the ever-renewed going out of style of the new that has become dead or passé viz. out of date. There is, however, a more fleshly side to fashion's deadly appeal. In his amazing account of the shopping arcades of fin de siècle Paris—*The Arcade Project*— Benjamin elaborates as follows:

Each generation experiences the fashion of the one immediately pre-ceding it as the most radical antiaphrodisiac imaginable. In this judge-ment it is not far off the mark as might be supposed. Every fashion is to some extent a bitter satire on love; in every fashion, perversities are sug-gested by the most ruthless means. Every fashion stands in opposition to the organic. Every fashion couples living body to the inorganic world. To the living, fashion defends the rights of the corpse. The fetishism that succumbs to the sex appeal of the inorganic is its vital nerve.[21]

---

21 Benjamin, *The Arcades Project*, translated by Howard Eiland and Kevin McLaughlin, (Cambridge, Mass.: The Belknap Press of Harvard University Press, 1999), p. 79.

Commingling the ideas of Benjamin and Freud, one might ask whether the satire on love is part of love's very nature in a way similar to how life paradoxically flourishes on and within the death drive. *Mad Men* depicts love as a satire on love: there is not one single love affair that remains stable; each and everyone is subject to infidelity, to falling out of fashion, to withering, to aging. No doubt, the high rate of relational break ups is part and parcel of the misogyny and homophobia that the series displays. It would certainly be wrong to describe its protagonists as embodying or purporting to embody an essential or authentic nature of humanity. In many ways *Mad Men* is a satire and not a realistic representation of life as it is or has been. There are, however, revealing moments in what may strike us as satirical exaggerations. In *Mad Men* these moments centre on the consistent persistence of what has been presumed to be over: be it the marriage between the two main protagonists which keeps being unbound and rebound, or the rise, fall and survival of the advertisement agency or the belief in the American dream despite its obvious demise in social collapse and personal misery, which paradoxically keeps all characters of the series going.

To keep going is itself a form of testing beyond the duration of a given test; to paraphrase a recent paraphrasing of Winston Churchill by the infamous CEO of a multinational energy company, 'if in hell, keep going'. What could be a tougher test than undergoing what we differently and variously imagine to be hell? Part of the fascination with the sixties (or the eighties) of the last century may be that we project some nostalgic energy or motivation into the commandment to keep going while witnessing the morphing of the American dream into a nightmare—a process similar to the transformation of the American pastoral to the 'American berserk' in the eponymous novel by Philip Roth. The daughter of the main protagonist of *American Pastoral*—the successful and highly assimilated Symour Levov, who on account of his assimilatory success is nicknamed 'the Swede'—'transports him ['the Swede] out of the longed-for American pastoral and into everything that is its antithesis and its enemy, into the fury, the violence, and the desperation of the counter pastoral—into the indigenous American berserk.'[22] A similar kind of concern with a radical and rapid turn from stability into instability, from the American dream into the American nightmare, may explain why Mad *Men* strikes a chord with its audience. The critical acclaim the series has enjoyed is, however, partly due to the fact that this is not a sentimental or nostalgic soap opera. As has been discussed above, *Mad Men* is more of a satire than it is a cheap melodrama about the

---

22 Roth, *American Pastoral*, (London: Vintage, 1998), p. 86.

endurance of relationships and the solidity of our world. Indeed as the series evolves, the taken for granted solidity evaporates. The test of the keep going consists in keeping up the appearance of solidity and endurance (i.e. the appearance of happy marriage or the American dream).

It is of course the job of the mad men in question here to present a world that is solid and at the same time superabundant with joy and indulgence. They are, as Don Draper puts it 'selling happiness' by reassuring the public that 'whatever you are doing, it's OK' thus reinforcing the keep going slogan. Advertisement's role is to keep up appearances for an otherwise unsavoury world. Advertisement is the lie of capitalism. The technology by which this lie operates is one of image presentation. The first episode of the series opens with a crisis in the public image of smoking: there is the health alert raising a red flag regarding the risks of smoking and members of the medical profession can no longer serve the advertisement agency in their promotion of *Lucky Strike*. What does the mad man in-chief do? He dismisses any talk about death, aging, health risks and re-enforces the image of the brand as source of luck and happiness. In the face of obvious long term catastrophes (in this case creeping illness due to smoking) advertisements display and reinforce a sense of certainty and simplicity, assuring and re-assuring us that our world is solid, ageless and can find fulfilment in smooth copies of ease and pleasure. The irony here is of course that such an easy and superficial world of appearance depends on the inhalation of what brings about death and destruction (i.e. smoke). Advertisements thus attest to the impact, representations have on the way we perceive aging, youth and mortality. The hazy veil generated by smoke represents and at the same time hides what it is about: death. As has been intimated above, the death drive persists precisely in the advertised image of a targeted and ever so brief blip of life's 'youthful' intensity as presented in the advertisement spot.

Here a consumerist form of biopolitics emerges: one that turns youth into a normative realm—into a duty—that demands endless copies of its image of bliss. Don Draper—the master advertiser—fantasizes about a 'magical machine' that is capable of producing identical copies of the advertised image of fulfilment (see first episode; series one). Clearly here bliss has become normative. Draper emphasizes the biopolitics of the advertisement industry when he says 'you are born, you die and in between you follow rules.' These rules are those of the fantasized 'magical machine' which endlessly reproduces identical copies of what 'happiness' should be.

The discussion in this section has shown that despite all appearances of ease, flourishing and creativity, representations which daily confront us in advertisements, reinforce a managerial concern with conformity and social norms. The case of smoking is quite striking, because it illustrates how the advertisement industry can reinforce established habits despite overwhelming evidence to the contrary: faced with health warnings, the image of smoking persists as key to a fulfilled life.

Mad Men are about the sixties of the last century and how public perception has changed. Part of the change of perception is also due to various advertisement campaigns to cease smoking. Yet smoking persists and this is at least partly due to the powerful images associated with it: images that hide while at the same time celebrate the death drive as an easy release from the pressures of life. Advertisements demand an infinite copying process of the serenity which they set out to evoke. This monotonous series of copies mirrors the endless repetition of restful moments of pleasure which characterizes the life of the death drive. The duplication of deceptive ease constitutes the monotony of flat mimesis: the promises of fulfilment may be met for a blip of a 'youthful' instance but they are certainly far from sustainable.

The crucial but hidden topic of *Mad Men* is that of mimesis defined as flat copy of norms, conventions and images. The biopolitical merging of life with a controlling apparatus may not necessarily be presented in normative terms. In the case of the advertisements with which we have become familiar within our post-twentieth century consumer culture, the control panels are switched in a more smooth and subtle manner. Advertisements present copies of copies, which in turn provoke the mimetic command to copy these series of copies. More importantly, the copying itself promises to offer fulfilment. Once we copy the smoke of the Lucky Strike advertisement, we are bound—so the flatly mimetic story goes—to find what we are looking for. As this chapter has shown, the allure of this fulfilment is the longing for rest; it is the pleasure principle of the death drive. Advertisements may be highly sophisticated and may be the product of impressive resources of creativity, but the sophistication and the creativity in question here creates images that streamline or shape our lives in a one-dimensional manner. It is precisely such streamlining of energy which produces quasi-identical copies of restive fulfilment which instantiates the pleasure principle of the death drive. As the discussion of this chapter has shown, the increased public desire for such pleasure illuminates its wornness at precisely the point where youth emerges as the norm to be copied. The urge to live the life of the prefabricated bliss of 'youthful' consumption, bespeaks and reveals the agedness of our aged age. The youthful dotage which manifests itself in our obsession with advertised copies of easy blips of bliss seems to preclude a readiness to face and to cope with change. Instead of becoming more resilient in an increasingly complex and changing world we cling to fictions which various representations—advertisements are one amongst many—evoke to be real. The first part of this chapter has discussed a notion of age that is not necessarily tied to the physical aging process but to a certain unwillingness to countenance change and thus remain stuck in a copy of already established representations of the true, the good, the youthful and the beautiful. One of the main contentions of this book is to argue that age is not primarily a condition of time passing, but a certain mindset that refuses to engage with discontinuity, transformation, disruption and interruption. In short, it is a mental outlook that remains stuck in various versions of flat mimesis.

As we have seen in this chapter, aging requires change. We start to age from the moment we are born. So the representational or standard opposition between aging and birth is actually fictitious. In order to analyze the fictitiousness of some forms of representation, we need to analyze the way in which, on a neuroscientific level, the mind tends to copy bodily impressions and affections. These copies of what the senses tell it may mislead our mind to take fictions to be realities. In the following chapter, we analyze Spinoza's innovative critique of such mental-bodily representations that misrepresent both us and our world.

2   Revisiting Torture and Torment

> You will be hollow. We shall squeeze you empty, and then we shall fill you with ourselves. George Orwell, *Nineteen Eighty-Four*

The preceding discussion of *Mad Men* is pertinent for a more nuanced understanding of life and death issues at the end of the twentieth and the opening of the twenty first century, because advertising—the subject matter of the series—instantiates an industrialized form of the traditional testing/ torturing of life. Traditionally and in quite a non-scientific sense, testing as torture was to do with proving the truth of certain and already established beliefs or goals. Torture sets out to test the validity of old and sacred truths. It thus aims to safeguard age from the forces of change (this will be a crucial topic of our discussion of Kazuo Ishiguro's *The Remains of the Day*).

In this way, religious opponents were tested in the form of torture to extract from them the truth one already knew: someone who was seen to be evil or satanic was tortured, until she or he confessed to being Satan or a witch or a Jew or a Protestant or a Catholic (each of this depending on a given circumstance of religious doctrine). The test as torture performs the violence of flat mimesis upon the bodies of its victims.

The test here consists not in the discovery of the new but in the replication of what has already been established as the truth. Torture does not test its victims to falsify truth but to verify a truth that might actually be false and yet must not be questioned (hence torture does not assist intelligence gathering). The violence of the torturer is aimed at hearing or seeing a copy of the world view to which he or she subscribes. The end of torture is to test the universal verifiability of a given doctrine. Torture perpetrates its violence to enforce its version of reality upon those who question it. In this sense, it enforces a rather graphic model of flat mimesis: mentally and physically it imposes its version of the world upon those who are seen to pose a challenge to this version.

As Elaine Scarry has shown, the torturer aims to unmake the world of the one who is the subject of torture. Torture inflicts aversive pain on its victims to destroy their sense of the world: 'the de-objectifying of the objects, the unmaking of the made, is a process externalizing the way in which the person's pain causes the world to disintegrate; and, at the same time, the disintegration of the world is here, in the most literal way possible, made painful, made the direct cause of the pain.'[1] An analysis of torture reveals how suffering—both mental and physical—is the outcome of having our world emptied out. This painful process of emptying out should turn us into copies that confirm and conform to the representation of the world which governs the mind-set of the torturer.

By unmaking human worlds, torture attempts to do away with human diversity. We are supposed to be representations that match with the coordinates of one monolithic conception of what it means to be alive. As the torturer and representative of Big Brother, O'Brien says to Smith Winston— one of O'Brien's victims—in Orwell's *Nineteen Eighty-Four* 'You will be hollow. We shall squeeze you empty, and then we shall fill you ourselve.'[2] Scarry describes this torturous process of flat mimesis as follows: 'the torturer and the regime have doubled their voice since the prisoner is now speaking their words.'[3] Orwell shows how torture can be handled in such an insidious way that it appears to be the workings of a free will rather than of an imposition. In this way, O'Brien explains the sophistication of Big Brother's smooth work of control thus: 'When you finally surrender to us, it must be of your free will. We do not destroy the heretic because he resists us: so long as he resists us we never destroy him. We burn all evil and all illusion out of him; we bring him over to our side, not in appearance but genuinely, heart and soul.'[4] We may wonder whether Big Brother performs the tasks of the magical machine—the object of Don Draper's professional longings as the master advertiser of *Mad Men* (see previous chapter). What I call flat mimesis is a doubling, or more extremely, a homogenization of one voice that attempts to de-individualize as many as it possibly can by turning them into its mouthpiece, its acoustic amplification. Torture thus attempts to erase the questioning of what it expects to be a flat mimesis of its creeds and aims. In a traditional religious context, the torturer demanded a copy of either a given perception of the Godly or the Satanic.

2.1 Spinoza's Post-Human Critique of Mimesis

As I have shown in *Spinoza and the Specters of Modernity*, one of the most promising aspects of the Spinozist enlightenment was to do away with

---

1 Scarry, *The Body in Pain: The Making and Unmaking of the World*, (Oxford: Oxford University Press, 1985), p. 41.

2 Orwell, *Nineteen Eighty-Four*, (London: Penguin, 1989), p. 293.

3 Scarry, *The Body in Pain*, p. 36.

4 Orwell, *Nineteen Eighty-Four*, p. 292.

perceived grand goals of either the Satanic or the Godly. What is crucial here is that, this questioning of the grand teleology of theology and philosophy goes hand in hand with Spinoza's radical revision of the mind-body problematic. Contradicting his philosophical godfather Descartes, Spinoza argues that God comprises both body and mind: '*God is a thinking thing*' (mind) as well as '*an extended thing*' (body).[5] This levels the philosophical playing field which is preoccupied with a hierarchical conception of the mind over and above the body. Spinoza takes issue with traditional philosophers who 'are so firmly persuaded that that the body now moves, now is at rest, solely from the mind's command, and that it does a great many things which depends only on the mind's will and its art of thinking'.[6] Spinoza breaks with the traditional notion of humanity according to which the mind is the undisputed sovereign enforcing a single and exclusively valid conception of the world.

Spinoza no longer thinks in terms of hierarchy but he attends to distortions within the work of human representations. These distortions arise from flat mimesis where the mind translates and copies the often misleading affections of the body and represents them as equivalence of truth. This recognition of corporeal inadequacies does not mean that Spinoza in good Cartesian fashion asks us to ignore the body or to control it by an act of mental will. His break with Descartes and much of the philosophical tradition is precisely to insist that we unavoidably rely on the life and work of the body, because the 'object of the idea which constitutes the human mind is the body'.[7] Spinoza radicalizes the parallelism between the corporeal and cerebral when he describes the mind as the idea of the body: 'The idea that constitutes the formal being of the human mind is the idea of the body.'[8] This means that if we want to understand our mind we have to understand the body. The divide between the two no longer makes sense because one is intrinsically dependent on the other and in a way each is coterminous with the other. As the neurologist Antonio Damasio has shown, via the workings of the brain, the body is indeed the object of the mind. Damasio pleads for a change in our understanding of the mind-body problematic:

> Working towards a solution, even a partial solution, requires a change in perspective. It requires an understanding that the mind arises from or in a brain situated within a body-proper with which it interacts;

---

5 Spinoza, *Ethics*, edited and translated by Edwin Curley with an introduction by Stuart Hampshire, (London: Penguin, 1996), p. 33.

6 Spinoza, *Ethics*, p. 71.

7 Spinoza, *Ethics*, p. 40.

8 Spinoza, *Ethics*, p. 44.

that due to the mediation of the brain, the mind is grounded in the body-proper; that the mind has prevailed in evolution because it helps maintain the body-proper; and that the mind arises from or in the biological tissue—nerve cell—that share the same characteristics that define other living tissues in the body-proper.[9]

Damasio argues that this change in perspective is crucial for an improvement in medical policies and medical practice. He acknowledges that 'changing the perspective will not itself solve the problem', but he doubts 'that we can get the solution without changing the perspective'.[10] He makes a strong case that such change in perspective is not the domain of medicine as a monolithic discipline but emerges from its interaction with the humanities.

Philosophy has, however, been too much in a mimetic relationship with what it understood to be the scientific. Medicine, on the other hand, has been mainly attentive to those voices in the humanities which endeavour to represent truths already established in scientific research. This is one reason why Spinoza's revolution in the perception of the mind-body problematic went largely unnoticed. As Damasio has put it: 'If my interpretation of Spinoza's statements is even faintly correct, his insight was revolutionary for its time but had no impact in science.'[11] Part of Spinoza's insight was not only to put the body on equal footing with the mind, but to emphasize the epistemological importance of our corporality. The latter insight is, however, quite ironic.

Let me unpack the irony. Our knowledge of ourselves and our world depends upon bodily input (the affects). This makes our epistemology rather fraught and flawed because our affects can indeed mislead us and according to Spinoza they cannot be avoided. Spinoza's critique of fictions is a critique of mimesis. While representing the neurological input it receives from bodily sensations or affects, the mind often (of course not always) fabricates fictions which it takes to be the truth. Here mimesis (as we shall see in Chapter 7, contrary to what Aristotle has maintained in his *Poetics*) does not yield knowledge of good and evil but propounds fictions of what is good and evil—fictions which claim to be the truth but actually are its distortion. Spinoza's famous analysis of static categories such as 'perfection' or 'goodness' unmasks the misleading stasis of such representations. Rather than being stable and static, our world is

---

9 Damasio, *Looking for Spinoza: Joy, Sorrow, and the Feeling Brain*, (London: Harcourt, 2003), p. 191.

10 ibid.

11 Damasio, *Looking for Spinoza*, p. 217.

constantly in flux and the mimetic capacities of our mind cannot keep up with the ceaseless change that characterizes us in all stages of our lives (whether we are young or old).

As I have shown in *Spinoza and the Specters of Modernity*, Spinoza is a rationalist with a difference and part of this difference is a, certain humility towards human epistemology, towards the adequacy of truth claims. As Damasio has pointed out, Spinoza 'suggested that the body shapes the mind's contents more so than the mind shapes the body's'.[12] This has serious repercussions for our understanding of consciousness and representational adequacy. To a certain extent, our consciousness is unavoidably false and our representations of ourselves and our world are up to a point the work not of truth but fiction.

The preponderance of the body is a fact that we cannot avoid but it is a fact we should not so much condone but try to understand in a self-conscious manner. The insight that our consciousness is to some extent unavoidably false demands of us a high degree of self-consciousness. In *Spinoza and the Specters of Modernity*, I have called this high degree of self-consciousness the 'mind's mindfulness', but of course it is a mindfulness here that is highly attentive to and dependent on the medical realm of our corporeality. The imagination that propounds fictions of the real is part of Spinoza's mind as the idea of the body. In this way we represent the sun as being near to us and concomitantly imagine the earth to be the centre of the universe (as it has been imagined in the biblical conception of the Ptolemaic universe), because of the way the sun affects our corporality. Where we go wrong is not so much in our lack of knowledge but in the way our knowledge is that of a mimesis of often misleading corporal affects.

The mind reads misleading neurological input uncritically, and thus represents corporeal affects as an adequate notion of reality. This misreading has disastrous political, intellectual and social consequences. In this way the religious dogma of the earth as the unchanging centre of the universe was seen to be substantiated by bodily or physical evidence. A substantial part of this evidence was the affect of the sun's closeness to the earth. The mind, by representing bodily affects, sees the sun to be in striking vicinity of the earth. This representation does not yield knowledge of the truth but, as Galileo (a contemporary of Spinoza) has shown, turns out to be a fiction: 'For we imagine the sun so near not because we do not know its true distance, but because an affection of body involves the essence of the sun insofar as our body is affected by the sun'.[13] Spinoza does not berate us for our inadequacy; inadequacy here describes our

---

12 Ibid.
13 Spinoza, *Ethics*, p. 54.

proneness to believe representations or fictions to be true. On the contrary he understands our representational dilemmas writing that we 'can hardly avoid this, because' we 'are continually affected by external bodies.'[14] What is crucial here is that we need to be aware that our knowledge derives from and represents our sense of being affected by external bodies.

This self-critical awareness may sometimes be lacking in neurological accounts that are preoccupied with the mind's all too often assumed independence from the body. In this way the neurologist Semir Zeki argues that 'a central and primordial function of the brain is the seeking of knowledge and that it does so through the formation of concepts'.[15] This is also what Spinoza maintains. However, Spinoza is not satisfied with delineating the mechanics of the mind as reaching out to gain knowledge of extended things (or bodies). More importantly Spinoza shows how such work of representation goes wrong and can lead us to take distorted images of the truth for the truth itself. According to Zeki such distortions make for the misery of the brain which he calls 'the failure of reality to match the synthetic brain concept that it has generated'.[16] Implicit in Spinoza's critique of flat mimesis is the attempt to dismantle the ideal of a match or equivalence between our affects or consequent mental concepts and the larger world of God or nature.

Our sense of misery results from our presumption to be able to represent the cosmos of which we are a significant part but, considered from the perspective of nature's infinite diversity, nevertheless only a tiny part. Spinoza therefore does not attempt to disqualify the knowledge gathering of the brain when it forms concepts. He does, however, limit the truth claims of such concepts, aligning them to the work of the imagination. In a sense Zeki does something similar when he discusses artistic achievement within the context of Michelangelo's and Cezanne's break with a flatly mimetic tradition. In different but related ways, Michelangelo and Cezanne break with a representational tradition within art. They depart from the prevailing view of mimesis which is 'that of an image impressed upon the retina and interpreted rather than constructed by the brain'.[17] Zeki appraises such construction as human creativity. Spinoza would agree but he would also warn against the deleterious and often lethal consequences of confusing such constructions with a monolithic

---

14 Spinoza, *Ethics*, p. 61.

15 Zeki, *Splendors and Miseries of the Brain: Love, Creativity, and the Quest for Human Happiness*, p. 1.

16 Zeki, *Splendors and Miseries of the Brain*, p. 103.

17 Zeki, *Splendors and Miseries of the Brain*, p. 117

conception of truth. It is such a monolithic and fictitious conception of truth which he criticizes as theology's anthropomorphic imagination of God.

Spinoza does not attempt to invalidate such religious or philosophical creativity which attempts to transcend a limited sphere of particularity. Our human condition is unavoidably trapped in the antagonism between the particular and the universal. On a micro-level our membership in one particular social group limits our sense of humanity's universality. On a macro-level humanity's limit is its position confined to one particular place of the universe from where it will never be able to gain a comprehensive and conclusive account of the world's vastness. Human creativity, culture, civilization—however we want to call the mind as trying to make sense of the extended world of bodies—attempt to reach out and understand themselves and their environment despite the odds of failure. As Scarry has put it: 'Every act of civilization is an act of transcending the body in a way consonant with the body's needs: in building a wall, to return to an old friend, one overcomes the body, projects oneself beyond the body's boundaries but in a way that expresses and fulfils the body's need for stable temperatures'.[18] This act of transcending the body is a form of 'benign power'.[19] We might also call it creativity.

Creativity becomes uncreative and painful when it refers to enforcing its version of the world onto others. We have seen how creativity is employed for fictitious representations of the world as static and monolithic. The preceding chapter has discussed how the advertisement industry employs creativity for non-creative ends which extol the simple bliss associated with the death drive. We have seen how the TV series *Mad Men* focuses on smoke and smoking to bring to the fore the hidden allure of blips of bliss which claim to represent youth but actually hold out the promise of rest if not death. The art of advertisement suggests that what we are doing is ok. Its representation thus proclaims the keep-on going nature of the copying process, where we do not need to face change but feel comfortable with what we think we are.

As has been intimated in the previous chapter, this wished for cessation of change manifests not only the death drive but also the true state of an aged society where we are old disregarding our actual age. When we no longer engage with change we are old, whether we are teenagers, adults or elderly. A clear sign of such cessation to interact with change is what I call flat mimesis. As will be discussed in the remaining part of this chapter, the aim of torture is to make people conform to—rather than

18 Scarry, *The Body in Pain*, p. 36.
19 Ibid.

disturb or disrupt—a changeless representation of the world where we are what we are supposed to be. In flat mimesis and, in an extreme form, in torture we witness 'a condensation of the act of 'overcoming' the body present in benign forms of power'.[20] Here benign forms of power turn into 'the fiction of power' which is 'the final product and outcome of torture'.[21] What is crucial here is that the fiction of power denies its fictitious character and hence refers to enact its will in the rather sensitive world of bodily sensations via the destructive form of pain. Through pain it unmakes the differing world of others.

Spinoza has haunted such fictions of power. His thought has posed a challenge—if not an outrage—to established ways of conceptualizing society, politics, medicine and religion. Central to this challenging and constructive work is his innovative reading of self-preservation as dependent on the preservation of the others. Spinoza defends the rights of the individual, while at the same time enmeshing these rights with the well being of human society as a whole. Here the flourishing of the individual relies upon the well being of the larger community.

Spinoza was the first thinker to appreciate difference not in terms of separation or segregation but as contribution to a diverse and interconnected understanding of well being. This made his thought such a challenge to theological, medical and political orthodoxies and perhaps accounts for Damasio's dismay about his small impact on science. In the Spinozan building of self and society opposites are not fundamental. Oppositions do not oppose each other but are complementary to each other. One of the tasks of this book is to render the oppositions between youth and age inoperable. The harm done by some representations is their production of static and mutually exclusive stereotypes. Spinoza's critique of the mind's reliance on misleading bodily or affective inputs turns fluid this otherwise static universe of representation.

No wonder Spinoza has often been represented in terms of the nonrepresentable and invisible: as a ghost on the move. Spinoza's legacy seems to be a ghostly one: it opens up a space where apparently incompatible entities visit each other as if one were haunting the other. The spectre that Marx conjured up in his *Communist Manifest* (1848) had already made an appearance in the hugely influential *On the Doctrine of Spinoza* with which Friedrich Heinrich Jacobi provoked the Spinoza controversy in 1785. Jacobi makes clear that he endeavours to put an end to the haunting which Spinoza's ghost seems to keep Europe enthralled. Jacobi attempts to turn the indefinable spectre of Spinoza into the clearly

20 Ibid.
21 Ibid.

definable doctrine of Spinoza. Jacobi sets out to clarify matters by pinpointing the exact structure and shape of Spinoza's teaching so that it can be opposed. Far from having put an end to Spinoza's legacy, Jacobi in fact provoked a controversy that hugely increased the appreciation of the writing, life and thought of the Dutch Jewish philosopher within the public sphere of the late eighteenth century and beyond.

Spinoza has outlined a blueprint for well being in the religious, political, cultural and medical sense. His work is concerned with human flourishing mainly because the driving motor behind Spinoza's rational inquiry is the discovery of ways through which humanity avoids the pain of torture which destroys human diversity. He attempts to undermine conditions of pain—be they psychological, religious, secular or political—by analyzing the deceptive nature of various fictions of power. Fictions of power do their deleterious and often lethal work in the real world of society to further the interests of human self-aggrandizement.

Spinoza's astounding achievement was to unmask concepts of the good and of God as self-aggrandizements of a given society as well as justifications to wage war on those who do not subscribe to its creed or were seen to undermine its sense of solidity and belonging. What Spinoza critiques is the keeping up of appearances in theology and philosophy: he unmasks societal self-glorification behind different appearances of God and the social Good.

Crucially for the discussion here, Spinoza unmasks conceptions of God not as a discovery of the divine or some elements of the divine but as copy—a flat mimesis—of a given human community. He does so in his groundbreaking critique of anthropomorphism in the first book of his *Ethics*. Here he first takes issue with the conflation of human notions of will and intellect with that of God, writing that 'if will and intellect do pertain to the eternal essence of God, we must of course understand by each of these attributes something different from what men commonly understand'.[22] We conflate the human with the divine as a result of what I call flat mimesis.

According to Spinoza mimesis operates via categories, via naming. He makes clear that the names 'will' and 'intellect' enforce an equivalence between the human and the Godly which in actual effect does not exist in reality but only in name: 'For the intellect and will which would constitute God's essence would have to differ entirely from our intellect and will, and could only agree with them in anything except the name'.[23] He illustrates the deceptive copying process of naming by pointing out

22 Spinoza, *Ethics*, p. 15.
23 Ibid.

the actual difference between the existence of a dog of our world and that which names a starry constellation. The categories of 'will' and 'intellect' are employed as copies of the divine in the same illusory way: 'They [i.e. human as differentiated from divine intellect and will] would not agree with one another any more than do the dog that is a heavenly constellation and the dog that is a barking animal'. [24] The political point of Spinoza's unbinding of the torturous copying of divine categories upon the human, is the denial that such divine categories exist in the first place. To say that a mundane dog is a copy of the starry constellation which is synonymous with it would be absurd. Spinoza argues that the same absurdity governs any attempt to see our human worlds as copies of divine entities. Will and intellect are human and thus fallible concepts rather than mimetic replication of what is presumably perfect or divine. If God is perfect and the world a copy of the perfection of its presumed creator, then everything that strikes us as imperfect must be copy of God too.

As a result of Spinoza's analysis, the word perfect turns out to be an empty projection of the purported divine upon our human condition so that 'God is not supremely perfect; because if things had been produced by God in another way, we would have to attribute to God another nature, different from that which we have been compelled to attribute to him from the consideration of the most perfect being'.[25] Spinoza's splitting of the copying process between the divine and the human has radical consequences for a revision of traditional theology and politics which were based on a flat aesthetics of mimesis. If the most perfect being imaginable is not perfect then perfection cannot exist. This holds true not only for the term 'perfect' but for every elevated category—like goodness, or the final cause of the good. These notions do not have an equivalent in reality as it has traditionally been proclaimed. Spinoza unmasks the purported equivalence of elevated and aggrandising notions with particular human realities not as copies of the truth but as fictions writing 'that Nature has no end set before it, and that all final causes are nothing but human fictions'.[26] This is the starting point of his critique of teleology as a veiled form of theology.[27]

Spinoza does not take issue with fictions as such but he questions a reading of fictions according to the aesthetics of flat mimesis. The classic

---

24 Ibid.

25 Spinoza, *Ethics*, p. 23.

26 Spinoza, *Ethics*, p. 27.

27 For a detailed discussion of Spinoza's critique of theology as teleology see Mack's, *Spinoza and the Specters of Modernity*.

biblical topos of mimesis is of course the creation of the human in the image of the God. Spinoza's stringent critique takes issue with precisely the mimetic projection from God to humanity. He does not dismiss the metaphor as metaphor but he admonishes us not to take the metaphorical and fictional in a literal way. He alerts us to deleterious conflations of flat mimesis and politics. Such conflation may have lethal consequences which occur when a particular group represents itself as image of the 'Godly and Good'. As result of flat mimesis different communities have touted rival self-conceptions of a fictitious God:

> Hence they [i.e. different human societies] maintained that the gods direct all things for the use of men in order to bind men to them and be held by men in the highest honour. So it has happened that each of them has thought up from his own temperament, different ways of worshipping God, so that God might love him above all the rest, and direct the whole of Nature according to the needs of their blind desire and insatiable greed. Thus this prejudice was changed into superstition, and struck deep roots in their minds. This was why each of them strove with great diligence to understand and explain the final causes of things.[28]

Spinoza here unmasks purported final causes as nothing else but copies of various interest groups which are projected upon the guarantor of omniscience and omnipotence: God. Far from being the image of God, humanity and its notions of God here emerge as the self-projection and self-aggrandizement of various human identities. Fictions of the divine are the foundations of such identities. Spinoza does not take issue with the construction of identities. Neither does he dismiss fiction. On the contrary, he asks us to take fictions seriously, as the ground on which we come to conceive of who we are. In contrast to the nineteenth-century philosopher Ludwig Feuerbach and his secular version of the essence of Christianity, Spinoza does not advocate a conflation of our image of God with the social/religious groups of which we happen or choose to be members.[29] Spinoza asks us to analyze fictions and group identities and he encourages us to separate the open-ended and diverse nature of our narratives from the certainty and absoluteness that goes with the notion of God.

Spinoza implicitly conceives of the human as an open-ended and not to be fully defined entity. From this perspective he is a post-humanist. In an important study, Thomas A Carlson has recently traced the origins of

---

28 Spinoza, *Ethics*, p. 27.
29 See Feuerbach's *Das Wesen des Christentums*, (Stuttgart: Reclam, 1984).

contemporary post-humanism to the mysticism of Gregory of Nyssa, John Scottus Eriugena and Nicolas of Cusa. Furthermore he argues that renaissance humanist thought—the era that preceded Spinoza's radical Enlightenment—radicalized a religious but non-doctrinal and non-mimetic understanding of the human as indefinable, which has already been developed by Cusa's notion of creativity not as copy of God but as an independent and free force: 'Cusa's theological and cosmic framing of the intellectual and human creativity that constitutes culture can be read to mark a decisive shift away from the logic of mimesis operative through much of Western metaphysics. Along these lines, the world-forming operation of the technological plays a notable role in expressing—and enabling—human freedom'.[30] Human freedom is premised on the lack of certitude, on the absence of quasi-divine omniscience and omnipotence.

By freeing the human from its mimetic bondage to various doctrinal and social conceptions of the divine, Spinoza does not stifle the scientific potential for inventions. Nor does he hamper creativity in the arts and the humanities. On the contrary his break with a dominant tradition of flat mimesis within Western metaphysics brings us to see our human condition as not only limited but also infinitely creative and with a non-fixed basis of flourishing. Our lack of absolute knowledge spurs us on to find an infinite variety of new forms of knowing and perceiving the world. Our diversity compensates for our lack of one single and absolute form of power.

Spinoza's critique of conceiving humanity as a copy of God thus highlights the problematic nature that characterizes endeavours to define or 'measure' what it means to be human. Partly as a response to disturbing bio-political practices within the twentieth century (Nazism, Stalinism and other forms of totalitarianism) traditional conceptions of humanity have been questioned. This has been the case, because, as Hannah Arendt has argued, various forms of totalitarian rule have made use of certain humanistic traditions while perverting these traditions. The bio-political definition of humanity in terms of species existence depends on certain conceptions of normativity and human essence. Recent debates about the 'posthuman' call these normative conceptions into question.

Is there a human essence and why should there be one? Definitions of human essence have been established with the understanding of humanity's centrality in the cosmos. Spinoza was the thinker who most explicitly and stringently analyzed various humanistic and theological attempts at defining the human as anthropomorphic conceptions of God. In this section, I have discussed how Spinoza's thought is of continuing relevance

---

30 Carlson, *The Indiscrete Image: Infinitude and Creation of the Human*, (Chicago: University of Chicago Press, 2008), p. 105.

in an age that the Dutch chemist Paul Crutzen has described as anthropocene, as new age 'defined by one creature—man—who had had become so dominant that he was capable of altering the planet on a geological scale'.[31] Through scientific-technological dominance, humanity is in the process of altering the conditions of life on planet earth.

While Spinoza encourages scientific inquiry and technological change, he is also wary of the anthropocentricism that is part of a Christian—albeit non-doctrinal—tradition as discussed in Carlson's *The Indiscrete Image*. In this non-doctrinal Christian tradition, we may not be direct and flat copies of God, but our creativity is nevertheless conceived as an image of the Divine. Spinoza is critical of such projections from the human onto God or Nature. The critique of anthropomorphism questions a certain mimetic paradigm. It is a paradigm of flat mimesis. Flat mimesis equates the presumed unity and perfection of God with humanity. This mimetic short-circuit violates our diversity.

Spinoza's critique is all the more relevant in our anthropocene age. As Crutzen has shown, humanity today has become a geological force. Spinoza's *Ethics* helps us in coming to terms with the theological and scientific-historical ideas that prepared for such a predominance of humanity within the ecological system of our planet. He attempted to remove man from the centre of the philosophical, theological and scientific universe.[32] He unmasked all attempts of grand human teleologies as a theology that equates humanity with God/nature. We have seen how from this perspective Spinoza—on the basis of his analysis of mimesis—could be considered a non-humanist thinker. This section has explored how his critique of theology and humanism may assist us in a critique of current medical, theological and political attempts at reinforcing the anthropocene nature of what our planet has become. This analytic work is not merely an academic exercise. On the contrary it performs an ethics of resilience by which we become aware of our changed world and are thus better prepared to cope with current and future changes in both geography and demography.

2.2 Nietzsche, Post-Humanism and back to the Biopolitical Economics of *Mad Men*

One of Spinoza's most famous intellectual heirs was of course Nietzsche who had his Zarathustra witness the declaration of God's death. Nietzsche was aware of the radical implications within Spinoza's uncovering of

---

31 This quote derives from a citation of Paul Crutzen in Elizabeth Kolbert's article 'The Climate of Man,' *New Yorker*, April 2005, p. 54.

32 See Mack's *Spinoza and the Specters of Modernity*.

teleology as anthropomorphic theology. Spinoza reduced not so much God or nature but the biblical image of God: humanity. Spinoza morphed humanity's grand goals and beliefs into ridiculous deceits. What energized and dignified and in fact divinized such grand goals and beliefs was of course God's omnipotence which Spinoza argued a given human society arrogated for itself while proclaiming the superiority of its religion, or its God, or its virtues over that of another society which it singled out as its opponent. As we have seen in the previous section, Spinoza is not interested in humiliating human self-respect. On the contrary he attempts to lay the grounds for an appreciation of our common humanity; one that is free from claims of superiority and practices of exclusion. He sees in the conflation of human diversity with the presumed stability and unity of the divine, a main cause for violence. A more modest understanding of our small participation within an infinite cosmos would further, less grand and violent societies.

Spinoza prepares for a twenty-first century version of post-human humanism; one that is truly non-doctrinal and sees humanity in terms of an ever-changing ground of diversity. Judith Butler has recently argued for a sense of mobile diversity, which avoids tying humanity to any form of certainty and sovereignty: She admonished us in this context: 'We make a mistake, therefore, if we take a single definition of the human, or single model of rationality, to be the defining feature of the human, and then to extrapolate from that established understanding of the human to all of its various cultural forms.'[33] Butler's post-Nietzschean position allows for a multi-dimensional perspective which encompasses justice and cultural diversity.

Her admonition can, however, also be applied to medical and societal conceptions of what it means to be born or of what it means to be young. We make a mistake if we impose a fixed image of age upon society. As will be discussed throughout this book, literature has the capacity to question a mimetic response to an established conception of what it means to be aged. Literature is a disruptive force that subverts one-dimensional perspectives on culture, aging, birth and identity. Nietzsche is attentive to the subversive nature of fiction, whereas Spinoza critiques them as mimetic projections of a given society's identity upon God or nature as guarantor of absolute value and truth.

It seems as if Nietzsche—having incorporated Spinoza's critique of theology and traditional philosophy as mimetic variations of what has been established as true and certain—could assist us in a novel under-

---

33 Butler, *Precarious Life: The Powers of Mourning and Violence*, (London: Verso, 2004), p. 90.

standing of literature not in terms of mimesis but as immaterial ground for heterogeneous creations. Post-Nietzschean thought seems to appreciate the 'heterogeneity of human values'.[34] Judith Butler is not hostile to democracy as Nietzsche may well have been.[35] Hers is also 'not a relativism that undermines universal claims', but is instead 'the condition by which a concrete and expansive conception of the human will be articulated, the way in which parochial and implicitly racially and religiously bound conceptions of the human will be made to yield to a wider conception of how we consider who we are as a global community'.[36] In this way the open-ended and uncertain vision of what it means to be human does not question the universal rights of any part of humanity. Instead it establishes a mobile ground, because human time and human space are themselves constituted by change and mobility.

Butler focuses on participatory communities when she writes that it 'is, we might say, an ongoing task of human rights to reconceive the human when it finds that its putative universality does not have universal reach'.[37] Butler's is a mobile reaching out, which does justice to the mobility and diversity of humanity. One of the main aims of this book is to make such reaching out for—rather than copying of an already established notion of—universality, the stepping stone for a reconception of not only literature but also current perceptions of birth and aging: here aging and youth are no longer opposed notions. Instead they turn complementary. Literature turns the categories of age and birth fluid. They become subject to change and in so doing they crisscross each other.

The loss of a firm ground of certainty enables such crisscrossing that does justice to both diversity and human heterogeneity. Such a loss enables us to gain democracy, as Butler has ingeniously argued. Nietzsche proclaimed such loss but he was also worried about it; he was not a committed democrat after all. As Alexander Nehamas has put it, 'the last thing he is is a social reformer or critic'.[38] While Spinoza deflates the ethical value of goals and final causes in order to diminish the injustices that are perpetrated in the name of grand schemes and religious convictions, Nietzsche fears that the disillusionment that accompanies Spinoza's radical Enlightenment could itself give rise to a void which could become the

---

34 Ibid.

35 For a divergent account of Nietzsche's politics and especially his defence of moral pluralism see Daniel W. Conway's *Nietzsche & Politics*, (London: Routledge, 1997).

36 Butler, *Precarious Life*, pp. 90–91.

37 Butler, *Precarious Life*, p. 91.

38 Nehamas, *Nietzsche: Life as Literature*. (Cambridge, Mass.: Harvard University Press, 1985), p. 225.

breeding ground of violence. Nietzsche is concerned not so much with violence as with the levelling consequences of Spinoza's radical Enlightenment. Nietzsche's preoccupation with hierarchy dismissively responds to what I have called elsewhere Spinoza's non-hierarchical vision.[39] Nietzsche's politics is not democratic—open for everyone—but restricted to the select few, the upper echelons of his hierarchical construct: 'Nietzsche's positive morality is not addressed to everyone. Perhaps it consists only in a code of conduct by which the select few can become, and come to be recognized as, 'higher' human beings, creators of their own values, true individuals'.[40] In contrast to Spinoza's, Nietzsche's individualism is exclusive, exclusively granting the right to be an individual to the elite. The elite are able to refashion a sense of hierarchy in the levelled space of the desert. Nietzsche's Zarathustra describes this void as the growth of empty space. Nietzsche realizes that Spinoza's critique of teleology (grand goals) as theology could have a rather destabilizing impact on us as we have traditionally (in the Biblical sense) come to see ourselves as special, as being created in God's image:

> He understands the dangerous rush that occurs with the removal of God and Goal, the ensuing depression of instincts and the unpredictable violence of a collapsed morality. Having proven capable of deconstructing "goals of action," can science refurbish them? Experimentation supplants the Goal, the collapse of telos and history, without escaping the precariousness that used to be associated with goals of action. Thought would no longer be bound to truth or falsity but turned into the interpretations and evaluations of non-finite experiments, summoned by interpretations of forces and evaluation of powers.[41]

The absence of grand goals could give rise to a sense of futility and of the absurd. It could make us weary and dreary. It could give rise to a culture of flat mimesis that governs the societal interactions of our aged age. A longing to become copies of advertised images pervades this aged age. As we have seen in the previous chapter the contemporary TV series *Mad Men* veils our consumerist and advertisement culture with the smoke of the death drive. The death drive is the core of the pleasure principle: it does not want to engage with an ever-changing and thus hurtful reality

---

39 For a detailed discussion of Spinoza's non-hierarchical vision see Mack's *Spinoza and the Specters of Modernity*.

40 Nehamas, *Nietzsche: Life as Literature*, p. 225.

41 Ronell, *The Test Drive*, p. 217.

and instead turns passive, morphing into the copy of something already established.

It was certainly not Spinoza's intention to help establish a society that lacks curiosity and tries to find fulfilment in blips of bliss that mark the death drive. On the contrary he set out to make us love God intellectually: to make us see how we are a small but significant part of the vast and to us in its totality incomprehensible universe which he calls god or nature. Spinoza's destruction of grand goals and concomitantly of our anthropomorphic conception of god (or nature) is part and parcel of his non-hierarchical vision of a society not based on exclusion but a sense of interdependence and inclusion. His aims are through and through ethical (committed to self-preservation—his *conatus*—as the preservation of the other) and democratic (in the participatory and non-discriminatory sense). He argues that we can promote social well-being by decreasing hierarchical divides of inequality and as the authors of *The Spirit Level* have recently shown the discrepancy between rich and poor in a given society finds indeed a clear correlation in high levels of mental and physical illness in such an unequal society: 'The problem in rich countries are not caused by the society not being rich enough (or even by being too rich) but by the scale of material differences between people within each society being too big.'[42] Spinoza's critique of mimesis addresses differences like this, because what 'matters is where we stand in relation to others in our society'.[43] A change in how such relations are established requires not a copy of what we have become to be familiar with, but a break in how we structure our social and economic life, making us less unequal and more democratic.

As has been intimated above, Nietzsche is not so much concerned with Spinoza's ethical and social thought but with the epistemological implication of a Spinozist critique of Goal and God. This is what Ronell in her reading of Nietzsche (quoted above) focuses on. What are the repercussions for our understanding of our cognitive powers, if we are only a small part of what is to us forever in its totality an infinite and impersonal universe which Spinoza calls *deus sive natura*? Will we be satisfied not with final answers but with constantly incomplete ones which are in need of revision? Modern science operates on the basis of the ceaselessly renewed testability and thus reversibility and re-visibility of its findings. Its methods are those of the unceasingly falsifiable. In this sense it has incorporated Galileo's and Spinoza's demotion of the earth and humanity as the centre of the universe and all this implies for human omniscience.

---

42 Richard Wilkinson and Kate Pickering, *The Spirit Level*, p. 25.
43 Ibid.

Nietzsche doubts whether we can be satisfied with such demotion of our cognitive status not as images of God but as an embodied part of the natural world. This may explain why he coined the notion of the eternal return in order to confirm rather than to question humanity's grandeur. As Nehamas has shown, Nietzsche equates life with literature. As we shall see throughout this book, such conception of life as copy of literature—and vice versa of literature as representation of life—is quite problematic. In Nietzsche's case difficulties are compounded by the fact that a rather traditional understanding of literature as harmonious, coherent and whole underlies his concept of the eternal return. Nehamas has critiqued Nietzsche's equation of literature and life's internal coherence as follows:

> And once we admit contents, we admit conflicts. What we think, want, and do is seldom if ever a coherent collection. Our thoughts contradict one another and contrast with our desires, which are themselves inconsistent and are in turn belied by our actions. The unity of the self, which Nietzsche identifies with this collection, is thus seriously undermined.[44]

Nietzsche's reading of life as literature is itself a fiction. While Spinoza critiques the fictitiousness of our lives, Nietzsche's 'eternal return' encourages us to celebrate our lives as fictions: as stylized harmonisations or even deifications of our humanity. The point of Spinoza's critique of revelation is precisely to question such equation of life with an idealized concept of literature or of God. That our minds are dependent not on God's creation but on the whims of our body—one of Spinoza's crucial findings—has serious ramification on how we are capable of verifying truth and of gaining knowledge (epistemology). It means that we have to keep testing truth; have to keep subjecting established truths to the test of ever new findings and ever new discoveries and ever new questions and questionings. This can be a rather exhausting process. Within our increasingly complex world, it is perhaps not that surprising to encounter public dissatisfaction with the open-ended and non-conclusive nature of scientific inquiry. The unease with the testable and revisable and thus incomplete status of intellectual finding is matched by a longing for easy and certain answers.

Advertisement is an answer to this call for ease and certainty: identification with a brand should make us feel special; creatures of a quasi-divine creator who is the producer of the brand and its marketing. In this way our consumer society is proof positive for Nietzsche's fear about the void left

---

44 Nehamas, *Nietzsche: Life as Literature*, p. 180.

behind by Spinoza's invalidation of Goal and God and ironically his notion of the eternal return seem to anticipate the endless—truly eternal—copying process that keeps going both advertisement and consumerism. Grand theological and philosophical conception have made room for the immanent grandness of economic power which is based, in the first instance, on the advertised attraction and subsequent consumption of brands as key to certain fulfilment of needs on a global and a bombastic scale.

Goal and God—the subject matter of Spinoza's critique of teleology as theology—has given way not to Spinoza's envisioned non-hierarchical and interdependent society but to one centred around a hierarchical divide in wealth, social recognition and status; one with which the authors of *The Spirit Level* take issue. The new goals are set according to the ambitious targets of wealth creation. The fulfilment of these targets promises a sense of certainty in the work place which is matched by the certainty of ease of consumption as promised in advertisements. The goal as target has moved from the doctrinal/theological to the economic and consumerist sphere. As we have seen, *Mad Men* is a spoof on this world of economic targets and yet it has a rather serious and realistic ring to it. Is not our society structured around a set of targets which in different ways measure economic success and viability? Enterprises employ advertisement agencies in order to ensure the successful marketing of their product and the success of an advertisement campaign is measured by the number of sales following its release.

The creativity and artistic expertise that may inform the production of a particular advertisement is one that is targeted to guarantee the attainment of a marketing goal. Creativity here is certainly not an independent force that could create a new cosmos but serves to copy and enhance the management targets of a given enterprise. The dreariness of our target culture has to do with its intellectual vacuity. This sense of the superficial may in some instances provoke its opposite—intellectual interests in complexity—but it can also produce impatience and disengagement with issues that do not fit into the certainty that the establishment of targets—as formulated in number sales or other forms of clear measurements—tend to evoke. In different ways our performance is tested in order to extract via wearying and dreary experiments our economic validity as measured against targets. What may innocuously appear as targets are of course norms which we have to meet if we want to do well within the workplace. The testing involved here is certainly not a question of life and death but rather one of success and failure, of social/economic recognition or exclusion. It takes place within a seemingly democratic context that appears to respect ethnic, religious and cultural diversity.

So we may ask whether we can employ the term biopolitics for a type of government that respects humanity's ethnic, religious and cultural diversity. Even though some might try to depict recent policies, which encourage individuals to conform to politico-medical regiments, as a new democratic form of biopolitics, I think we have reason to be suspicious of the defence of our contemporary managerial culture. Biopolitics in its democratic form might indeed be soft power, dependent not on external enforcement but on internalization of norms.[45] Big Brother wants us to love rather than fear him. Orwell's *Nineteen Eighty-Four* closes with 'He Loved Big Brother'.[46] The soft power in question here may, however, as Orwell's *Nineteen-Eighty-Four* strikingly shows, undermine the diverse constitution of human creativity.

To take one example outside the immediate sphere of health care: what are the social replications for mental and creative well being of a policy that prescribes one uniform delivery of teaching via a centrally approved and pre-formatted programme which every teacher has to deliver in his or her field? The teacher must not deviate from the rigid structures of what the government tells him or her to conform to. Uniformity and conformity are of course defended in the name of standards: in order to make sure that every pupil receives the same standard of education, teachers are not allowed to make use of their particular skill and their particular creativity. Even though this is certainly not a question of life and death—as in totalitarian forms of biopolitics which will be discussed in the following chapter—it nevertheless concerns the quality of our lives as creative beings who are keen to engage with the life of the mind. Creativity turns dreary if it is at the beck and call of an exclusively mimetic imperative because it narrowly addresses only one aspect of our human potential for flourishing. The target culture of neo-liberalism reduces our diverse capacity to one function: to meeting the aims of wealth creation. In this we are asked to turn into the targets we have to meet. We become copies of advertised bliss in our so called leisure time but we also have to copy copies of economic achievement in our work space.

The issue is not mimesis as such: we cannot but in one way or another represent the world we live in and even the most radically detached

---

45 Nikolas Rose has recently described this kind of internalisation of a biopolitical paradigm as follows: 'In the field of health, the active and responsible citizen must engage in a constant monitoring of health, a constant work of modulation, adjustment, improvement in response to the changing requirements of the practices of his or her everyday life.' Rose, *The Politics of Life itself: Biomedicine, Power, and Subjectivity in the Twenty-First Century*, (Princeton, NJ: Princeton University Press, 2007), p. 223.

46 Orwell, *Nineteen Eighty-Four*, p. 342.

work of art relates to its context precisely by the radical detachment from it. It would be silly to question the validity of the relationship between the word and the world, the text and its context. Indeed the social benefit of art is premised precisely on such relationship. Far from taking issue with what connects the work of art to the larger world, an aesthetics that goes beyond mimesis, questions not representation as such but the exclusivity of a mimetic paradigm that is imposed onto creativity. Most important it is a paradigm that circumscribes creativity, because our inventive energies have to be channelled into the production of mimetic images or *memes* that help increase consumption and thus guarantee meeting the demands of certain economic or political targets.

The imperative to be nothing but a copy or a representation of some external agency's idea or plan (be that a company in the case of advertisements or a government in case of education), deprives creativity of the ground of diversity on which it could truly flourish. The diminution of idiosyncratic forms of creativity brings about a shrinking of our world. As we have seen in the discussion of torture within this chapter, this abatement of the full range of mental and physical life characterizes the occurrence of pain. As we shall see throughout this book, it also has become a stereotypical characteristic of the aging process. This may be perhaps one reason why our age feels aged: there is a closing down of worldly experience due to the managerial command to circumscribe our life to the attainment of certain economic or biomedical targets. In this context the shrinking of our world takes place within a market economy that does not necessarily exclude or discriminate against its members on ethnic or religious grounds. As will be discussed in the following chapter, totalitarian forms of biopolitics are premised on the reduction of human diversity to the fiction of a monolithic entity. The arts and humanities have the capacity to reveal what such ideological doctrines of homogeneity really are: fictions which we have been forced to treat as if they were realities. As twentieth century history has shown, such fictive constructs have shaped real life experiences in the most deleterious way.

3 Revisiting Clones: Change and the Politics of Life

'Nostalgia is the pain of an old wound. ... It is a place where we ache to go.' *Mad Men* Series 1; last episode

3.1 Cloning and Art as Mere Copy in Ishiguro's *Never Let Me Go*

The previous chapter has analyzed the shrinking of worldly experience as a hallmark of torture, suffering and pain. This diminution of one's world has become a criterion by means of which we can identify the process of aging. There is, however, the danger that we quasi-automatically identify aging with pain and a shrinking world. Representations of age may thus actually determine the actual occurrence of aging. Biomedical advances have been pushing the physical onset of senility ever further into an extended life span. Yet earlier and rather antiquated representations of the aged persist in the public domain. Do these stereotypical representations of age partake of certain biopolitical structures?

In order to address this question, it is helpful to define the term biopolitics. It literally means 'The Politics of Life'. This may sound rather innocuous and indeed in his book *The Politics of Life Itself*, Nikolas Rose presents a rather benign account of biopolitics in terms of the political, medical and social management of illness. As we will see in this chapter, the term biopolitics, however, signals more sinister connotations. Michel Foucault, who coined the word, employed it to analyze modernity's attempt to control the body via various forms of power.[1] In biopolitics the body has become one with politics.

Here our life has any worth or meaning only when we embody the ideological norms and commandments that certain forms of politics impose on us. Biopolitical forms of control may be assisted by physical force and violence (as they have been in the totalitarian regimes of the

---

1 For a detailed discussion of the history and meaning of the term biopolitics see Roberto Esposito's, *Bios: Bioplitics and Philosophy*, translated and with an introduction by Timothy Campbell, (Minneapolis: University of Minnesota Press, 2008).

past century) or they may operate in a more subtle manner. The more elaborate forms of biopolitics do their work not so much in violent ways. Instead they try to establish a type of mental control through a sophisticated political or managerial usage of representation. Representations here have the function of *memes*, which replicate standard types of behaviour within a given community (this will be further examined below in an analysis of Ishiguro's *Never Let Me Go*). As we have seen in the discussion of *Mad Men* in Chapter 1, here artistic creativity is employed solely for the attainment of economic or medical targets and the perpetuation of the status quo. Representations that exclusively depict aging as the opposite of youth and birth partake of this attempt to subsume corporeality under a preordained social or political category. As we will see in the concluding chapter of this book, literature and arts are capable of changing the way we think about aging. They do so by interrupting and disrupting the way we consign physical phenomena to their pre-ordained representations.

In this chapter, I maintain that the closing down of worldly experience characterizes—not necessarily aging—but various forms of biopolitics. This argument may surprise some readers because the biopolitical may have come to be seen as the exclusive domain of totalitarian power. In the course of this chapter, we will briefly discuss totalitarianism in the context of Hannah Arendt's philosophy of birth which she developed as an alternative to the racist obsession with youth, beauty and procreation of Nazi Germany. The first part of the chapter continues the discussion of the previous two chapters about more subtle and more contemporary forms of biopolitics: the managerial control of representations and images (of which the advertisement industry in *Mad Men's* is a striking example). The focus here is on Kazuo Ishiguro's *Never Let Me Go*. It is a novel about cloning set not in a science-fiction like future but rather within the imaginary setting of post-world war II Britain. The political scenario is thus not that of totalitarianism but of liberal democracy. The British government has ordered the cloning of citizens with the aim to enhance the health of the population. The agenda is thus in keeping with the benign form of biopolitics as appraised in Rose's *The Politics of Life Itself*. Rose argues that such novel and harmless type of biopolitics promotes hope rather than fatalism or despair: 'Crucially, it is a biopolitics in which references to the biological do not signal fatalism but are part of the economy of hope.'[2] In Ishiguro's *Never Let Me Go*, we encounter an economy of hope but it only applies to those who are in receipt of organ donations

---

2 Rose, *The Politics of Life Itself: Biomedicine, Power, and Subjectivity in the Twenty-First Century*, (Princeton: Princeton University Press, 2007), p. 167.

rather than those who are excluded from full participation in such a society focused on the management of health. The clones participate in a rather one-sided way in such an 'economy of hope'. They are born not to give birth, in return, but to serve as donors for the non-cloned and procreative part of the population.

Here we witness the complete separation between birth and age because the clones exist solely for the purpose of aging and dying prematurely. Theirs is an ever shrinking world: due to the single minded and socio-political purpose of their life—that of donating organs for the non-cloned part of the population—their life is foreshortened. They thus instantiate the stereotype of aging: they are set apart, they are incapable of procreation and their world is a closed and continually declining one. While describing an imaginary community that is circumscribed by the stereotypical perimeters of age, deprivation, non-procreation and death, the novel's hidden heart is that of birth. The title of the novel *Never Let me go* is a quotation from a pop song by which its narrator, Kathy H., is captivated. 'What was so special about this song?' she queries and goes on to say that it was what she read into it that made the song special for her:

> Well the thing was, I didn't use to listen properly to the words; I just waited for that bit that went: 'Baby, baby, never let me go…' And what I imagined was a woman who's been told she couldn't have babies, who really, really wanted them all her life. Then there's a sort of miracle and she has a baby, and she holds this baby very close to her and walks around singing: 'Baby, never let me go…' partly because she is so happy, but also because she is so afraid something will happen, that he baby will get ill or be taken away from her. Even at the time, I realized this couldn't be right, that this interpretation didn't fit with the rest of the lyrics. But that was not an issue for me.[3]

As we will find out a couple of pages later, the issue is that, like all clones, Kathy cannot have babies. Remembering her endearment to the lines of the song, she recalls: By then [the time of her captivation by the song], of course, we all knew something I hadn't known back then, which was that none of us could have babies.'[4] The significance of the song for her is that of a delusion that keeps her going. She thinks the song represents the miracle of birth for someone who—similar to her— has been excluded from procreation. Miracles do not happen, at least not in *Never Let Me Go*.

---

3   Ishiguro, *Never Let Me Go*, (London: Faber and Faber, 2005), p. 64.
4   Ishiguro, *Never Let Me Go*, p. 66.

The novel depicts, however, the way in which we submit to social and political forms of control without being physically forced to do so. The clinging to delusions, to various fictions and to a belief that the fictitious will turn real in a miracle-like fashion make us avoid reality. As will be discussed in the next chapter, this avoidance of reality gives us pleasure—in a fetishist way, we do not acknowledge the grimness of a given situation but collaborate with it in the delusional hope that it will turn out not to be so bad.

The cloned protagonists of *Never Let Me Go* willingly do what is expected of them because they avoid both recognizing and believing the reality of their lives' pre-ordained purpose. Instead they fabricate fictions and trust miracles. Similar to his *The Remains of the Day* (as will be discussed in the closing section of the following chapter), Ishiguro's *Never Let Me Go* critiques the way fictions come to shape our socio-political reality. The subject matter of *The Remains of the Day* is the collaboration with Nazi totalitarianism. *Never Let Me Go* focuses on the biomedical as well as biopolitical topics of aging and birth.

The spheres of aging and birth are indeed a mine field where the medical and the political overlap. The imposition of a pre-ordained socio-political model upon the life of the cloned community characterizes the plot of the novel. As teenagers, the cloned are not allowed to be young. They are forbidden to plan their own life itineraries. They are interdicted to interact with the world on their own terms—leaving for America, working in a supermarket or being film stars, for example. Miss Lucy—one of the educators or guardians—at the Hailsham boarding school for the cloned—attempts to be clear about what cannot be fully spelled out and acknowledged:

> The problem, as I see it, is that you've been told and not told. You have been told, but none of you really understands, and I dare say, some people are quite happy to leave it that way. But I'm not. If you are going to have decent lives, then you've got to know and know properly. None of you will go to America, none of you will be film stars. And none of you will be working in supermarkets as I heard some of you planning the other day. Your lives are set out for you. You will become adults, then before you're old, before you're even middle-aged, you'll start to donate your vital organs. That is what each of you was created to do. You're not like the actors you watch on your videos, you're not even like me. You were brought into this world for a purpose, and your futures, all of them have been decided.[5]

---

5   Ishiguro, *Never Let Me Go*, p. 73.

Miss Lucy's message is that of the *meme*: it does not so much explicitly impose but it spreads a preordained life from which there seems to be to no way out. The aim of her message is mimetic: it tries to represent the future of the community of cloned teenagers. The representation makes claims to be accurate but the phrasing is highly euphemistic and distorts the bleak reality of the life that has been pre-arranged for the clones. The euphemism mainly consists in depicting their biography as being free from aging. They will never reach old age. This bleak prospect euphemistically turns into its opposite. Instead of being subject to the forces of aging, the clones—so the euphemistic account goes—will live decent lives. The hope of decency depends on their willingness to copy what the pre-ordained representation of their life tells them to do: namely to find their sole purpose and fulfilment in the donation of their 'vital organs' for the non-cloned community. Decency here denotes the voluntary embrace of life as copy, as a clone. If nothing else, the word 'vital' betrays the euphemism. How can someone have a 'decent life' with the near or pre-ordained prospect of missing ones vitality? More importantly, life which is that of a representation is static and lacks the unpredictability that comes with growth. Growth is another word for aging. By being deprived of growth, the clones are already at their endpoint, close to death. They are fixed and indeed their life has been pre-arranged (as Miss Lucy makes clear in the quote above).

Strikingly, Miss Lucy's revelation about their pre-fabricated biography does not strike the students of Hailsham as new or surprising: 'And it's curious, when we were older and the guardians were giving us those talks, nothing came as a complete surprise. It *was* like we'd heard everything somewhere before.'[6] This testifies to the power of the *meme*: it spreads in so subtle ways that those it affects are not even aware of it. The content of the flat mimesis which advertises its message in *meme* like fashion is that of a fiction which nevertheless determines socio-political life: the Britain depicted in *Never Let Me Go* is indeed divided into the sphere of the human non-clone population and those who are considered to be clones and thus non-humans. The name of the boarding school for the clones is telling: Hailsham literally means the counterfeit or fraud (sham) of glory or acclaim (Hail).

Part of the hoax at Hailsham is the guardian's focus on the creativity of the students (i.e. the clones). The students have to paint and to write poetry. The product of their creative efforts is then collected by the guardians of Hailsham. The students read much into such apparent appreciation of their creativity. They see in it the attempt of a romantic or lamp-like

6   Ishiguro, *Never Let Me Go*, p. 75.

insight into the workings of their inner life. As we find out at the end of the novel, such interest is driven by a political agenda as one retired former guardian makes clear: 'You said it was because your art would reveal what you were like. What you were like inside. That's what you said, wasn't it? Well, you weren't far from wrong about that. We took your art because we thought it would reveal your souls. Or to put it more finely, we did it to *prove you had souls at all*.'[7] Proof of the clones' inner life would support the claim that they are humans. This means that the touchstone of our humanity is that of a unique or idiosyncratic core which is sometimes called 'soul' or 'inner life'. The clones, by contrast, are defined and represented not as singularities but as mere copies that lack psychic complexity.

Art and literature here—for a brief moment at least—promise to disrupt the workings of flat mimesis. The well meaning guardians could now go to their superiors and dispute that the clones are mere copies, mere representations of someone else: 'Look at this art! How dare you claim these children are anything less than fully human?'[8]—they could exclaim. Yet the power of socio-political representations seems to be insuperable. The guardian could not change the public image of the clones. The status quo resists the idea that the marginalized and excluded—in this case the clones—are humans: 'But I have to tell you, my dear, it wasn't something commonly held when we first set out all those years ago. And though we have come a long way since then, it's still not a notion universally held, even today.'[9] Here clearly literature does not have the ability to disrupt the status quo. This is so because creativity is seen not as a disruptive political force but rather as yet another mimetic or representational device. The public perception of the arts remains that of mimesis and representation: they merely copy the world rather interacting with it.

The poetry and the paintings of the students at Hailsham are nothing more than a lamp-like copying of the otherwise not to be seen regions of their inner life. The arts are segregated and separated from the medical and political management that governs society. This is why creativity cannot disrupt the biopolitical paradigm that condemns Hailsham's students to live solely for the purpose of organ donations. As one retired guardian makes clear, a deferral of their bleak fate would not have been granted under any past and current circumstances: 'But this dream of yours, this dream of being able to *defer* [i.e. being able to defer the

---

7   Ishiguro, *Never Let Me Go*, p. 238.
8   Ishiguro, *Never Let Me Go*, p. 239.
9   Ishiguro, *Never Let Me Go*, p. 238.

donations of their vital organs]. Such a thing would always have been beyond us to grant, even at the height of our influence.'[10] The guardians—even the most well intentioned ones—are also shaped by the public representation of their students as clones. Their response therefore mirrors that of their society at large. It is one of disgust and revulsion—despite their protestation of empathy and admiration of a mimetic kind of creativity. Even the best inclined of the guardians admits: 'We're *all* afraid of you. I myself had to fight back my dread of you all almost every day I was at Hailsham. There were times I'd look down at you all from my study window and I'd feel such revulsion..'[11] Ishiguro's *Never Let Me Go* focuses on the all pervasive power of public representations that divide our society into the included and the excluded. This division characterizes biopolitics in it totalitarian as well as in its more subtle medical and free market version as depicted in Ishiguro's presentation of an imaginary post- world war II Britain where clones serve to increase the health of the nation.

Serving the health of the nation is of course a euphemism for the biopolitical demotion of those who provide the service. As we have seen, the 'persistence of this euphemistic language'[12] that pervades the novel is only one aspect of a larger critique of mimesis. The title *Never Let Me Go* refers to the capacity for birth or creativity as a potential disruption of representations that have come to shape the status quo. Were the clones allowed both to procreate and to age, they would have outdone their public representation as that of clones who are mere copies rather than individuals. They as well as their guardians and their society at large are held captive by the perimeters of what they have come to represent. This is why they cannot find a way out of victimization. A non-mimetic-natal form of creativity would have disrupted the status quo. Birth as the creation of something new would have unsettled their public representation as mere copies, as clones.

The term birth has, however, rather dark connotations. In the last century, birth has all too frequently been linked not to the individual and the diversity of new beginnings but to the increase of a given racial and ethnic entity. Here life and birth became subservient to the killing of social groups who propaganda for genocide proclaimed to be undermining and endangering life like an illness or disease. The Nazis

---

10 Ishiguro, *Never Let Me Go*, p. 238.

11 Ishiguro, *Never Let Me Go*, p. 246.

12 See Mark Currie's 'Controlling Time: *Never Let me Go*,' in Sean Matthews and Sebastian Groes's (eds), *Kazuo Ishiguro: Contemporary Critical Perspectives*, (London: Continuum, 2009), pp. 91–103 (p. 100).

indeed abused life, birth and biomedicine for a justification of mass murder. We have to attend to this abuse of life to do justice to a new understanding of the humanities and the arts within a philosophy of birth. Strikingly, the Nazis did not use the term birth in a metaphorical but in a radically literal sense: they were concerned with the increase of fertility within the species they named and categorized as 'Aryan'. Nazism as the most shocking form of bio-politics we have yet witnessed concocted life or the biomedical with the literal usage of categories by means of which it made the lie of its ideology a lethal reality.

3.2 The Market Verifies the Truth of Life: Foucault's Biopolitics of Free Market Liberalism

The philosophy of birth focuses on the creative force that gives rise to the life of a new cosmos. Birth here therefore denotes not only the literal act of giving birth but, in a translated or metaphorical sense, activities of creation more broadly speaking. As will be discussed in this section, the term birth has become rather problematic within modern politics because it has all too frequently been used within the context of population control and worse still racism and genocide. Birth and biopolitics seem to be closely associated fields. Michel Foucault has described biopolitics as 'the attempt, starting from the eighteenth century, to rationalize the problems posed to governmental practice by phenomena characteristic of a set of living beings forming a population: health, hygiene, birth rate, life expectancy, race.'[13] The Lectures on *The Birth of Biopolitic* do not discuss issues of hygiene, health, birth rate, life expectancy and race. Instead they analyze the economic theory of liberalism. Liberalism is closely related to the discussion of more subtle forms of biopolitical rule which are much more insidious and effective than those which refer to physical force.

As we have seen in the previous section, as well as in the discussion of the TV series *Mad Men* (in Chapter 1), these more subtle forms of biopolitics solely operate via representations. Representations here are like advertisements—they spread like *memes* throughout a given population and attempt to predetermine what we find to be truthful and beautiful. In the introductory lecture to *The Birth of Biopolitics*, Foucault does not use the term representation or mimesis. He discusses his method with reference to a certain analysis of how societal practice comes to

---

13 Foucault, *The Birth of Biopolitics: Lectures at the Collège de France 1978–1979*, (ed.) By Michel Snellart and translated by Graham Burchell, (Basingstoke: Palgrave Macmillan, 2008), p. 317.

verify something as either true or false. I would argue that what has been established to be 'true' turns into the object of broadly publicized representation (i.e. advertisements etcetera) which then, in turn, becomes a copy to be imitated by the population at large.

We have to copy those kinds of behaviours that have been confirmed to be sane or normal rather than mad or pathological. Foucault argues that such biopolitical verification of 'truth' is itself a convention or social construction which manifests itself as truthful through societal practice. Foucault describes his method as follows:

> It was a matter of showing by what conjunctions a whole set of practices—from the moment they become coordinated with a regime of truth—was able to make what does not exist (madness, disease, delinquency, sexuality etcetera), nonetheless become something, something however that continues to exist. That is to say, what I would like to show is not how an error—when I say that which does not exist becomes something, this does not mean showing how it was possible for an error to be constructed—or how an illusion could be born, but how a particular regime of truth, and therefore not an error, makes something that does not exist, able to become something. It is not an illusion since it is precisely a set of practices, real practices, which established it and thus imperiously marks it out in reality.[14]

The societal practice of what has been verified as truth—even though it is something, as Foucault emphasises, that does not exist—subjugates a given population to a certain regime of life as shaped by a power-knowledge apparatus.

From Aristotle onwards mimesis has been allocated the role to represent knowledge. The traditional cognitivist aesthetics is precisely premised on such mirroring of the true (and the beautiful). With the birth of biopolitics in the eighteenth century, however, we witnessed a change in the meaning of truth. Truth is now no longer the prerogative of traditional religion and traditional philosophical or metaphysical inquiry. Rather the verification of what is truth increasingly depends on the immanent realm of both ever growing populations and global markets. From now on the market verifies the truth or falsehood of knowledge. Mimesis—the representations of knowledge—is thus linked with market predilections (which grow out of as well as shape fashions within the population at large).

---

14 Foucault, *The Birth of Biopolitics*, p. 19.

The market thus turns from an instrument of jurisdiction—deciding the right price for a given good etcetera—to being the arbitrator of what holds true in societal or governmental practice. Foucault emphasizes this point as follows: 'In simple and barbaric terms, let's say that from being a site of jurisdiction, which it remained up to the start of the eighteenth century, the market, through all the techniques I discussed last year with regard to scarcity and grain market, etcetera, is becoming a site of veridiction.'[15] From now on economics—rather than religion or meta-physics—decides what is true or false. The image of truth generated by the market then becomes the subject matter of representations that repli-cate social practice in advertisements (the topic of the *Mad Men*): 'The market must tell the truth (*dire le vrai*); it must tell the truth in relation to governmental practice.'[16] The market lives from consumers.

As we have seen in the discussion of Ishiguro's *Never Let Me Go*, the truths of consumerism may be closely related to biomedical issues: the clones exist to satisfy a health market—a non-cloned population that consumes their vital organs. Liberalism coincides with an immanent or biopolitical control of freedom: 'The new governmental reason needs freedom therefore, the new art of government consumes freedom. It con-sumes freedom, which means it has to produce it.'[17] Going back to our previous discussion of *Never Let Me Go*, the production of free consumer goods here clearly coincides with the creation of clones whose very exis-tence depends on the consumption of their vital organs by the larger population. The clones are not physically forced to do what they have to do. Rather their lives freely turn into a copy of what has been pre-or-dained for them: not to procreate as well as not to age and instead to die prematurely due to the donation process. The previous discussion of Ishiguro's *Never Let Me Go* thus illustrates what Foucault means when he analyzes biopolitics within the context of liberalism's free market of free choice.

There is, however, one striking difference between Foucault's approach and mine. Foucault, as he acknowledges, is not interested in how an error or how an illusion could be born.[18] Our preceding analysis of *Never Let Me Go* precisely concerns the ways in which an illusion is born. Hence we have been preoccupied with representations that operate like *memes*— *memes*, which both represent and advertise various illusions with a view of marketing these illusions as truthful. As product of a successful

---

15 Foucault, *The Birth of Biopolitics*, p. 32.

16 Foucault, *The Birth of Biopolitics*, p. 32.

17 Foucault, *The Birth of Biopolitics*, p. 63.

18 See the quote above from Foucault's, *The Birth of Biopolitics*, p. 19.

advertisement campaign they thus shape social practice. In *Never Let Me Go* we do not find advertisements as such. However, the way the guardians—in the form of various messages or speeches—represent the pre-arranged life of clones, is similar to the manner in which advertisements work: they confirm the status quo and more importantly, they attempt to make us freely embrace things as they are because of the pleasure—the 'decent life' which the guardians promise (see previous section)—we may derive from them.

While the discussion in this book is concerned with the aesthetic or literary devices that help market biopolitical as well as biomedical norms, Foucault's concern is how these rules and ways of life manifest themselves in societal practice. His archaeological perspective is a vital compliment to our discussion of representations of aging, birth and other biomedical issues as they then shape social attitudes and government policies. In *The Will to Knowledge*—the first volume of *The History of Sexuality*—Foucault has provided a thorough analysis of new types of rule that subject bare life to the absolute control of political dictates. Foucault has prepared for the analysis found in this slim and important book which offers the first account of biopolitis, in the 1977–1978 lectures at the Collège de France on *Security, Territory and Population*. In these lectures, he uncovers the shift from the traditional notion of sovereignty that is concerned with both the territorial and the juridical to the one that attempts to regulate the circulation and the behaviour of the population.

This shift from a sovereign grid on a territory to one in control of the population introduces the modern paradigm of biopolitics. It goes hand in hand with a methodological or technical change from law to life: the legal professions recede in importance and what take their place are those who attempt to gather knowledge about life itself. They are concerned with how life can be represented and thus regulated and ruled and ultimately made subservient to the will of the sovereign. The traditional separation between the private and the public increasingly evaporates. Life itself becomes a question not of the individual or a idiosyncratic growth but of conformity to a pre-established and absolute political rule: 'For the first time in history, no doubt, biological existence was reflected in political existence; the fact of living was no longer an inaccessible substrate that only emerged from time to time, amid the randomness of death and its fatality; part of it passed into knowledge's field of control and power's sphere of intervention.'[19] Life here turns into a copy of a

---

19 Foucault, *The Will to Knowledge: The History of Sexuality: Vol. 1*, translated by Robert Hurley, (London: Penguin, 1998), p. 142.

given political norm. Everything that does not conform to this norm has to be excluded from the sphere of the living. The purported rendering knowledgeable of so far arcane/hidden process of life so that life itself can become a subject of certainty and predictability—in short a subject of rule and subjected to rule—eventuates into the equation of the biological with the politically normative: 'A normalized society is the historical outcome of a technology of power centred on life.'[20] The normalized society of biopolitics is particularly disturbing if the knowledge on which it is founded is not that of science but that of the pseudo-science and pseudo-theology of racism.[21] Here the focus is on life too: on what distinguishes a racial definition of human life, from what racism excludes from belonging to humanity (i.e. groups against which it discriminates).

The most glaring and horrid form biopolitics has yet taken is the unprecedented death machinery of the Nazi genocide. This may sound paradoxical. How can biopolitics—which is, as the term bio indicates, concerned with life—be employed for the management of mass-murder? As recent historiography has shown, the Nazis were primarily concerned with life rather than with death. As Boaz Neumann has put it:

> The Nazi starting point, therefore, was life, and not death. They did not offer an ideology of death. Death was the by-product of a certain philosophy, religion and revolution of life that preceded and conditioned it. The tidings to humanity were not of death but of life, that determined the fate of those who, by a historical contingency, did not belong to life.[22]

Crucial to this deadly bio-political set-up is the categorization of humanity in terms of species. As I have shown in *Spinoza and the Specters of Modernity* the bio-politics of racism depends on the division of humanity into those that are truly human and those who are not.[23] As the quote above indicates, Nazi racism radicalized this division by demarcating it in terms not just of who is truly human but of who is truly alive.

The Nazi categorization made birth or rather the pre-natal a decisive turning point. In this context Roberto Esposito has analyzed birth as

---

20 Foucault, *The Will to Knowledge: The History of Sexuality: Vol. 1*, p. 144.

21 For a detailed discussion of how racism pseudo-science is founded upon a pseudo-theological paradigm see Mack's *German Idealism and the Jew: The Inner Anti-Semitism of Philosophy and German Jewish Responses*, (Chicago: University of Chicago Press, 2003).

22 Neumann, 'National Socialist Politics of Life' in *New German Critique* 85 (Winter 2002): pp. 107–130 (126).

23 See Mack, *Spinoza and the Specters of Modernity*, pp. 125–138.

the lynchpin around which Nazism rotated. Esposito refers to what he calls 'three Nazi *dispositifs*: the *absolute normativization of life*, the *double enclosure of the body*, and the *anticipatory suppression of birth*'.[24] As will be discussed below, Nazism's obsession with the categorization and normative regulation of life grows out of its complete disregard of human contingency and idiosyncrasy. Nazism allowed for the multiplication of one standard copy which it marketed as truthful and beautiful. The conception not of an individual but the species to which his or her conception belonged was the decisive factor: 'The new Nazi humanism was a pre-natal Humanism. It redeemed the human beings at their moment of birth, in contrast with the Christian concept of salvation after death. As such, Nazism did not offer humanity salvation from life after death, but salvation during life.'[25] What is crucial here is that the pre-natal state determines not the idiosyncratic constitution of individuality but the belonging to a species. The definition of species is itself of course subject to the grid of categorization (in the Nazi case 'Aryan' or 'Jewish').

Every particular birth is thus completely subordinated to a politically established norm of racial belonging or non-belonging which, on a natal or pre-natal basis, equates existence with either life or death. What we witness here is the biopolitical subsumption of an embodied individual under a given category or norm of the (in this case) Nazi body politic. Nazism focuses on the management and radical control of life. It does so via a vast and effective totalitarian system. This totalitarian as well as managerial system categorizes various ethnic groups within Germany and throughout the European continent according to the political norms of its racial hierarchy. Foucault has analyzed the management of biopolitical modernity as follows:

> If one can apply the term *bio-history* to the pressures through which the movements of life and the processes of history interfere with one another, one would have to speak of *bio-power* to designate what brought life and its mechanisms into the realm of explicit calculations and made knowledge-power an agent of transformation of human life. It is not that life has been totally integrated into techniques that govern and administer it; it constantly escapes them. Outside of the Western world, famine exists, on a greater scale than ever; and the biological risks confronting the species are perhaps greater, and certainly more serious, than ever before the birth of

---

24 Esposito, *Bios*, p. 11.
25 Neumann, 'National Socialist Politics of Life', p. 123.

microbiology. But what might be called a society's "threshold of modernity" has been reached when the life of the species is wagered on political strategies. For millennia, man remained what he was for Aristotle: a living animal with the additional capacity for a political existence; modern man is an animal whose politics places his existence as a living being into question.[26]

The alignment and, worse still, merging of life with political strategies— what Foucault calls the 'threshold of modernity'—tends to be a de-individuating process that sacrifices cultural and personal diversity to the commandment to conform to a political norm.

Foucault's phrase 'modern man is an animal whose politics places his existence as a living being in question' is highly illuminating, because it establishes not so much collaboration between life and politics but a collision between the two entities. Clearly Foucault sees humanity from a post-Spinozan and post-Darwinian perspective: we are not creations of an elevated supernatural or transcendent God but we are part of an immanent natural sphere; we belong to the animal kingdom rather than being representative of a transcendent or divine one (even though we of course also differ in some characteristics which distinguishes the rest of the animal sphere). Politics as bio-politics attempts to question and outdo our embodied and natural existence. The modern element of bio-politics is its endeavour to transform and reshape our human condition as heirs not of God but of apes. It does so via the either, the free—working solely on the basis of representations that are to be copied, as has been discussed in the previous section—or violent imposition of norms. In the totalitarian case these norms require the implementation of categories that spuriously—but within the highly controlled setting of terror regimes validly—divide life into what belongs to life and what does not. Here we witness novelty and transformation that has rather lethal and indeed genocidal consequences.

In this sense Nazism and totalitarianism is premised on a non-metaphorical notion of birth too. Here, however, it is not the birth of individuality that contributes to a diverse humanity but one that radically sets out to erase our human constitution as frail and vulnerable. Yeats's phrase 'a terrible beauty is born' comes to mind here. The terrible beauty has to do with the deceptive order or symmetry and spurious consistency of norms that are violently enforced upon our unpredictable and irregular existence as inhabitants of a contingent world.

---

26 Foucault, *The Will to Knowledge: The History of Sexuality: Vol. 1*, p. 143.

3.3 The Nazi Genocide, Hannah Arendt and the Philosophy of Birth

> 'On the stroke of midnight', as a matter of fact. Clock-hands joined palms in respectful greeting as I came. Oh, spell it out, spell it out: at the precise instant of India's arrival at independence, I tumbled forth into the world. Salman Rushdie *Midnight's Children*.

The norms in question may of course be more benign than the racial ones established by Nazism. What is nevertheless problematic in, if there is such a thing, 'ethically valid biopolitics'—the one espoused by Rose's *The Politics of Life Itself*—is the normative grid that tends to undermine the foundation of diverse human flourishing. It may well be such a normative grid that wears down the creative fabric and texture of our society. The autocracy of such grid reinforces a sense of dreariness and disillusionment with public culture and engagement.

Issues of creativity, democracy, citizenship and diversity lies at the heart of the contemporary relevance of what I call the 'philosophy of birth'. While subverting Nietzsche's notion of literature and the eternal return (see the last section of the preceding chapter), Hannah Arendt has brought the notion of birth into the philosophical arena as response to the biopolitical usage to which it has been put by Nazism. As we have seen in the second section of this chapter, Nazi racism was premised on the natal/pre-natal selection of who is truly alive (or deserves to live) and who not. The Nazis were of course obsessed with birth in the literal sense. They established a number of policies that promoted the increased production of "Aryan" babies. In a sense their idea of an enlarged life space (*Lebensraum*) originated in the desire to increase the birth-rate: the phenomenally huge increase in the "Aryan" population would thus necessitate an increased territory to be occupied by this ever-growing race. The Nazi case clearly proves Foucault's analysis of biopolitics: the population is the primary focus; and questions of territory are only raised to serve Nazism's political target or norm of an ever-expanding population.

Arendt's philosophical appraisal of birth is provocative especially when we take into account the historical context in which it evolves. As Esposito has shown, she developed her notion of natality as response to Nazi racism and biopolitics:

> Wanting to institute a political thought that is radically counter posed to Nazi biopolitics, Arendt, like Freud before her (but in more explicit fashion), attacks precisely the point at which Nazism

had concentrated its own deadly power. As Nazism employed the production and with it the suppression of birth so as to dry up the source of political action, so does Arendt recall it in order to reactivate it.[27]

One might therefore question Giorgio Agamben's charge against Arendt (and also against Foucault) accusing her of having ignored the Nazi genocide in her political thought. Agamben does so in the introduction to his ground breaking book *Homo Sacer*, no doubt, to emphasize the distinctiveness and originality of his own approach as follows:

Almost twenty years before *The History of Sexuality*, Hannah Arendt analyzed the process that brings *homo laborans*—and with it, biological life as such—gradually to occupy the very center of the political scene of modernity. In the *The Human Condition*, Arendt attributes the transformation and decadence of the political realm in modern societies to this primacy of natural life over political action. That Foucault was able to begin his study of bioplitics with no reference to Arendt's work (which remains, even today, practically without continuation) bears witness to the difficulties and resistances that thinking had to encounter in this area. And it is most likely these very difficulties that account for the curious fact that Arendt establishes no connection between her research in *The Human Condition* and the penetrating analyses she had previously devoted to totalitarian power (in which a biopolitical perspective is altogether lacking), and that Foucault, in just as striking a fashion, never dwelt on the exemplary places of modern biopolitics: the concentration camp and the structure of the great totalitarian states of the twentieth century.[28]

Agamben is certainly right in drawing attention to the curious fact that Foucault in his discussion of bio-politics never mentions Arendt's pioneering work in this field. Nor does Foucault establish the rather obvious connection between biopolitics and the Nazi genocide. Agamben's analysis of an apparent disconnection between Arendt's philosophical work on the reduction of human capacities to the narrow tasks of

---

27 Esposito, *Bios*, pp. 178. For a detailed discussion of how Freud responds to Nazi anti-Semitism see Mack's *German Idealism and the Jew: The Inner Antisemitism of Philosophy and German Jewish Responses*, (Chicago: University of Chicago Press, 2003), pp. 136–154.

28 Agamben, *Homo Sacer: Sovereign Power and Bare Life*, translated by Daniel Heller-Roazen, (Stanford: Stanford University Press, 1998), p. 10.

merely biological life—what she calls *homo laborans*—and her analysis of totalitarian power, however, is accurate on the surface level only. Arendt does not establish explicit connections between her historical and, literary as well as philosophical work: she does not make cross-references via footnotes or other scholarly methods between *The Human Condition* and *The Origins of Totalitarianism*. Yet her writing itself performs the hybridisation of literary, journalistic and philosophical modes of inquiry. As I have shown elsewhere she does not engage one exclusive discourse: her philosophical work is not narrowly philosophical, and her historical work is shot through with philosophical as well as literary ideas.[29]

She implicitly asks the reader both to continue her writing by connecting different aspects of her work and in doing so to reconfigure as well as deform—if not de-figure—aspects of her ideas. This deformation instantiates a new beginning: it animates as well as reshapes her writing and thought within the ambience of new constellations. This is partly what the present book sets out to achieve. There are clear connections between Arendt's discussion of life turning superfluous under totalitarianism and her critique of the biopolitics that give rise to what she calls *homo laborans*. The following discussion will focus on her philosophy of birth as non-mimetic divergence from a biopolitical paradigm of life. What Agamben critiques as a disconnection in Arendt's work instantiates not so much an absence of relationship but the creation of new fields of thought which are not representative of each other but interconnected nevertheless. This interconnection of the diverse, calls into question established ways of perception and one crucial aspect of this questioning approach is the critique of certainty as philosophical norm and economic target. Diverging from Nietzsche's understanding of coherence, Arendt appreciates politics as the literature of the incoherent, as the embodiment of a diverse as well as diverging—in other words forever changing—unity.

Arendt establishes this interconnection between literature's inconsistency and that of a democratic form of politics not only in her later work but in earlier writings, starting roughly with the essays that led to the composition of *The Origins of Totalitarianism*. Agamben is wrong when he claims that Arendt's arguments in her work on totalitarianism differ from her more philosophical book *The Human Condition*. *The Human Condition* spells out her notion of natality. Arendt has, however, already discussed the notion of birth in *The Origins of Totalitarianism*.

---

29 See Mack's "The Holocaust and Hannah Arendt's Philosophical Critique of Philosophy: *Eichmann in Jerusalem*," *New German Critique* (Winter 2009): pp. 35–60.

In her analysis of totalitarian terror she distinguishes between what she calls a single-minded and consistent concern for a given population or species—what Foucault and later Agamben would declare to be biopolitics—from the threat of disruption that the birth of a single individual might pose to the ideological consistency of race thinking:

> Terror as the execution of a law of movement whose ultimate goal is not the welfare of men or the interest of one man but the fabrication of mankind, eliminates individuals for the sake of the species, sacrifices the "part" for the sake of the "whole." The superhuman force of Nature or History has its own beginning and its own end, so that it can be hindered only by the new beginning and the individual end which the life of each man actually is. Positive laws in constitutional government are designed to erect boundaries and establish channels of communication between men whose community is continually endangered by the new men born into it. With each birth a new beginning is born into the world, a new world has potentially come into being.[30]

When Arendt employs the term birth she has in mind the Greek notion of *bios*. *Bios* denotes the idiosyncratic way of life of a particular group or a particular person. It is a unique journey of life and our word biography derives from this semantic field.

Zoe, on the other hand, expresses 'the simple fact of living common to all human beings (animals, men, or gods)'.[31] *Bios* poses a threat to a homogenous form of politics which is totalitarian. In order to counter this threat biopolitics renders *bios* indistinct from *zoe*. The precondition for totalitarianism is biopolitics, because the reduction of idiosyncratic life—what Arendt calls "new beginning"—to the homogenous phenomenon of mere life—the mechanical functions common to all biological systems—renders humanity (or at least large parts of it) superfluous: 'Only where great masses are superfluous or can be spared without disastrous results of depopulation is totalitarian rule, as distinguished from a totalitarian movement, at all possible.'[32] If we are no longer valued for our distinctive contribution to humanity (either as individuals or as groups) we are expandable and thus superfluous.

---

30 Arendt, *The Origins of Totalitarianism*, with a new introduction by Samantha Power, (New York: Schocken, 2004), pp. 599–600.
31 Agamben, *Homo Sacer*, p. 1.
32 Arendt, *The Origins of Totalitarianism*, p. 414.

Bios denotes this distinction and Arendt—recalling and reworking Augustine's notion of *initium*—calls it birth or new beginning. A striking example of rendering a distinct group valueless and expandable is Paul de Man's wartime writings about Jews. In these writings de Man argued that humanity would lose nothing if Jews were transported away from 'Western civilisation'. As John Banville has put in his novel (*Shroud*) meditating about some de-Manean themes: 'that nothing of consequence would be lost to the cultural and intellectual life of Europe, really nothing at all, if certain supposedly assimilated, oriental elements were to be removed and settled somewhere far away, in the steppes of Central Asia, perhaps, or on one of Africa's more clement elements'.[33] Arendt's notion of birth or new beginning counters this hierarchical opposition between expandable and valuable people. Her form of politics is thus democratic and Charles Mathewes is right when he calls her political outlook participatory rather than elitist or agonistic as some of her critics claim.[34] Mathewes, however, misreads her philosophy as subjectivist. He argues that her 'work remains captive to a subjectivist account of the human's agency in the world,' and he accuses her of 'irrationalist voluntarism'.[35] Arendt distances herself from a subjectivist position. Indeed (and as we will see below) she analyzes the ways in which totalitarianism confuses the subjective with the substantive. In order not to fall prey to irrationalism, Arendt appraises democracy's legal system as mediation between the subjective and the substantive.

In order to distinguish her position from subjectivism and "irrationalist voluntarism", Arendt argues that new beginnings can turn out to be double-edged affairs. She seems to be more wary about the interruption of the new than Walter Benjamin (as will be discussed in Chapter 5). When new beginnings destroy the past in its entirety, they are likely to introduce a reign of terror. Samantha Power has argued that the very title of Arendt's book about totalitarianism describes a break of sorts: 'In *Origins*, which might better have been titled "The Originality of Totalitarianism" Arendt 'argued that totalitarianism constituted a colossal rupture with all that had come before'.[36] As Power acknowledges this statement is a half-truth at best, because Arendt indeed 'presented what

33 Banville, *Shroud*, (London: Picador, 2003), p. 214.

34 See Mathewes, *Evil and the Augustinian Tradition*, (Cambridge: Cambridge University Press, 2001), p. 191. For a view that presents Arendt's political philosophy as agonistic see Bonnie Honig's "The Politics of Agonism," *Political Theory* (16, 1993): pp. 520–32.

35 Mathewes, *Evil and the Augustinian Tradition*, p. 174.

36 Power "Introduction" in Arendt, *The Origins of Totalitarianism*, p. xii.

she saw as evidence of historical continuity'.[37] It is better to stick with Arendt's title *Origins*, especially as it has a certain relationship to Walter Benjamin's *The Origin of German Tragic Drama*. In Benjamin's oeuvre, the term 'origin' denotes the historical continuity of what is harmful and thus keeps producing suffering and a sense of the tragic or mournful. As we will see in Chapter 5, according to Benjamin, art establishes a new beginning that departs from history's catastrophic continuity.

Nazism therefore is not so much a new beginning but a break with or departure from the life enhancing aspects of past traditions. Break is not the right word either because Nazism proudly connects with the past— the history of what it calls the 'Aryan species'. It establishes connections with traditional religion or ethics by inverting traditional religion or ethics—in this way Nazism turns the commandment not to kill into the duty to murder. So rather than manifesting a new beginning, Nazism does not introduce something novel but rather destroys the constitution of our world.

Nazism destroys and corrupts past traditions. In so far it is not a substantive new beginning. As Charles Mathewes has shown, Arendt reactivates an Augustinian tradition not only in her notion of natality but also in her account of evil as a privation and corruption of ethics: 'Germany, and large parts of occupied Europe, suffered not a moral collapse, but moral inversion.'[38] In order to prevent such work of both destruction and corruption, democracy's legal system attempts to guarantee stability in an otherwise fluid society:

> The stability of the laws corresponds to the constant motion of all human affairs, a motion which can never end as long as men are born and die. The laws hedge in each new beginning and at the same time assure its freedom of movement, the potentiality of something entirely new and unpredictable; the boundaries of positive laws are for the political existence of man what memory is for his historical existence: they guarantee the pre-existence of a common world, the reality of some continuity which transcends the individual life span of each generation, absorbs all new origins and is nourished by them.[39]

Here Arendt clearly does not dismiss the traditional role of the mimetic imagination: to represent an absent past and thereby to yield knowledge

---

37   Ibid.
38   Mathewes, *Evil and the Augustinian Tradition*, p. 187.
39   Arendt, *The Origins of Totalitarianism*, p. 600.

that has been gathered by past generations. It is important, however, to emphasize that the past has itself been a new beginning. The past is not to be opposed to the present in a way similar in which age is not to be opposed with youth (and vice versa). Both in different ways contribute to the infinity and unpredictable plurality that constitutes the human world.

Totalitarianism and other forms of biopolitics set out to either destroy or diminish humanity's diversity. They want to produce a flattened out version of us where we conform to one will or desire; or to one racial construction of a species. In the quote above Arendt warns against a loss of substance which is precisely the destruction of diverse subjectivities: the substantive heritage of the past grows out of a diversity of new beginnings. The latter constitute our human world. Nazism's destruction and corruption of traditional ethics and religion, is consistent with its genocidal undertakings: both genocide and the annihilation of a heritage reduce human diversity to a wished for monolithic entity.

Countering such biopolitical homogeneity Arendt discusses the interchange between subjectivity and substance that characterizes both her notion of politics and—as we shall see later—her understanding of the arts and the humanities (literature in particular). Totalitarianism and other forms of biopolitics attempt to reduce the gulf between the subjective and the substantial until they form one apparently consistent whole. In the case of Nazism, one subjective version becomes translated—reinforced by terror—into a substantive reality. Totalitarianism strikes its adherents as consistent as well as predictabe because its autocracy precludes the disruptive inconsistency and the unpredictable diversity which accompanies the event of new beginnings.

The world has become predictable and consistent because a disruptive or interruptive form of subjectivity has been exiled or eradicated. In this way totalitarianism claims to be substantive rather than subjective. This appearance of its substantiality has been achieved by eliminating both 'the distinction between fact and fiction (i.e. the reality of experience) and the distinction between true and false (i.e. the standard of thought)'.[40] As we have seen in the first section of this chapter and as will be discussed in the chapters that follow, literature critiques fiction. The fictions that shape our lives are driven by desires for simplicity; for establishing a sense of the predictable and the consistent. Literature and the arts connect us with the unpredictability and inconsistency of our human condition.

---

40 Arendt, *The Origins of Totalitarianism*, p. 610.

In *The Human Condition* Arendt calls natality our unavoidable confrontation with the reality principle of unpredictability, decay and dissolution (yet another word for inconsistency). The premise of Arendt notion of natility is action: 'Moreover, since action is the political activity par excellence, natality, and not mortality, may be the central category of political, as distinguished from metaphysical thought.'[41] In acting as well as in thinking the subjective and the substantive meet. Arendt distinguished her action-based notion of politics from Heidegger's metaphysical being-towards-death. While not denying dissolution and aging, Arendt's focus on birth includes our physical contingency which in turn embraces dissolution and mortality. It commingles the ethereal sphere of thought (the subjective) with what thought encounters in the sphere of action: substance. This coexistence of the subjective and the substantive constitutes both the uncertainty of our everyday life, and, as we shall see in the following chapters, that of literature too. It is worth emphasizing that Arendt's as well as Benjamin's notion of both literature and politics substantially differs from Nietzsche's where it is a harmonizing narrative which eternally returns rather disrupts the eternal return of the status quo. The new is the occurrence of what has not been predicted—or in a darker sense it is the event with which we have not reckoned but for which we have to prepare if we want to be resilient:

> The new always happens against the overwhelming odds of statistical laws and their probability, which for all practical, everyday purposes amounts to certainty; the new therefore always appears in the guise of a miracle. The fact that man is capable of action means that the unexpected can be expected of him, that he is able to perform what is infinitely improbable. And this again is possible only because each man is unique, so that with each new birth something uniquely new comes into the world.[42]

Arendt writes 'in the guise of a miracle'. The new appears to be fictitious or miraculous, because it is not necessarily logical and not necessarily consistent. The guise is, however, deceptive. Far from being miraculous, the uncertainty of the new characterizes our ordinary lives. The certainty of stability and predictability distinguishes a totalitarian or biopolitical society which pursues the collective—albeit unsustainable—life of a fiction where a subjective craving for predictability has assumed the

---

41 Arendt, *The Human Condition*, second edition; with an introduction by Margaret Canovan, (Chicago: University of Chicago Press, 1998), p. 9.

42 Arendt, *The Human Condition*, p. 178.

position of substantive reality. The substance of our messy embodied life will come home to roost and will haunt our lived fictions—be they totalitarian or 'free-choice' —in the form of suffering.

Thinking with Hannah Arendt we could say that suffering in its mental and its physical manifestations arises from the pressure to deny or abandon our unpredictability. A substantial part of this unpredictability is our creativity. Removing the term birth form its literalist, species-like connotation which prevailed during the Nazi reign of terror, Arendt implicitly developed a philosophy of birth, which defines the human as the non-definable and not to be programmed or predicted life that flourishes within a contingent world through its nascent capacity to begin anew. What is literature but infinite versions of new beginnings? Arendt quotes the theologian Augustine as the foundation of her literary understanding of politics: '*Initium ergo ut esset, creatus est homo, ante quem nullus fuit*' (That there might be a beginning, man was created before whom nobody was). According to Augustine, who might rightly be called the father of all western philosophy of history, 'man not only has the capacity of beginning, but is the beginning himself'.[43] As will be discussed in the following chapter, we inhabit the space opened up by the splitting of subject and substance. A split assumes divergence and yet we unite what is divergent. By living a subjective life that encompasses as well as encounters divergent and contradictory substances we embody the unpredictability of new beginnings.

As we will see in the following chapter, literature does justice to our unpredictable constitution, because, from a removed position, it reinforces the splitting and, at the same time, it engages the subjective in a dialogue with the substantive. It also sheds light on the predicament that may go hand in hand with our unpredictability. The uneasy overlap between substance and subjectivity can make room for a conflation of the two. Then the subjective proclaims to be the only form of substance. This is the case in the totalitarian rendition of life as a lie. Why, however, choose nations (the German nation under Hitler is the most striking example) to give credit to such lies? Arendt accounts for such deleterious choice with what Freud calls the avoidance of the reality principle. As we have seen in the previous chapter, the advertisement industry thrives on such wilful ignorance of our complex world. While remaining at some distance to psychoanalysis, Arendt implicitly evokes the easy satisfaction craved by the death drive. She makes the desire to find easy answers to the contingency of our world responsible for the popularity of totalitarian forms of politics. The illusion of consistency renders the world benign

---

43 Arendt, *Essays in Understanding* 1930–1954, p. 322.

and beyond the reach of suffering. As Spinoza has shown, our sense of importance and self-esteem seeks succour in fictions of teleological consistency.

In the middle of the twentieth century, Arendt argues that totalitarian rulers momentarily turn reality into such a fiction: 'Before they seize power and establish a world according to their doctrines, totalitarian movements conjure up a lying world of consistency which is more adequate to the needs of the human mind than reality itself; in which, through sheer imagination, uprooted masses can feel at home and are spared the never-ending shocks which real life and real experiences deal to human beings and their expectations.'[44] Here a fictitious kind of subjectivity does violence to substance: it attempts to eliminate the inconsistency of the world wherein it has been strategically placed in order to count as true the fiction of a non-contingent and predictable universe. Such easy comfort comes home to roost, precisely because we are not substance less subjects. The proof of this is not least to be found in suffering. Totalitarian regimes can only enforce their fiction of a consistent reality at the cost of substance itself. People purchase 'the most rigid, fantastically fictitious consistency of an ideology "while paying" for it with countless sacrifices'.[45] Suffering is the price of a fictitious reality. As we will see in the following chapter, literature as a critique of societal fictions may promote our future awareness of simple or consistent but ultimately destructive as well as self-destructive biopolitical fictions; fictions of biopolitics that attempt to turn real by representing autocracy and homogeneity as inescapable realities.

---

44 Arendt, *The Origins of Totalitarianism*, p. 464.
45 Ibid.

4 Rethinking Suffering: Self and Substance

You're craving depths that don't exist. This guy is the embodiment of nothing. Philip Roth, *American Pastoral*

4.1 Literature's Mediation between Substantive and Subjective Suffering, or the Critique of Žižek: Can we do Justice to Suffering Without a Notion of Substance?

This chapter focuses on the way in which the uncertainty and contingency of our world provokes its imagined and wished for opposite: consistency and certainty. Literature's truthfulness consists precisely in its consistent inconsistency: in its persistent alertness vis-à-vis fictions of certainty. From this novel perspective, literature is not merely fictitious because it has the implicit capacity of disrupting the fictitious. Relating to the preceding argument concerning mimesis, the following discussion moves from a theoretical exposition of Žižek's, Paul de Man's and Martin Heidegger's and Hannah Arendt's thought to a more literary analysis of Ishiguro's *The Remains of the Day*. In this way, it prepares for the development of a nascent theory of literature which will be the task of the following two chapters.

Chapters 5 and 6 offer a new approach to the study of literature during a discussion of Benjamin's work on poetry and art in the age of mechanical reproduction. In this chapter, the analysis of Hannah Arendt's notion of natality will contribute to a new literary theory that combines ethics with aesthetics. The combination of ethics and aesthetics forges a tie between life and literature. The reading of literature in terms of life is of course not new. The distinctiveness and innovation of my approach consists in shedding light on how literature does not so much represent or copy existing life as it establishes the ground for a new polis where humanity can break with harmful practices of the past and the present. The following paragraphs will continue the analysis of contemporary anxieties which underline harmful social practices and beliefs.

We live in a world that does not acknowledge its constitution. What is certain about its constitution is its uncertainty. We seem to be suspended between subjectivity and substance, between the New Age form of a spurious spirituality and a pressing sense of suffering that of course has to do with the issue of substance (be they physical or mental). As the father figure of Hanif Kureishi's novel *The Buddha of Suburbia* has put it:

> We live in an age of doubt and uncertainty. The old religions under which people have lived for ninety -nine point nine percent of human history have decayed or are irrelevant. Our problem is secularism. We have replaced our spiritual values and wisdom with materialism. And now everyone is wandering around asking how to live. Sometimes desperate people even turn to me.[1]

Here the aging father of the young protagonist offers a self-deflating diagnosis of the contemporary split between the spiritual and the material, between the subjective and the substantive, between the age old traditions of the religious and the secular loss of tradition. The acknowledgement that 'desperate people even turn to me' underlines the extent of how despairing our situation has become: the only alleviation of suffering seems to reside in a-would be Buddha or would be Messiah of suburbia. The antagonism between the subjective and the substantive is here enmeshed in intergenerational dissonance. As Sander L Gilman has pointed, for Kureishi 'the religious conflict is a conflict of generations'.[2] Could various tensions between generations reflect the mutual exclusion of substance and subjectivity which lies at the heart of the would-be Buddha's complaint? In other words, is the fictitious world of New Age spirituality not the mirror image of materialist overload? Instead of confronting the issues that shape much of our societal suffering and unease, our society escapes into various substitutes of substance (be it New Age or other forms of spurious intellectual gratification).

Ours seems to be an age that avoids a confrontation— at least on a consciously reflective level—with changes that are in the making or have already come to shape the way we live. This avoidance of the reality principle in representations of simple blips of bliss—which determine our culture of advertisement and consumption—has been analyzed via a discussion of the TV series *Mad Men* in Chapter 1. Žižek has recently called fetishism the psychological mechanism involved in such refusal to engage with reality. In his application of psychoanalysis to political and

1   Kureishi, *The Buddha of Suburbia*, (London: Faber and Faber, 1990), p. 76.
2   Gilman, *Multiculturalism and the Jews*, (London: Routledge, 2006), p. 142.

cultural criticism, Žižek argues that we succumb to fetishism, when we know the rather pathetic consequences of our actions and yet perform them nevertheless.

Fetishism is the persistence of forms of behaviour that have become deprived of their validity and yet are still in force. The question of validity is bound up with that of a certain positioning. This will become apparent in a more detailed discussion of fetishism's cultural itinerary. The term fetish 'derives from the Portuguese *feitiço* and was applied first by the fifteenth-century Portuguese traders to describe the cult objects of West Africa used in witchcraft'.[3] Seen from the vantage point of its history, the usage of the word goes with a certain perspective and the perspective in question can shift: what from a Christian point of view may strike you as superstitious may appear to a non-Christian as superstitious or fetishist in Christian practice (the wearing of crosses as talisman and so forth).

The term 'parallax' describes this shiftiness in perspective which characterizes the perception of what constitutes fetishism. Žižek has enmeshed his critical theory in a certain mobility of the perspective that the term parallax denotes: 'Parallax', according to its common definition, is the apparent displacement of an object (the shift of its position against a background) caused by a change in observational position that provides a new line of sight.'[4] In a discussion of Salman Rushdie's postmodernism, Wendy Steiner has shown how 'parallax' is a constitutive feature of a liberal (and postmodernist) coexistence of diverse and often contradictory traditions: 'Instead of a definitive, secure world, we have the parallax shifting of perspective.'[5] Criticizing the 'fetishism' of contemporary society, Žižek has recently taken issue with our contemporary 'parallax', bearing 'witness to how, in postmodernism, the parallax is openly admitted, displayed–and, in this way, neutralized: the antagonist tension between different standpoints is flattened out into an indifferent plurality of standpoints'[6] Here Žižek does not attempt to do away with a multiplicity of perspectives but he rather wants to alert us to the loss of such plurality if it derives from a perspective of indifference.

The gap between different points of view can only be sustained through an engaged observer. An indifferent (as opposed to engaged) perspective flattens out the difference of antagonism which nourishes

---

3   Wendy Steiner, *The Scandal of Pleasure: Art in an Age of Fundamentalism*, (Chicago: University of Chicago Press, 1995), p. 81.

4   Žižek, *Living in the End Times*, (London, Verson, 2010), p. 244.

5   Steiner, *The Scandal of Pleasure*, p. 119.

6   Žižek, *Living in the End Times*, p. 253.

the life of diversity. In his most recent work, Žižek implicitly corrects some aspects of his appraisal of philosophical parallax which deflates any substantive account of our existence and instead enthrones the subjectivity of perspective as the sole motor of our existence in the shadow of Descartes's *cogito*, maintaining that 'the status of the Real is purely parallactic and, as such, non-substantial: it has no substantial density in itself, it is just a gap between two points of perspective, perceptible only in the shift from the one to the other'.[7] According to Žižek, it is such a radical parallactic account of our humanity that empties the world of substance, which accounts for the plurality of our postmodern universe.

Previously, Žižek has made a strong case for the paradoxically consubstantiality of substance's disappearance and the multiplicity of our radical subjectivism, writing that 'the parallax Real is, rather, that which accounts for the very *multiplicity* of appearances of the same underlying Real—it is not the hard core which persists as the Same, but the hard bone of contention which pulverizes the sameness into a multitude of appearances'.[8] The hard bone of contention goes back to Hegel's famous equation of the spirit with the bone. According to Žižek, 'Hegel converts the Fichtean I=I into the absolute contradiction Spirit=Bone, i.e. into the *point of absolute non-mirroring*, the identity of the subject *qua* void with the element in which we cannot recognize his mirror image, with inert leftover, the bone, the rock, the hindrance which prevents the absolute self-transparency of the pure performative: the subject is posited as correlative to an object which precisely cannot be conceived as the subject's objectivation'.[9] The absence of mimesis here coincides with the absence of any substance that could be mirrored. A radical contingency marks Žižek's non-substantive subject. It is a contingency born out of the void, which can be filled by so many contingent inert leftovers, by what Hegel calls the bone.

In his most recent work, Žižek alerts his readers to the danger that the coexistence of various contingent and contradictory leftovers, which fill our subjectivity (having been emptied out of substance), may give rise to indifference and cynicism. When this happens, then there is not so much a plurality of contingent worlds but rather a flattening out of difference where nothing matters any longer.

---

7   Žižek, *The Paralax View*, (The Massachusetts Institute of Technology Press, 2006), p. 26.

8   Žižek, *The Paralax View*, p. 26.

9   Žižek, *Enjoy your Symptom! Jacques Lacan in Hollywood and Out*, Second Edition with a new preface by the author (London: Routledge, 2001), p. 102.

We may, however, ask how something can matter if matter (substance) does not exist in the first place. As we have seen via a brief glance at the history of its usage, the term fetishism adumbrates parallax: one object appears to be a fetish from a certain perspective, but is a holy relic seen from the insider's point of view. When Žižek criticizes contemporary society in terms of fetishism, he presupposes some notion of substance that is either disavowed or extolled into a quasi-sacred realm. He argues that we know what is wrong with us, but nevertheless cannot believe in what is right. In this way, we cling to the status quo and thus perpetuate what is harmful.

Fetishism precludes change in the face of obvious recognition to the contrary: 'The most basic coordinates of our awareness will have to change, insofar as today, we live in a state of collective fetishistic disavowal: we know very well that this will happen at some point, but nevertheless cannot bring ourselves to believe that it will.'[10] It is this gulf opening up between knowledge and belief—which characterizes Žižek's usage of the term fetish—that presupposes, however, a notion of substance—a matter of knowledge or a matter of belief.

The moot point is that Žižek has disavowed the validity of any substantive form. Žižek's work certainly partakes of a Heideggerian mode of thought that turns around the abyss of absence and the impossibility of full presence. This mode of thought has determined much postmodernist theory in literature, philosophy, architecture and jurisprudence. The logic of postmodernism is 'in keeping with a Heideggerian or existential analysis of modernity in which the awareness of the departed meaning is all we can aspire to'.[11] In literary studies, Žižek's approach may well come closest to Paul de Man's rigorous demystification of literature as the absence of referential meaning (as will be discussed in the following chapters). From his early wartime writings in the 1940s to his tenure as Sterling Professor at Yale, de Man and his adoring followers have insisted on the self-foiling of any form of enjoyment or meaning that literature may appear to evoke in its audience. As Wendy Steiner has put it, 'throughout his career de Man reiterated his early idea that literature is independent of life'.[12] Literature achieves this autonomy or independence from life, by dint of its referential void; signifying nothing. While we may be grateful to de Man for his rigorous insistence on the differentiation between life and art, he nevertheless succumbed to a literalism of sorts when he confused the empirical with the artistic: 'Far from

10 Žižek, *Living in the End Times*, pp. x-xi.
11 Steiner, *The Scandal of Pleasure*, p. 202.
12 Steiner, *The Scandal of Pleasure*, p. 195.

mistaking art for reality, as he criticized modernism for doing, he—sometimes—mistook reality for art.'[13] In de Man's case, this confusion of reality with art results in emptying life of substance. Reality turned into de Man's deconstructionist art is nothing else but the void of the signifier; signs rather than bodies.

The polymath Žižek may appear to be far removed from the 'expert' literary critic de Man and yet they both share a post-Heideggerian or postmodernist hostility towards substance or matter. In de Man's case the subject's referent foils the fulfilment of a substantive reference. In a similar way Žižek insists on the void that is the real of our existence as substance less subjects. How can we know and believe something within the abyss of the void? As we have seen Žižek's critique of our postmodern fetishism hinges upon knowledge and belief.

Here we reach the crux of the impasse: Žižek's is a postmodernist logic of the substance less but in order to substantiate knowledge we cannot do without substance. In order to overcome this impasse, Žižek has resurrected the traditional Marxist notion of class struggle. The class struggle should give substance to something that is without substance. The proletariat comes to embody that which has no body, no substance: 'The first figure, corresponding to the enclosure of external nature, is unexpectedly perhaps, Marx's notion the proletariat, the exploited worker whose product is taken away from him, reducing him to a subjectivity without substance, to the void of pure subjective potentiality whose actualization in the labour process equals its de-realization.'[14] The de-realization of the labour process is part and parcel of what Marx critiques as capitalism's status quo. It is hardly an outline of a better state of society. Idealizing this process comes close to what Benjamin criticized as the social democratic infatuation with the bourgeois work ethic of labour.

Žižek refers to the term proletariat, however, to bring into relief his defence of social antagonism: we need proletarians to have a class struggle. Žižek's focus is political, Hegelian and Lacanian in its concern for the unacknowledged antagonisms and the spectre of social unrest and suffering that is not anticipatory but already present in the current condition and conditioning of the ecology and economy. The missing issue here is that about what the struggle could be about. There need be some form of matter about which we can argue or over whose possession we may struggle. The economy concerns the distribution of wealth and the class struggle is about such spreading of the goods of this world.

13 Steiner, *The Scandal of Pleasure*, p. 205.
14 Žižek, *Living in the End Times*, p. 313.

According to Žižek, the proletariat is 'subjectivity without substance', precisely because it has been disenfranchised. Its loss of substantive power is what deprives the proletariat of substance. Deprivation does, however, presuppose something of which we could be deprived. Marx's point is precisely to remedy this state of affairs. So Žižek's recent discussion of fetishism and social antagonism reflects an unacknowledged missing link in his thought which revolves around substance and its lack. This is not to deny the importance of parallax for addressing suffering, aging and illness within our mobile cosmopolitan society. We should rather bring the radical positioning of parallax together with what constitutes the increasingly mutating substance of our society. The substance in question here is not single but is itself split during transformations into ever new forms.

It is one of the central contentions of this book that we can only think in terms of bringing together a new form of mobile as well as diverse substance with the creative freedom of Descartes's *cogito* (and of Kantian autonomy too) via a novel understanding of art's social validity. Literature and art embody the paradoxical and hybrid state of residing in between the substantive and the non-substantive, the real and the non-real, the subjective and the objective: 'Art is *of* reality and it is not.'[15] More importantly, literature's interstitial location outside and at the same time inside substance prepares it not just for the narration of what is fictive but in doing so for a critique of the fictions that may have come to shape reality (this will be discussed in some detail in last section of this chapter).

The interstices of literature question the all too simplistic and often misleading divide between the real and the constructed. When politicians admonish us to get real, they often promulgate their constructions of reality as the objective state of things. The reality projected by some politicians involves suffering and some form of sacrifice which asks us 'to get real'. One example of financial sacrifice has been Gordon Brown's insistence that Britain's multibillion expenditure for Trident—a renewal of a highly costly nuclear weapons programme—is necessary to meet the threat of terrorism. Any opposition to such dear military spending in the face of huge cost cuts in public finances (cuts in the range between twenty five and forty percept in the education, health and home office budget) is met by the admonition to get real.

What is the real in question here? Žižek empties the real out of any substance and concomitantly inflates pure subjectivity as the arbiter of what matters. His argument is accurate to a certain extent: up to a point the real is without substance and therefore radically dependent on the

15 Steiner, *The Scandal of Pleasure*, p. 119.

position of the observer. Humanity makes its world. It gives birth in various non-literal manifestations: in the form of buildings, artworks, technical innovations and so forth. Our constitution is indeed a constructivist one. Modern philosophy from Descartes' onwards has alerted us to our constructivist nature.

Descartes's cogito as well as Kant's autonomy seem to do justice to our capacity for autonomous world creations. Postmodernism, however, has reflected upon both the history of modernity—in particular on the biopolitics of totalitarianism which has been analyzed in the previous chapter—and on Heidegger's existentialism. Consequently, postmodern writing and thought has given an account of how such creative plans can fail or even turn into their opposites: into sites of mass murder and limitless destruction (Derrida's work on autoimmunity is a case in point here).[16]

Heidegger's existential analysis of our being drawn towards death shows that creativity flourishes on the abyss of radical contingency, of meaninglessness, of the nothing without substance. His famous notion of a secularized or, in other words, god-less guilt describes 'an owning up both to the radical contingency of one's thrownness and to the inescapability of an ever-threatening death, as well as to the practical necessity, in acting at all, of fleeing in some way from such nullity, of "erring" in the ontological sense in order to be, in order to "stretch one's existence along in time"'.[17] The feast of our world making—as celebrated from a Kantian or Hegelian perspective—gives rise to fear and turns out to be so many escape routes from the inevitable lack of substance which is our being drawn onto death.

We keep constructing our different versions of the world on the post-Heideggerian abyss of nothingness as manifested not in the world of our constructions but in the endpoint, or, ironically, in the aim viz. telos of our life which is death. As Robert Pippin has shown, Heidegger thinks within a Kantian framework of human autonomy while turning it upside down. He dwells on what Kant and Hegel would not bear to countenance: the failure of meaning and practical sense making. The issue here is not death but the lack of substantive meaning which death represents: 'The failure that Heidegger is trying to account for is not a failure to "make sense" of death but an occasion on which the failure to

16 For a detailed discussion of Derrida's writings on autoimmunity see Mack, *Spinoza and the Specters of Modernity: the Hidden Enlightenment of Diversity from Spinoza to Freud*, (London: Continuum, 2010).

17 Pippin, *The Persistence of Subjectivity: On the Kantian Aftermath*, (Cambridge: Cambridge University Press, 2005), p. 71.

make sense of, be able to sustain reflectively, sense making itself happens.'[18] Our autonomous construction of the world reveals itself as being premised on its failure. Temporality highlights the potentiality of such failure.

Now Žižek reads German Idealism through post-Heidggerian eyes. Our seemingly substantive constructions of different forms of world are essentially and existentially empty, without substance. The only thing remaining is the pure form of Descartes's *cogito* or Kant's and Hegel's notion of autonomy. Yet how can Žižek refer to issues of knowledge and belief from the position of a substanceless subject? The fact that our attempts to create worlds are subject to failure does not necessarily invalidate such attempts. Some might fail and some might prevail. The eventual loss of substance in death, on an individual level, or on a species level, 'in the end of times', does not impinge on our contemporary needs as embodied rather than substanceless subjects. There are clearly substantial issues and the contemporary cost cutting exercise concern issues of substance that affect the lives and minds of millions (health, education and so forth). Žižek implicitly addresses these issues when he castigates our society for avoiding them, or disavowing their existence in fetishist behaviour.

We could read Žižek's critique of contemporary society's fetishism, as an unacknowledged acknowledgement of substance, of matters of knowledge and belief. We know that there is climate change underway and yet we refuse to believe it. Climate change is a question of substance because it has a huge impact on the material condition of our world (sea levels rising, severe storms and the massive increase in global temperature). Climate change is only one example for our fetishist disavowal of matters we know but refuse to believe.

Literature might be what Žižek is looking for. One of the main arguments developed in this book is that literature is capable of changing the most basic coordinates of our awareness. With literature we enter an avenue where we come to believe what we know. This is due to its capacity to change the way we approach our world. It is capable of transforming our consciousness. In doing so, literature benefits citizenship: it transforms our interaction with each other and with our environment. In this way, fiction might ironically have a much more realistic stringency and valence than the get real admonitions of some politicians. Indeed, literature's fictions may critique the way in which we believe in what we know not to be true (as will be discussed in the concluding section of this chapter).

18 Pippin, *The Persistence of Subjectivity*, p. 75.

4.2 Aging, the Changing Demography, and Literature's Transformation of Consciousness

Mutatis mutundis, we have to move beyond 'a state of collective fetishistic disavowal' when we face current and future demographic challenges. What is crucial here is that these challenges are part of the larger economic and social antagonisms that we consistently try to avoid. The truth here is apparent but we cannot face up to it. This reluctance of facing up to truth, however hurtful it may be, is intricately bound up with what I have called a culture of flat mimesis in Chapter 2. We attempt to copy the image of easy bliss, of simple fulfilment, of 'youth' as presented in political slogans and advertisements, because we long for simplicity in a world that is increasingly complex and quick in its transformations. Biomedical advances drive much of the changes whose social repercussions we desperately try to disavow.

As has been discussed in Chapter 1, biomedical advances have transformed the actual inception of aging: we are capable of working much longer than current coordinates of retirement would acknowledge. In addition huge changes in demography and new economic necessities are increasingly enhancing the working life of an apparently aging population. Due to biomedical advances new forms of aging have less to do with a decline in cognitive capacities. Within a knowledge-based economic system, however, the stable functioning of cognition in those who are deemed to be 'old' is a crucial factor. It should be a red flag alerting us to the dangers that go with denying those who physically appear to be old the capacity and the right to contribute to the welfare of society at large. The forces behind such demotion of the apparently 'old' are fictitious because due to tremendous medical advances the facts of aging are in the process of startling transformations that no longer warrant the application of out-dated standards and categorization. The persistent clinging to passé standards and categorization is the product of flat mimesis and ironically manifests an aging process irrespective of age: the copying of what we are familiar with but what no longer holds true debilitates the young and old.

In this context, we may wonder whether Žižek's notion of 'fetishism' may be better described by what I have called 'flat mimesis'. As we have seen the history of its usage, indicates that the word 'fetish' depends on the perspective of those who employ it in order to invalidate the religious and social practices of a culture other than their own. This emphasis on the position of the observer enmeshes the term fetishism within the conceptual field of the notion 'parallax' and, as has been discussed in the previous section, parallax describes the change within the same object if perceived from different points of view. A fetishist approach clings to one perspective and in doing so confers on an ordinary thing the sacred or the supernatural status. Endowed with such status, the thing must not be seen in any other light. It has become incapable of change and undergoes a serious of copies that are aimed to provide a seemingly identical replication of the thing itself (crosses as talisman in a Christian context).

The mimesis is a flat one, because the thing (the cross around the neck) has the fetishist capacity to be consubstantial with the supernatural power it arguably represents. This coincidence of the ordinary thing of representation with the sacred Thing represented, characterizes the single minded and rather flat perspective which characterizes fetishism. The conviction that goes with such flat perspective hinges upon a certain disregard of substantial properties: the ordinary thing can only transmute into the sacred Thing of fetishism, if its rather sobering material qualities are disavowed and not taken in account. This is a perspective and a concomitant consciousness which the fetishist rejects at least apropos the object in question here. A change in perspective would work for a change in consciousness. This transformation of the way we perceive and think about certain issues of our world is precisely the intellectual domain of literature, the humanities and the arts.

It is crucial here to emphasize that such transformation of perception and cognition is not limited to a cerebral or subjective sphere. On the contrary it has a tremendous impact not just on subjectivity but also on embodied substance. The transformation of perception and cognition concerns both our subjectivity and our substance. We are clearly substantial—rather than 'substanceless'—subjects who relate to a given exterior or societal context in which we absorb as well as create the different texts and textures that shape our lives. Literature and the arts have a two pronged and radically divergent field of activity: one is ethereal or non-substantial—what the term fiction may denote in this context—and the other transmogrifies the way we relate to issues of substance in the embodied sphere of society.

Literature's independence from life paradoxically provides a new lease of life. It operates in a free mental sphere beyond substance and yet impinges upon our embodied existence in a way that is capable of alleviating suffering. This alleviation is not an immediate or direct one but rather does its work via a change of perception and consciousness. This change may seem ethereal and ephemeral but its subject matter is substantive. According to Elaine Scarry this state between non-material cognition and its materialization characterizes the sphere of human culture as whole:

What gradually becomes visible (by inversion in its deconstructed form in torture and war and straightforwardly in its under constructed civilized form), is the process by which a made world of culture acquires the characteristics of "reality", the process of perception that allows invented ideas, beliefs, and made objects to be accepted and entered into as though they had the same ontological status as the natural given world. Once the made world is in place, it will have acquired the legitimate forms of "substantiation" that are familiar to us. That an invented thing is "real" will be ascertainable by the immediately apprehensible material fact of itself: the city (not the invisible city asserted to exist on the other side of the next sand dune, but one within the sensory horizon) has a materialized existence that is confirmable by vision, touch, hearing, smell; its reality is accessible to all the senses; its existence is thus confirmed within the bodies of the observers themselves.[19]

Literature certainly differs from the built environment as manifested in cities. Scarry's argument about the interaction between the non-substantial construct and its substantiating realization is nevertheless pertinent for a discussion of literature and its complex relationship with reality. Literature self-consciously sets itself apart from any pretension to be a substantial part of our material existence. If it is read in this way (i.e. as a substantial part of our material existence), the reading in question is a literalist one and as such affiliated with various forms of political as well as religious fundamentalism. Seen as literature, the Bible does not lay claim to be literally true. Only a literalist reading of the Bible would affirm that, say, the apocalypse, as outlined in the book of revelations is going to take place (or is going to take place in the way described therein). Literature is a form of make belief and as such it differentiates itself from forms of embodied truth.

Literature does, however, lay claim to truth in a non-literalist fashion. In this non-literalist way it impinges on our reality while being set apart from it. It is fictitious in the sense of being separate from the materialized and thus substantiated reality of culture as instantiated in the architecture and the skyline of our cities (as discussed by Scarry in the quote above). Being fictitious in the sense of being separated from the reality we encounter on an everyday basis does not mean that literature tells lies about our world. On the contrary, its mental space has the capacity to change our ways of perception and cognition in a uniquely powerful

---

19 Scarry, *The Body in Pain: The Making and Unmaking of the World*, p. 125.

manner precisely by dint of its separation from what we are used to see as presentations or representations of our world.

The creativity of literature thus differs from the reality making activity, which is the focus of Scarry's writing in the above citation: it does not create a mental construct to translate it literally into a materializing and eventually materialized form; rather literature's truth keeps a distance from the literal and materialized world of human culture to change the way we coordinate and live our lives within this world. This is what I mean by its consciousness changing capacity: a mental space that is distinct from the materialized space of other arts and sciences and yet one that helps create a more fulfilling life within our embodied world due to the new perspectives it provides on how we can better coordinate our attitudes, beliefs and ways of interaction within the ever changing material conditions of our society.

A substantial part of the changing conditions within contemporary culture and society are biomedical and are thus due to scientific advances. In order to be able to keep up with the biomedical revolution we have to change the way we engage with reality and in order to do so we need to attend to the transformational rather than merely representational work of literature. Literature turns out not so much *to produce fictions but to critique the fictional work of our perception of birth, youth and aging*. Literature's achieves this critical stance not via mimetic techniques but through a transformation of our ways of thinking. It confounds oppositions and turns them complementary rather than mutually self-exclusive.

This work at the transformation of the ways we perceive us and our world is the so far un-acknowledged core of the critical expertise that has emerged in recent attempts to understand postcolonial literature. In his classic study *The Location of Culture* Homi K Bhabha has employed the term hybridity— as 'a strategy of ambivalence in the structure of identification that occurs precisely in the elliptical *in between*, where the shadow of the other falls upon the self'[20]—in order to describe the complementary rather than mutually exclusive relationship between the colonizer and the colonized, between East and West. What is hybrid is ambiguous, is difficult to pin down, in short, it is uncertain. While the agenda of colonizers was to create clear cut distinctions between the "civilized West" and the "savage East", the actual colonial experience, as Bhabha shows, confounds such distinctions.[21]

---

20 Bhabha, *The Location of Culture*, (London: Routledge, 1994), p. 60.

21 For an analysis of the anthropology of colonialism and its bearing on post-Holocaust writing and thought see Mack's, *Anthropology as Memory: Elias Canetti's and Franz Baermann Steiner's Responses to the Shoah* (Tübingen: Niemeyer, 2001).

To be more precise, literature outdoes the oppositional structure with which the social norms of the colonizers set out to colonize what they desire to be marked as deficient: 'The colonial signifier—neither one or the other—is, however, an act of ambivalent signification literally splitting the difference between the binary oppositions or polarities through which we think cultural difference.'[22] It has been rather underappreciated that Bhabha derives his notion of the ambivalent and the hybrid from Hannah Arendt's theory of action and inter-subjectivity, which, as I have shown elsewhere, is part of her philosophy of diversity.[23] Bhabha points out that Arendt's notion of action is premised on the acknowledgement of uncertainty and contingency as the foundation of our shared—and thus social or political—human condition:

> Agency, as the return of the subject, as "not Adam," has a more directly political history in Hannah Arendt's portrayal of the troubled narrative of social causality. According to Arendt, the notorious uncertainty of all political matters arises from the fact that the disclosure of the *who*—the agent of individuation—is contiguous with the *what* of the intersubjective realm. This contiguous relation between *who* and *what* cannot be transcended but must be accepted as a form of indeterminism and doubling. The *who* of the agency bears no mimetic immediacy or adequacy of representation. It can only be signified outside the sentence in that sporadic, ambivalent temporality that inhabits the notorious unreliability of ancient oracles that 'neither reveal nor hide in words but give manifest signs'. The unreliability of signs introduces perplexity in the social text.[24]

Bhabha ingeniously reads Arendt's notion of politics in terms of a splitting between *who* and *what*. This links up with the previous discussion of this chapter: the *who* is of course subjectivity and the *what* is the substance of the material world of our political-social interaction. Now this splitting is not actually separating two different entities. Instead the split raptures and fractures one substance: our substantial world experience is split between the non-substantiality of the subjective *who* and the

---

22 Bhabha, *The Location of Culture*, p. 128.
23 For detailed discussion of this point see, Mack's 'Hannah Arendt's Philosophy of Plurality: Thinking and Understanding and *Eichmann in Jerusalem*', in Andrew Schaap, Danielle Celermajer and Vrasidas Karalis (editors.) *Power, Judgment and Political Evil. In Conversation with Hannah Arendt*, (Farnham, Surrey: Ashgate, 2010), pp. 13–26.
24 Bhabha, *The Location of Culture*, p. 189.

substantiality of the *what*. As Bhabha points out these two realms are not disconnected but contiguous with each other and this very contiguity between ethereal subjectivity and the materialized body of the exterior world makes for the uncertainty and contingency of the human condition. We may be able to ascertain some of the *whats* that constitute our world. We are, however, unable to represent the *who*, the kernel of our substanceless subjectivity.

The contiguity of the *who* and and the *what* shapes the paradoxical non-factual factuality of intersubjectivity. Our situation is more complex than what Žižek's notion of the 'substanceless subject' may insinuate: we are substantive subjects and at the same time we inhabit a sphere of endlessly subjective substances. The interaction between subjectivity and substance (and vice versa) constitutes the intersubjective realm of politics and accounts for its tendency to fall prey to various fictions that are taken to be real with often deleterious if not lethal effects. This tendency of reality to be shaped by and sometimes to be subsumed by fictions has a significant bearing on issues of substance such as suffering. Spinoza was the first philosopher who took seriously the role fictions play within our societal lives.[25] As we have seen in Chapter 2, his critique of final causes and teleology is a critique of fictions: 'all final causes are nothing but human fictions.'[26] Spinoza does not berate us for the constructions of fictions. Constructing fiction (of teleology and final causes and so forth) is part of our subjectivity and is an inalienable aspect of our humanity. He does, however, admonish us not to confuse fiction with reality, not to mistake subjectivity for substance. This is of course difficult to achieve in our world where, as Bhabha's reading of Arendt has suggested, subjectivity is contiguous with substance.

Within a Heideggerian context of radical contingency, Spinoza's rationalist hope to separate substance from subjectivity seems to be doomed to failure. Spinoza's critique of the fictions of teleology gives, however, already some purchase on understanding contingency as substantial fact of our world. Arendt's writing and thought has been heavily informed not so much by Spinoza as by Heidegger's phenomenology. She keeps faith with Heidegger's attempt to do justice to substance as we encounter it not only in our embodied subjectivity but also in our sense of being placed within a particular context, within what Jeff Malpas has called *Heidegger's Topology*. Arendt calls that fictitious which distorts and potentially attempts to destroy, the unpredictability of our individual and

25 For a detailed discussion of this point see Mack's *Spinoza and the Specters of Modernity*.

26 Spinoza, *Ethics*, edited and translated by Edwin Curley with an introduction by Stuart Hampshire, (London: Penguin, 1996) p. 27.

highly idiosyncratic locations within the diverse and contingent cosmos of the human. She calls politics what sustains the plurality of our lives. Against this background, could it be that Arendt's notion of politics is akin to that of literature?

This may appear to be a rather odd, if not disingenuous idea. Does not Arendt insist on the importance of factual truth in political discussions? The central notion of natality, or new beginnings in Arendt's work has helped to strengthen the appeal of her political philosophy. I am concerned with idea of bringing ethics and aesthetics together. Arendt's work on the factuality of the social sciences is most helpful for the development of a new approach to the study of literature which highlights its social benefit in a non-utilitarian way. Her theme of natality, of new beginnings is indeed closely connected to an innovative appreciation of literature. The account of literature I am proposing here does not clash with the concern with facts, which is the hallmark of the social sciences. Literary studies from this perspective engage in a critique rather than confirmation of various fictions that keep us enthralled in our everyday lives. Literature prepares for new beginnings by revealing the non-obligatory, or, in other words, fictitious nature of that which has shaped social practices in the past and in contemporary society. From this standpoint, Arendt's emphasis on actions and their materialization does not call into question her literary and humanistic approach to political science and to the social sciences in general. It has been noted that narratives are of central importance to Arendt's work. Her post-Spinozan conception of the human condition has generated a shift away from grand philosophical schemes and systems to a concern with the particularity of literature. As Simon Swift has recently put it, 'the fact that the human condition is limited allows that condition to be the subject of story and narrative'.[27] Is literature nothing more than the subject and the subject matter of our limitations?

The recognition of epistemological limits may indeed make us wary of grand theories that presume to offer the key for the understanding of the universe and this wariness may help us appreciate the more limited sphere of literary narration. No wonder that post World War II thinkers from Arendt, via Paul Riccoeur to Alasdair McIntyre and Martha Nussbaum have turned their attention to the philosophical value within

---

27 Swift, *Hannah Arendt*, (London: Routledge, 2009), p. 28. For a brilliant discussion of the role of narrative in the work of Arendt see Lisa Jane Disch's *Hannah Arendt and the Limits of Philosophy* (Ithaca, NY: Cornell University Press, 1994) as well as Robert C. Pirro's *Hannah Arendt and the Politics of Tragedy*, (DeKalb, IL: Northern Illinois University Press, 2001).

literature. Yet Arendt differs from these theorists in a crucial respect. Her approach to literature is not primarily a mimetic one. Neither does she read literary text, as Ricoeur does, in terms of 'a vast laboratory in which we experiment with estimations, evaluations, and judgments of approval and condemnation through which narrativity serves as a propaedeutic to ethics'.[28] She does not question such an approach and would not necessarily dispute its validity.

Arendt abstains, however, from seeing literature exclusively as mimesis of reality. Her reading together of ethics, politics and literature goes much further: she implicitly reads purportedly non-literary, or, in other words, non-contingent or logical forms of political governance in terms of fictitious fabrication. Rather than upholding the common view of literature in terms of a representation of reality, she argues that reality is itself subjected to fictitious distortions of itself that result in forms of self-destruction. Within her writing and thought we may find an implicit conception of literature as a critique of fiction. We find this unacknowledged literary theory of Arendt only spelled out when we read, as I am suggesting here, her rather idiosyncratic notion of politics as another word for literature. Partaking of, while at the same being removed from a single-minded position within the *polis*, literature is best endowed to critique fictions of the non-contingent and the limitless that come to shape political life when it turns tyrannical or totalitarian.

It might be better to more adequately and clearly define what Simon Swift calls 'limited' as the contingent or inconsistent. In *On the Nature of Totalitarianism: An Essay in Understanding* Arendt argues that 'ideologies are systems of explanation of life and world that claim to explain everything, past and future, without further concurrence with actual reality'.[29] It is quite clear that she is far from conflating fact with fiction. Politics turns totalitarian, however, when it conflates the two and in doing so renders life a lie. The lie of totalitarian politics is a consistent one. It has eradicated contingency from the social realm. As has been argued above, the inconsistence of the public realm derives from the messy and pluralistic contiguity between substance and subjectivity. Totalitarianism reduces the plurality of subjectivity to one single point of view which claims to represent the truth. Through its monopoly of power totalitarian politics sets out to eliminate everything in substantial or real life that

---

28 Ricoeur, *Onseself as Another*, translated by Kathleen Blamey, (Chicago: University of Chicago Press, 1992), p. 115.

29 Arendt, *Essays in Understanding 1930–1954: Formation, Exile, and Totalitarianism)*, edited with an introduction by Jerome Kohn (New York: Schocken, 1994), pp. 349–50.

could question or contradict its monolithic stance. Arendt explains this insidious form of politics that renders substance congruent with the fictitious as follows:

> The point here is that the ideological consistency reducing every-thing to one all-dominating factor is always in conflict with the inconsistency of the world, on the one hand, and the unpredictabil-ity of human actions, on the other. Terror is needed in order to make the world consistent and keep it that way; to dominate human beings to the point where they lose, with their spontaneity, the specific unpredictability of thought and action.[30]

Via the infliction of tremendous suffering (i.e. terror), totalitarianism forces its fictitious world view upon the world. What it proclaims to be 'truth' is nothing but an opinion and yet, through terror the fictions of opinion are capable of shaping our embodied reality, if the terror in ques-tion is all-comprehensive viz. the totalitarian within a given society. In this context, Arendt draws attention to the dark aspects within the notion of the laboratory with which Ricoeur later on attempts to fathom the ethical value of literature. She reads Nazi concentration camps as 'labo-ratories in which human beings of the most varied kinds are reduced to an always constant collection of reactions and reflexes'.[31] Ricoeur's term 'ethical laboratory' differs from the context in which Arendt uses the word. It is, however, important, to emphasize how Arendt refrains from a scientific nomenclature (to which "laboratory" belongs) to do justice to humanity's unpredictability and the world's contingency (here she writes and thinks from the perspective of Heidegger's phenomenology).

On this view, literature's inconsistency and notorious refusal to be subsumed under logical or quasi-logical formulas that would predict-ably explain it—as outcomes of laboratory research are often exhibited in terms of predictable laws of behaviour or sequences of chemical reac-tion— are key elements of its realistic truthfulness. The truthfulness at issue is, however, not merely a mimetic one. Literature does not so much represent or copy our lives but provides a mental space in which we may come to realize how our subjectivity is contiguous with our substance and vice versa. In other words literature questions the coordinates of the consistent but untrue life to which we have to conform as professionals, as family members, as functionaries or managers and so forth. It not so

---

30 Arendt, *Essays in Understanding 1930–1954*, p. 350.
31 Arendt, *Essays in Understanding 1930–1954*, p. 304.

much or it not only represents the pressure to coincide with such de-individualized roles; instead it reveals how such conformity renders our lives a lie. The rendition of life into a lie is premised on narrowing down and eliminating human diversity through the demand to behave in a predictable manner.

4.3 Literature's Critique of Fiction: Ishiguro's *Remains of the Day*

Maybe it's time that we moved on, accepted more the unpredictable, unaccountable nature of the human being, and that will be apparent at the level of form and voice and structure in the novel. Ishiguro, 'I am sorry I cannot say more' in Kazuo Ishiguro (London: Continuum), p. 117

The following concluding section discusses a novel that critiques the way reality turns fictitious if we ignore the unpredictable and forever changeable constitution of our condition. Critique does its work here in a theatre beyond representation. Kazuo Ishiguro's novel *Remains of the Day* to some extent represents traditional English society. It is, however, striking that it does so in a way that turns representation against itself. Matters represented become subject to a narrative gaze that makes visible wounds and fractures in what appears to be 'normal' and wholesome. Here we witness the split between subjectivity and substance (as discussed on a more theoretical level in the preceding section). The narration unfolds from the position of subjectivity: it is a first person narrative. More precisely, it is an unreliable narrator who conflates his subjectivity with the substance of his narration. Subjectivity here assumes the place of substance and this presumption puts reality at the risk of turning fictitious.

The narrator is at pain to establish his authority as an objective and impartial observer. He reassures us that he is in the best position to provide a substantive account of all there is. It soon becomes apparent that there is more to it than meets the eye of the narrator. The narration oscillates in a tension between the certainty of its formal presentation and the questionability of what it represents. This vacillation between certainty and uncertainty characterizes many of Ishiguro's unreliable narrators. As Sean Matthews and Sebastian Groes have put it:

A curious paradox operates within the texts [i.e. of Ishiguro]. The writing, which seems so sure of itself and never puts a foot wrong, leads the reader away from the certainties rather than, affirming them. The role of language is important within this process: it is both a source with which to construct reality while its very constructedness leads us away from any notion of 'authenticity' of that reality. Indeed, despite the clarity of Ishiguro's texts, the language sometimes becomes overstrained and constructed to the point of collapse, so that 'reality' too gives way to possibilities that are dangerous and contingent.[32]

What has not been sufficiently discussed is the way in which such collapse of our ways of perceiving and reflecting about our world plays an important social and ethical role in Ishiguro's texts and perhaps within literature more broadly speaking. On this view, literature's stylistic refinement does not remain within the text but rather collapses the boundaries that separate the text and the world. It does so not to confuse literature with reality. On the contrary the tension between formal certainty and the uncertainty of what the literary form attempts to represent brings to the fore the rather confused and unstable ground on which we tread ordinarily, on an everyday basis. The disintegration of the represented world highlights the sometimes shaky, rather fictitious matter which we take to be truthful in real life. The tension between subjectivity (first person narrator) and substance (subject matter of narration) renders apparent the way in which we may tend to cling to fictions in our everyday lives (similar to Stevens the narrative voice of *The Remains of the Day*).

Literature thus critiques fictions; fictions which we accept as certainties outside the literary realm in the fields of medicine, politics and economics (the focus of *Remains of the Day* is politics and foreign relations in the Britain of the 1930ies). In a recent interview Ishiguro has made clear that his literary skills are not focused on literature or self-enclosed reflections about literature (so called metafictions). Instead his formal mastery attempts to disrupt the illusions and delusions which may come to shape our account of ourselves and our world. Ishiguro emphasizes:

I'm personally not interested in 'metafiction', in writing books about the nature of fiction. I've got nothing against such books, but for me there are more urgent questions than the nature of fiction. So in that sense I am not interested in writing about storytelling, but I *am* interested in storytelling in the sense of what a community or a nation tells itself about its past and by implication therefore where it is at the moment and what it should be doing next.[33]

---

32 Matthews and Groes, 'Introduction: Your words open windows for me: the art of Kazuo Ishiguro' in Matthews and Groes (eds), *Kazuo Ishiguro: Contemporary Critical Perspectives*, Preface by Haruki Murakami, (London: Continuum, 2009), pp. 1–8, p. 7.

33 Ishiguro, 'I'm sorry I can't say more': 'An interview with Kazuo Ishiguro' (conducted by Matthews) in Matthews and Groes (eds), *Kazuo Ishiguro*, pp. 114–125, p. 117.

Here Ishiguro outlines his concern with literature as a social and ethical art; one that is not engaged in 'navel gazing' but instead has an important role to play in society at large. This role is certainly reflective. Reflection here turns outward and changes the way we think. Literature transforms our cognition in a non-abstract way: via storytelling. The way in which it tells stories does, however, not simply replicate a given course of action; it rather makes us critical of such replications. Its representation calls into question what is represented. In doing so it alerts us to the questionability of various stories we assume to be truthful outside the literary realm, where, we are not necessarily sensitive and sensitized to the uncertainty of what we are sometimes asked to accept as certain. Literature sheds light on the fictitious aspects of our society. It is important to emphasize that literature operates on this level not with a view to turn reality into fiction. Instead it sets out to change our thinking about as well as our interacting with what is truth and fiction in our everyday context.

Literature thus transforms our cognition by undermining (rather than simply representing) the way fictions keep us enthralled, thus paralyzing our scope for action. Literature's disruption of the fictitious has the potential to disassociate us from various forms of acting in accordance with the spirit and script of pre-formulated stories which, as the saying goes, we have bought into. Literature's disruptive force grants us the freedom and impetus to reformulate what we otherwise submit to. As we have seen throughout this book, Spinoza's critique of religion is a critique of narratives. Spinoza takes both narratives and religions seriously, because they have come to shape our society. Ishiguro sees a similar affinity between the social force of religion and fiction. He raises questions about storytelling not in literature but in politics and society. Human reality has always been shaped by stories. In previous centuries they were the stories of religion—which is the focus of Spinoza's critique of flat mimesis—and in contemporary society different media cast and broadcast various fictions which confront our lives:

The stories that people tell each other within a community , they could literally be stories, but in the modern age it would tend to be TV programmes, journalism, all of that commentary that follows every event and dresses it up for us, interprets it for us, and tells us what it might actually mean. What are the tools by which we tell these stories? What exactly are these stories that we tell ourselves? When we tell ourselves stories as a nation about why we did something, what is the motivation? What drives the process? Are we trying to be honest or are we trying to deceive, or comfort ourselves? These are very much the same questions that apply to the function of religion in society.[34]

Strikingly Ishiguro does not neglect the classic tool of hermeneutics: interpretation. Interpretation—the quasi accurate or mimetic attempt to do justice to a text or event—is implicated in fiction making. The telling us of what an event 'might actually mean', is part of the motivation that drives a particular storyline in modern media culture. So is the interpretative act of public memory. What interests Ishiguro in all these hermeneutic and mimetic endeavours of our contemporary society is their potentially illusionary and self-deluding quality. Literature does not merely represent such societal self-delusions: instead it detects these illusions as what they are: fictions that have become reality but need not be part of reality.

Literature offers us a choice to either continue to live these fictions or to sever our subservience to them, thus changing our cognition and potentially our behaviour. As Hélène Machinal has shown, Ishiguro's *When we were Orphans* establishes an intriguing equation between 'detection and fiction.'[35] I would revise Machinal formulation and would argue that it is precisely fiction which literature detects in our 'real world'. Similar to Spinoza's critique of religion, literature's critique of fiction is not hostile to its subject matter. The writer does not dismiss our need for emotional attachment, for comfort and for narratives—be they religious or secular. Indeed the stories of literature are about how stories can be either an honest attempt to come to terms with suffering, failure and other forms of mishap or can, by contrast, perpetuate the narratives that were conducive to the concurrence of these as well as other calamities.

Literature represents the ways in which we deleteriously buy into representations. How representations take over our lives. How we turn into empty vessels to be filled by life stories which ruin our lives. Ishiguro describes his work as a critique of such passivity where we attempt to become copies of a flat and mimetic story line. This is particularly true of his *Remains of the Day*. Ishiguro elaborates as follows:

'Many of my' character tend to go with the flow, and even an outsider like Stevens in *The Remains of the Day* to some extent isn't an outsider. He's deeply somebody who thinks like a member of

---

34 Ishiguro, 'I'm sorry I can't say more': *An interview with Kazuo Ishiguro*, pp. 117–18.

35 Machinal '*When we were Orphans*: Narration and Detection in the Case of Christopher Banks' in Matthews and Groes (eds), *Kazuo Ishiguro*, pp. 79–90, p. 88.

his class, and he can't quite get out of that. I started writing *The Remains of the Day* because of my suspicion that to some extent we are all in some sense butlers. We don't stand outside of our milieu and evaluate it. We don't say, 'Wait, we're going to do it this way instead'. We take our orders, we do our jobs, we accept our place in the hierarchy, and hope that our loyalty is used well, just like this butler guy.[36]

The novel has been read as a study in repression which it certainly is. However, this is not its main subject matter (though it has become just that in the Hollywood film *The Remains of the Day*). Neither is it a historical novel: as Barry Lewis has pointed out, 'Ishiguro does not intend the England he presents there to be a historically accurate portrait'.[37] *The Remains of the Day* thematically fits into Ishiguro's oeuvre with its focus on how we become passive copies of roles, fashions or ideals—the stories gathered together in his most recent *Nocturnes* continue this theme revolving around the social pressure to hide (via cosmetic surgery and other fashionable devices) aging and the marks it leaves. A sign of this passivity is the longing for a fusion of subjectivity and substance. This holds true of *The Remains of the Day* where the 'I' of narration claims to represent its substance. The first person narrator establishes his authority as a quasi adequate copy of one of its main themes: Englishness.

The first part of the novel—entitled Salisbury—claims to represent 'all there is' without any distortions such as exaggeration might bring about. The narrator presents himself and his English heritage in terms of objectivity, professionalism and calmness. Even the English landscape surfaces as perfect representation of Englishness, of the famous stiff upper lip. The narrator elaborates:'I would say that it is the very *lack* of obvious drama or spectacle that sets the beauty of our land apart. What is pertinent is the calmness of that beauty, its sense of restraint'.[38] This 'sense of restraint' serves as a guarantee of accurate representation and the narrator appeals to his reader's ideal position as 'objective viewer'.[39] The 'I' announced at the beginning of the quote profiles itself as non-subjective, as a model of restraint, keeping subjectivity at bay.

The narrator is a butler, Stevens, who devotes his life to the idea of service and loyalty. This might be in keeping with the hierarchical ethos

36 Ishiguro, 'I'm sorry I can't say more': *An interview with Kazuo Ishiguro*, p. 115.

37 Lewis, *Kazuo Ishiguro*, Contemporary World Writers Series, (Manchester: Manchester University Press, 2000), p. 78.

38 Ishiguro, *Remains of the Day*, (London: Faber and Faber, 1989), pp. 28–29.

39 Ishiguro, *Remains of the Day*, p. 29.

of traditional values as they have come to shape class society in the United Kingdom. Much of Stevens's letters elaborate on the exclusive importance of reproducing traditional English ideas in the servitude to a master, who, in this case, is Lord Darlington. So far we might call the narrator a conservative who attempts to be faithful to the ideals that has shaped the life of his family and his country over centuries. The narrative voice clings to the innocence of tradition and yet the substance of the narration itself radically calls this innocence into question.

Representation here turns against itself: we cannot trust the narrator's authoritative judgments and ideals the further we delve into the novel. The tone of the novel is thus ironic: it says more than what it says, and what it says is not what it seems. In a sense there is an irony of irony in the self-defeat of representation: the narrator claims to be professional to the point of having moved beyond the sphere of subjectivity and yet the internal inconsistency of what he represents is precisely its consistency. Another word for this consistency is the certainty of representation. The subject matter of representation is, however, highly inconsistent and ethically dubious. In his letters Stevens presents himself as the perfect representative of what a butler and good Englishman is. Indeed he defines himself not as an individual but as the copy of a specific ideal type: that of the butler per se.

Stevens aims to be a copy of a copy. He tries to incarnate the butler persona, which has been that of his father. His father lived the life of flat mimesis by presumably becoming flat at once with the image of a professional English servant. After having narrated a brief story of the exemplary life of his father, Stevens comments on the representative truth-value of this episode of loyalty and professional service: 'In any case, it is of little importance whether or not this story is true; the significant thing is, of course, what it reveals concerning my father's ideals. For when I look back over his career, I can see with hindsight that he must have striven throughout his years somehow to *become* that butler of his story'.[40] The word 'become' is emphasised in the original and rightly so, because, within this context, the verb delineates the movement towards congruence of an individual with the copy of an already drawn image or already established storyline.

There is even a fictional society that guard over such standard. Stevens mentions the Hayes society—the guardians of conformity—as the objective guide by which to measure his father's successful representation of his role not as a literary character but as a person alive. He appeals to his reader to take his words literally concerning the accuracy of the literal

---

40 Ishiguro, *Remains of the Day*, p. 37.

copy of a butler which his father surely has become as guaranteed by the judgment of the Hayes society: 'I hope you will agree that in these two instances [i.e. as provided by two anecdotes about his father's exemplary service] I have cited from his career—both of which I have corroborated and believe to be accurate—my father not only manifests, but comes close to being the personification itself, of what the Hayes Society terms 'dignity in keeping with his position.' Dignity here denotes the complete coincidence of personality with a copy of a pre-given, standardized role: Steven's father lives the life not of his subjectivity; instead he attempts to immerse and abolish his subjectivity in the substantive role of his profession. As a literary character (the protagonist of the two 'instances' or episodes to which the quote above refers) he is not so much a distinct individual; rather his being 'comes close to' the non-personal personification of a role.

The literary representation is itself a representation; the doubling at work here ironically outdoes the flatness of the copying process. Stevens consistently describes the workings of flat mimesis when he says that a butler has to inhabit the role of the butler story (which of course has also been that of his father): 'A butler of any quality must be seen to *inhabit* his role, utterly and fully; he cannot be seen casting it aside one moment simply to don it again the next as though it were nothing more than a pantomime costume.'[41] Here Stevens implicitly rejects any possible criticism of his lack of independent thinking vis-à-vis the expulsion of Jewish refugees by his master. We will discuss the role of anti-Semitism and Nazism within the novel at the end of this chapter. Here it is important to emphasize that Stevens appraises his representative role model as a changeless one; as one that does not reflect upon the aging of time.

There is a tension between this fictional ideal of constancy or loyalty and change unfolding with the passing or, in other words, aging of the narration. The substance of this representative life becomes increasingly troubling throughout the course of the novel that consists precisely of these representative letters of Stevens addressed to someone who presumably should become yet another copy of the 'perfect servant' (a butler in waiting as it were). At the end of the first part of the novel there is a hint of trouble to come when Stevens equates the virtue of restraint with the superiority of 'the English race'.[42] Stevens proclaims that by virtue of their dignity and restraint the English are superior to foreigners: 'In a word, 'dignity' is beyond such person. We English have an important

---

41 Ishiguro, *Remains of the Day*, p. 169.
42 Ishiguro, *Remains of the Day*, p. 43.

advantage over foreigners in this respect and it is for this reason that when you think of a great butler, he is bound, almost by definition, to be an Englishman'.[43] The irony is that the novel's underlying theme—rather than that of Englishness—is our universal butler-like propensity to serve as tool within a grander storyline. The novel critiques our liability to pliability—to becoming substanceless subjects that assume roles like those of Stevens; and thus presume to be subjectless representations of substance.

The role of Stevens as representative of a butler's 'greatness' becomes more troubling within the course of the narration. We learn that within the thirties the main part of his service is dedicated to the appeasement and support of Nazi Germany. His master—Lord Darlington—attempts to do the gentlemanly thing by 'assisting' a former and seemingly vanquished enemy. Lord Darlington explains his ethics of the gentleman as follows: 'It is unbecoming to go on hating an enemy like this once a conflict is over. Once you've got a man on the canvas, that ought to be the end of it. You don't then proceed to kick him.'[44] This approach may be apposite the Weimar Republic but certainly not apropos the Third Reich.

Lord Darlington seems to realize some form of change from one to the other (from the Weimar Republic to the Third Reich). Rather than adapting to this change of Germany's political circumstances, he, however, extols Nazism's novelty over the outmoded model of democracy. This is strange and very inconsistent indeed: Lord Darlington, the novel's representative of old English upper class virtues, conscientiously and consciously extols Nazism's break with tradition. In this way he complains to Stevens about England's agedness:'We're really so slow in this country to recognize when a thing's outmoded. Other great nations know full well that to meet the challenges of each new age means discarding old, sometimes well-loved methods.'[45] Such well-loved methods would be the Biblical prohibition against killing and the liberal secular undertaking not to discriminate against people on the basis of religion, ethnicity or disability. Here is a clear instance of the clash between the formal certainty of narration and the dubiousness of what is represented. Lord Darlington seems to represent the traditional English gentleman and yet in his espousal of Nazism he clearly does away with an 'aged English democracy' in favour of Nazi totalitarianism: 'Always the last to be clinging on to outmoded systems. But sooner or later, we'll need to face

---

43 Ibid.

44 Ishiguro, *Remains of the Day*, p. 87.

45 Ishiguro, *Remains of the Day*, p. 197.

up to the fact. Democracy is something for a bygone era.'[46] How does this square with traditional English virtues?

Lord Darlington's son Reginald Cardinal attempts to alert Stevens to the danger of betraying political age (democracy) for the apparent youth and health of the new (Nazism) saying that his father is 'being manoeuvred. The Nazis are manoeuvring him like a pawn'.[47] Stevens, however, clings to his story line, extolling Lord Darlington as 'a gentleman, a true, old English gentleman'.[48] Both Lord Darlington and his obedient servant Stevens reject an ethics of resilience which, as has been discussed in the introduction to this book, is capable of resisting nefarious changes by precisely engaging with and understanding how matters are evolving. Reginald Cardinal seems to be aware of this destructive as well as self-destructive rejection of resilience in both his father and Stevens. He berates Stevens for his lack of curiosity, for his refusal to take into account the changed circumstance of a Germany that has become a Nazi state: 'Are you not, at least, *curious* about what I am saying' he asks him and goes on to mention the changed political reality: 'No one with good judgment could persist in believing anything Herr Hitler says after the Rhineland, Stevens.'[49] It is this lack of curiosity that keeps Stevens stuck in his role where he is unable to depart from the fiction—or set storyline— his life has become.

Against this background it is worth asking whether Kwame Anthony Appiah's philosophical appraisal of Stevens as representative of *The Ethics of Identity* does not stand on rather unstable ground. Appiah appreciates Stevens's dedication to Lord Darlington in terms of an authentic identity that combines tradition with individualism: 'Mr Stevens's individuality is far from arbitrary because it is a role that had developed within a tradition, a role that makes sense within a certain social world: a social world that no longer exists, as it happens, which is one of many reasons why none of us wants to be a butler in the way Stevens was.'[50] As we have seen, Stevens's narrative does not make sense: it depicts the way in which his 'tradition' self-destructs by not keeping ahead of its time.

Aging needs change (see the discussion in Chapter 1) but the change in question must be a circumspect one that is aware of why and how it does what it does. Ishiguro has made it clear that *The Remains of the Day* is not only about Stevens, the butler, but, also metaphorically, about us

---

46 Ishiguro, *Remains of the Day*, p. 198.
47 Ishiguro, *Remains of the Day*, p. 222.
48 Ishiguro, *Remains of the Day*, p. 223.
49 Ishiguro, *Remains of the Day*, p. 225.
50 Appiah, *The Ethics of Identity*, (Princeton, NJ: Princeton University Press, 2005), p. 16.

being 'all in some sense butlers.' In this metaphorical sense, the service is a dedication to a storyline or fiction out which we refuse to step—similar to Stevens's refusal to step out of Lord Darlington's plot. Literature makes us aware of the fictitious nature of our services and missions in the 'real world'. Appiah has defended Stevens against any charge of being a butler in the metaphorical sense which Ishiguro has in mind, protesting: Stevens's 'conservatism is decidedly not that of conformity'.[51] As we have seen, Ishiguro has emphasized that in his conception Stevens is not a conservative outsider but someone who goes with the flow. For a discussion of a truly revolutionary conservatism that goes against the flow and gives birth to a less harmful world while preserving all that has been excluded or marginalized in the old one, we need to turn to the literature as well as the theory and poetry of romanticism. This will be the task of the following two chapters.

---

51 Appiah, *The Ethics of Identity*, p. 13.

5 The Birth of Literature

5.1 From the Market Economy of the Romantic Genius to Art's Disruption of the Status Quo

'This anxiety is grounded in the idea of creating a sovereign textual subject, one which purports to double mimetically the authoritative and self-contained subjectivity of the author'. The cult of the individual, then, and its concomitant insistence on uniqueness are at work long before the rise of the bourgeoisie and are implicit in any originary economy. The early European romantics (Friedrich von Schlegel, Novalis, Wackenroder, and Tieck in Germany; Coleridge and Wordsworth in England) did, however, articulate the notion of 'original genius,' which, as several scholars have noted, complicated things immensely if only because the great literati were required to demonstrate both originality and genius in spontaneous and utterly convincing ways recognizable only to literary criticism. What emerges in the requirements for greatness in literary authorship is a paradox: the demand for spontaneous creativity on the one hand (proof of natural "genius"), and a work ethic that insists upon earning acquired goods or status on the other.[1]

Romantic literature has been predominantly interpreted within the traditional context of mimesis. The quote above highlights a shift of mimetic representation in early romanticism: the focus on representing the poet's originality which increasingly becomes associated, if not equated, with both economic value and the moralistic worthiness of work within a growing capitalist system. The paradox in question is the clash between the artist's individualistic and natural "genius" and the conformity to the work ethic of bourgeois society.

Mimesis is the common thread that combines these seemingly paradoxical opposites. The work of the natural "genius" is a copy of his or her inner depth and the representation of the psychic profundity of the individual is precisely its economic value: the proof of its genial individuality

---

1 Meltzer, *Hot Property: The Stakes and Claims of Literary Originality*, (Chicago: University of Chicago Press, 1994), p. 4.

is the value of its exchange rate in the market place. As we have seen in Chapter 3, the eighteenth century witnessed a shift in the meaning of truth, knowledge and mimesis: the verification as well as representation of truth is no longer significantly informed by traditional religion and metaphysical philosophy. From now on global markets decide what is worthy of knowledge for an expanding population.

The markets select who is a genius (or a celebrity) but paradoxically the mark of genius precisely consists in the spontaneous and creative break with market expectations. This paradox calls into question the individuality of the natural "genius", unmasking it as being grounded within bourgeois norms at the exact moment at which it flaunts these standards of conformity. That is to say, by deviating from common standards through a startling stance of instantiating "genius", it becomes attractive to the general public and in so doing confirms to the general rules of the 'original and thus valuable work', thereby conforming to the work ethic of capitalist society in general.

This book does not take issue with mimesis as such. Indeed it acknowledges its importance for literary studies. There is of course no such thing as an accurate copy: the representation always differs from what is represented. The moot point is, however, the posited ideal of a coincidence between the sign and signified. This coincidence of the sign and signified—or, in other words, of subjectivity and substance— seems to fulfil the promise held out by flat mimesis, as practiced by the advertisement industry and as satirized in the TV series *Mad Men* (see Chapter 1).

The relation between representation and what is represented has also informed divergent approaches to literature from Aristotle to Paul de Man. Erich Auerbach's masterly study *Mimesis* has traced the divergent lines of this understanding of literary studies. Auerbach's concern is mainly historical: a given text under discussion tends to represent the historical context which gave rise to it. In this way, Dante represents not so much his conception of the Inferno, the Purgatory or Paradise but takes 'earthly historicity into his beyond'.[2] In a classic study of romanticism, M. H.Abrams has developed this mimetic paradigm, which, arguably, Auerbach has defined, in a different direction: Abrams's *The Mirror and the Lamp* places the emphasis on the representation of the poet's inner life. As the above quote (from Meltzer's *Hot Property*) shows, this increasing focus on the artist's genius-like individuality has come to characterize the substance of mimesis in romanticism.

---

2 Auerbach, *Mimesis: The Representation of Reality in Western Literature*, translated by Willard R. Trask, (Princeton, NJ: Princeton University Press, 1953), p. 193.

The mirror in the title of Abrams's book denotes the mirroring of the external world, which is mainly the subject matter of Auerbach's *Mimesis*, whereas the lamp illuminates the inward life of the writer. The lamp sheds light on the psyche of the poet and the poem represents this inward scene which is not to be seen from the simple mirror perspective on the common world of the everyday. Abrams indeed points out the congruency of the romantic perspective with the twentieth century discovery of psychoanalysis. In this vein, Abrams characterizes one strand of romanticism as 'disguised wish-fulfilment',[3] Another strand is more conservatively preoccupied with revealing the writer's 'moral character'.[4] That aside, Abrams detects in romanticism a radicalization and culmination of the always present but latent 'doctrines which imply some limited correspondence between the nature of the artist and the nature of his production'.[5] Whether it functions as a mirror or as a lamp, literary criticism has tended to be concerned with the forms of representations.

This chapter prepares for an analysis of Benjamin's reading of the romantic poet Hölderlin in the following chapter. The argument advanced here does not attempt to break with mimesis as such but aims to draw attention to a so far neglected element that we shall uncover in a close reading of Benjamin's early essay on *Two Poems by Friedrich Hölderlin* (see the following chapter). This essay has been rather marginalized in theoretical discussions of romanticism.[6] Benjamin's interpretation of Hölderlin is significant for an innovative reading of romanticism: he emphasizes the public relevance of art while affirming its autonomy. In so doing Benjamin shifts critical attention away from the focus on the lamp-like illumination of the poet's profound interiority toward the socially liberating potential of romantic poetry. He insists on the poem's detachment from the status quo. It is precisely this radical disconnection between art and society that has the capacity to release us from the stifling confinement of harmful practises that have become normative (Blake's 'mind-forged manacles'). As Paul Celan's reading of Hölderlin shows, this disjuncture between art and society may go under the name of madness.

---

3   Abrams, *The Mirror and the Lamp: Romantic Theory and the Critical Tradition*, (Oxford: Oxford University Press, 1953), p. 147.

4   Abrams, *The Mirror and the Lamp*, p. 229.

5   Ibid.

6   A curious exemplification of this marginalization is Andrew Bowie's study *From Romanticism to Critical Theory*. Bowie invokes the title of Benjamin's Hölderlin essay only to quote a part from this essay that is concerned with a Novalis quote within this essay and then quickly moves on. See Bowie's *From Romanticism to Critical Theory: The Philosophy of German Literary Theory*, (London: Routledge, 1997), p. 195.

Here, however, madness has a healing potential that makes possible human flourishing, liberating the derogatory term of 'mental illness' from its clinical denomination.

Madness in this sense offers a fortuitous break from the status quo. Benjamin separates the work's originality from the work ethic that dominates our and his society.[7] The poem's novelty neither mirrors the societal expectation of genial profundity nor does it replicate society's obsession with youth, originality and outdoing competitors for the first place. Instead of mirroring or re-enforcing aspects of the existing cosmos or the existing inner life of the poet, the poem creates a new one. As a new creation it breaks with conventions, rules and forms of exclusion. It thus releases us from a competitive work ethic and a hierarchical stratification of relationship. This is romantic poetry's social benefit: one not premised so much on traditional understandings of mimesis (either as mirror or as lamp) as on the principle of birth or natality.

Can a similar kind of nascent theory of literature be detected in the work of Martin Heidegger and Paul de Man? The approaches of these two thinkers are indeed related. We will see how Martin Heidegger and following him Paul de Man remain caught in a representational framework. Jerome McGann has argued that de Man accepts 'referential verification as the norm of truth'.[8] De Man's influential approach towards the study of romanticism has indeed been shaped by Husserl's, Heidegger's and Sartre's phenomenology which is grounded in the notion of intentionality. Intentionality denotes a state of consciousness and 'consciousness is never pure consciousness, but is always consciousness *of* something'.[9] In this way it aims to mirror that of which it is conscious. De Man analyzes the ways in which such intention of mimesis fails and keeps failing in romantic literature. He thus 'sees language as a form of

---

7   As Meltzer has put it: 'In what we loosely refer to as Western culture, work is inextricably tied to the notion of identity. The connection already appears in the Church fathers (acedia prevents you from doing your duty, thus from participating in the divine good, in allowing the full development of the soul). It is clearly in Hegel: the slave in that dialectic ultimately becomes master because he *produces*; while the master, who can only consume, becomes prey to melancholy.' Meltzer, *Hot Property*, p. 150.

8   McGann, *Social Values and Poetic Acts: The Historical Judgment of Literary Work*, (Cambridge, Mass.: Harvard University Press, 1988), p. 3. For a critique of McGann's criticism of de Man see Seán Burke's *The Death and Return of the Author: Criticism and Subjectivity in Barthes, Foucault and Derrida*, (Edinburgh: Edinburgh University Press, 1992), p. 203.

9   Tilottama Rajan, 'Displacing Post-Structuralism: Romantic Studies after Paul de Man,' in *Studies in Romanticism* (24) (Winter, 1985): pp. 451-474 (458).

desire enmeshed in its own de-realization'.[10] This chapter will show another avenue to the study of romanticism one that is not ensnared by representation, realization and de-realization. The poem here does not so much aim at a mimetic form of realization but performs a new creation. It does not so much mirror consciousness and its objects of contemplation but sets out to change the coordinates of consciousness. As such it does not operate like a mirror or a lamp but as an interruption with existing forms of consciousness. The new cosmos created by poetry helps preserve aspects of our history and of our contemporary world but it does so in changed form. This change of form is of course already part of traditional types of representation, however, it is crucial that the emphasis here lies not with capturing something existent (in whatever mutated shape within its representational realization) but on transformation. We are thus concerned with a shift from existence (things as they are) to insistence (action to change things as they are for the good of the society).

5.2 A New Cosmos of Poetry—Walter Benjamin's Alternative to Martin Heidegger's and Paul de Man's Approach to Literature and its Implications for Cultural Studies (Slavoj Žižek)

The topic of this and the following chapter is the relationship between poetry and philosophy. It focuses on Benjamin's, Celan's and Heidegger's respective readings of Hölderlin. This is no doubt a much traversed field of inquiry. It nevertheless warrants further attention and rethinking. Why is this so? Partly because of the enigmatic character of Benjamin's early (1914-1915) essay *Two poems by Friedrich Hölderlin* which saw the light of publication posthumously in Gershom Scholem's and T. W. Adorno's first edition of his essays (1955). Stanley Corngold has described Benjamin's 'proud refusal to produce immediate insight or aesthetic pleasure'.[11] He characterizes the essay as 'hieratic, cryptic, and high-flown'.[12] What has not been sufficiently discussed is how this cryptic and high-flown style has a significant bearing on its content matter.

Why does the author refuse to yield to the reader the simple gratification of immediate insight? I will analyze how this stylistic gesture of refusal partly enacts Benjamin's idiosyncratic political stance as implicitly articulated in this essay. As we will see this early stance in fact shapes Benjamin's extraordinary understanding of communism in his major

10 Rajan, 'Displacing Post-Structuralism', 454.
11 Benjamin, *Collected Writings. Vol 1*, (ed.) By Marcus Bullock and Michael W. Jennings, (Cambridge Mass.: The Belknap Press of Harvard University Press, 1996), p. 36.
12 Ibid.

treatise 'The Work of Art in the Age of Mechanical Reproduction'. One of the main wagers of the argument developed in the following discussion is that Benjamin's early philosophical, or, as he calls it, 'aesthetic' work on Hölderlin (and then of course on romanticism in general as the topic of his doctoral dissertation) contributed to, what I have called elsewhere, his 'political romanticism'.[13] This term is provocative and runs counter to Philippe Lacoue-Labarthe's recent take on Heidegger's and Benjamin's respective encounters with Hölderlin's poetry.

In what appear to be stark terms Lacoue-Labarthe opposes Heidegger as a romantic with Benjamin as a modernist. He goes so far to equate Heidegger's Nazism with the essence of romanticism saying plainly 'Heidegger's poetico-political program is virtually indistinguishable from the Romantic program'.[14] The equation of National Socialism with Romanticism seems to be quite persistent,[15] and a more nuanced discussion of Benjamin's approach towards Hölderlin's poerty and its divergence from Heidegger's is crucial for a better understanding of diverse issues that lie at the heart of both the Enlightenment and Romanticism.[16] Far from being an uncritical defender of modernity, Benjamin insists on poetry as a self-sufficient yet incomplete form that resists various attempts at appropriation by modern ideologies.

The work of art's incompletion is a major theme in his thesis on the romantic notion of criticism.[17] It is this element of the incomplete that seems to call into question aesthetic autonomy: art does not speak on its own or, to be more precise, it only speaks fragmentarily when it speaks on its own and as a fragment it appears to ask for the endless work of interpretation, which is the task of criticism. In his early Hölderlin essay, Benjamin grounds the notion of the unfinished not so much in the relationship between art and its

---

13 See Mack, 'Modernity as an Unfinished Project: Benjamin and Political Romanticism' in Andrew Benjamin and Charles Rice (eds), *Walter Benjamin and the Architecture of Modernity*, (Melbourne: re.press, 2009), pp. 59–75.

14 Lacoue-Labarthe, *Heidegger and the Politics of Poetry*, translated and with an introduction by Jeff Fort, (Urbana: University of Illinois Press, 2007), p. 86.

15 Starting with Max Rouché's introduction to J. G. Herder' *Une autre philosophie de l'histoire*, bilingual edition, trans Rouché, (Aubier: Éditions Montaigne, 1943) romanticism has often been associated with Nazism.

16 For further discussion of this point see Mack's *Spinoza and the Specters of Modernity: the hidden Enlightenment of Diversity from Spinoza to Freud*, (New York: Continuum, 2010).

17 For a discussion of this topic see both Andrew Benjamin's *Disclosing Spaces: on Painting*, (Manchesters: Clinamen Press, 2004), pp. 1-14 and Andrew Benjamin's *Style and Time: Essays on the Politics of Appearance*, (Evanston, Illinois: Northwestern University Press, 2006), pp. 5–39.

criticism but within the infinite unfolding of what he calls the 'poetic law'. The 'poetic law' is a law that seems to be enclosed within the hermetic structure of the work and yet is not so much a self-enclosed hermetic principle but a transformative force: 'Only the power of transformation will make it clear and appropriate to declare that the poetic law has not yet fulfilled itself in this Hölderlinian world'.[18] The poem is self-enclosed and at the same time incomplete, that is to say, in need of transformation. At this point the transformation in question does not concern the relationship to an outside world (the poem and its different readings in works of criticism), but rather denotes the different stages of its composition. Indeed Benjamin compares two versions of the same poem—an earlier and a later one—to exemplify the self-enclosed process of poetic transformation. This sounds like an attempt at a philological analysis of literary composition. This impression is deceptive: at the opening of his essay Benjamin makes clear that his concern is not that of philology but aesthetics.

Aesthetics, at least from Benjamin's perspective, is a sub-discipline not of literary criticism but of philosophy. As a sub-discipline of philosophy it is concerned not so much with the genesis of a text but with its "truth". This pre-occupation with the truth of a work of art characterizes both Benjamin's and Heidegger's approach toward Hölderlin, in particular, and to poetry, in general. Their respective understandings of truth differ, though, as we shall see. This difference in their respective approaches towards what truth is in literature has important ramifications for their divergent interpretations of art's relationship to politics and society. In contrast to Heidegger, Benjamin discusses the truth of poetry within an intra-poetic sphere that seems to be detached from the conflicting demands and exclusionary pressures of competing political truth claims. Rather than addressing an extra-aesthetic realm, the poem ostensibly traces the development of its idiosyncratic itinerary:

> This sphere, which for every poem has a special configuration, is characterized as the poetized [*das Gedichtete*]. In this sphere, that peculiar domain containing the truth of the poem shall be opened up. This "truth," which the most serious artists so insistently claim for their creations, shall be understood as the objectivity of their production, as the fulfilment of the artistic task in each case.[19]

There seems to be a progressive development of truth, a *telos* of some sort, but crucially this teleology resides within the work of art rather than

---

18 Benjamin, *Collected Writings. Vol 1*, p. 24.
19 Benjamin, *Collected Writings. Vol 1*, pp. 19–20.

representing, as mimetic principle (or principle of mimesis), some external progress—be that the progress of history or that of a people or an economic system or science or political idea.

Benjamin's break with ideas of mimesis and representation is significant. My reading of Benjamin offers a new perspective on literary theory as well as on central issues within the emergent field of medical humanities. While literature's medical or healing capacity has often been understood in terms of the mimetic preservation of what is or has been, Benjamin emphasizes poetry's revolutionary potential, which he interprets as the non-commoditized promise of modern technology in his late essay 'The Work of Art in the Age of Mechanical Reproduction.' Diverging from the mimetic approach that tends to conceptualize literature as continuous representation of the past and the present, Benjamin's nascent theory of literature provides a novel perspective on art: as a break away from the continuity of harmful practices. As we shall see, Benjamin perceives the poem as a form of birth. It creates a new cosmos that differs radically from the societal structures that have shaped human history.

In my reading, Benjamin emphasizes literature's non-representational dimension, to appreciate it as a birth of the new and discontinuing. On this view, literature's reparative or healing work is not so much mimetic but nascent: it provides a mental space where humanity can truly flourish. What I call a nascent theory of literature differs from the so far prevailing mimetic one in that it does not subordinate the literary to the historical or economic or the political but rather makes it the ground for a radical re-conceptualisation of other disciplines (i.e. history, politics, economics etc.). Within the twentieth century, the mimetic approach to literature has largely been shaped by hermeneutics and phenomenology. Mimesis is a form of interpretation: by representing the world we interpret it. Poetry and its criticism engage in the interpretation of human existence. This is exactly Heidegger's approach to the philosophy of literature.

Heidegger has indeed had a tremendous impact on literary theory and criticism. He has shaped various modern and postmodern readings of literature. Let me briefly discuss his influence on a critic who has played an important role within the English reception of Hölderlin, in particular, and of romanticism, in general: Paul de Man. He has argued that 'poetic language interests Heidegger because it is not less but more rigorous than the philosopher's, having a clearer consciousness of its own interpretative function'.[20] He goes on to define humanity as the

---

20 Paul de Man, 'Heidegger Reconsidered' in de Man, *Critical Writings 1953-1978*, edited and introduced by Lindsay Waters, (Minneapolis: University of Minnesota Press, 1989), pp. 102–106 (p. 105).

'being that interprets itself by means of language'. As Karl Marx understood, interpretation is a form of representation. Traditional philosophy has interpreted the world, but Marx set out not so much to interpret as to analyze and change the world. As he put in *The German Ideology*, 'in reality and for the *practical* materialist, i.e. the *communist*, it is a question of revolutionizing the existing world, of practically attacking and changing existing things'.[21] Marx is of course concerned with economics. Benjamin attempted to do something similar for literature and art.

What I call a nascent literary theory shifts the emphasis from questions of mimesis, representation and interpretation, to a re-conceptualization of literature as creating a new cosmos that has the potential to disrupt the continuity of harm and suffering within the existing one. It differs from the prevailing approach that has been shaped by Heideggerians such as Paul de Man, who have established a mimetic link between the non-literary act and its literary/philosophical interpretation. Interpretation helps preserve what is and has been. As Paul de Man avers apropos of the poetry of Wordsworth and Hölderlin:

> 'It is thus possible for certain poetry to achieve the transition from the Titans to the interiority of interpretation, and to preserve in itself the traces of both these elements'. The heroic and the prophetic elements that are found in many romantic poets derive from this Titanic origin. But poetry never allows this power to rush blindly to meet the unknown future of death. It turns back upon itself and becomes part of a temporal dimension that strives to remain bound to the earth, and that replaces the violent temporality (*reissende Zeit*) of action with the sheltering temporality (*schützende Zeit*) of interpretation.[22]

Through its various rhetorical figures—as analyzed by de Man in *Allegories of Reading*—literature attempts to achieve an interpretative feat of preservation. From this Heideggerian perspective, literature does not break away from but offers a ground for established forms of selfhood.

Literature as representation struggles with the gap that opens between signifier and signified, between the thing and its image, between the act and its interpretation: 'To the extent that language is figure (or metaphor, or *prosopopeia*) it is indeed not the thing itself but its representation, the

---

21 Robert C. Tucker (ed.), *The Marx-Engels Reader*, Second Edition, (New York: Norton, 1978), p. 169.

22 Paul de Man, 'Wordsworth and Hölderlin,' in de Man *The Rhetoric of Romanticism*, (New York: Columbia University Press, 1984), pp. 47–65 (63).

picture of the thing and, as such, it is silent, mute as pictures are mute'.[23] The represented face appears to be a defacement of the original face of which it aims to be a copy but with which it cannot fully coincide and thus fails to be an exact equivalent. Radically departing from this mimetic approach to art, Benjamin does not mourn the gulf dividing the thing and its image. Indeed he argues against any attempts at such mimetic endeavours.

5.3 Excursus: Agamben, Doctorow, and the Biopolitics of Representation

Benjamin's critique of representation has important repercussions for a new understanding of politics because as Giorgio Agamben has shown there is a biopolitical agenda that informs the demand to form an identity via representative strategies. It is in the interest of the state to pin down our behaviour—to anticipate it, as it were—via the recognition of our various self-representations. In other words, mimesis is closely associated not only with the act of torture (as discussed in Chapter 2) but also with the aimed outcome of this act: the confession where an identity is re-confirmed (yes, I am a witch or a Catholic, Muslim, Protestant, or Jew and so forth).

According to Agamben, the biopolitics of the state cannot endure the presence of the unrepresentable: 'But what the state cannot tolerate in any way is that singularities form a community without claiming an identity, that human beings co-belong without a representable condition of belonging (being Italian, working-class, Catholic, terrorist etc.)'.[24] In order to subject life to the commands and demands of a political programme, the state asks us to represent ourselves in terms of clearly defined identities which it can use to play off one against the other. By identifying ourselves with a fixed and clearly marked category, we represent ourselves. In so doing, we reproduce ourselves as mimetic equivalents of the category under whose rubric we subject our life.

In this act of identification and representation, we abandon our singularity and turn into a clearly identifiable and thus controllable entity. Agamben analyzes the counterintuitive move by which processes of identification and representation do not enhance but diminish human plurality. Our membership within a given group is a copy of that group's

---

23 Paul de Man, 'Autobiography as defacement,' in de Man *The Rhetoric of Romanticism*, pp. 67–81 (80).

24 Agamben, *Means without Ends. Notes on Politics*, translated by Vincenzo Binetti and Cesare Casarino, Minneapolis: University of Minnesota Press, 2000, p. 87.

posited identity. We turn into such copy and thus abandon our singularity and non-conformity. The act of representation thus undermines what Agamben calls the '*factum pluralitatis*—a term etymological related to *populous*, with which I would like to indicate the simple fact that human beings form a community'.[25] Following Arendt's understanding of politics as another name for human plurality (and as I have maintained in the present book, another word for literature), Agamben relates the notion of people not to an issue of identity but community. Singularities constitute community thus understood. The notion of the *popuolus* from which plurality etymologically derives is ambiguous. One meaning of the term people denotes 'a fragmentary multiplicity of needy and excluded bodies'.[26] This is what Agamben has in mind when he talks about communality: a non-consistent and non-identifiable group which in its non-identity is truly plural (having many diverse shapes and outlooks).

There is, however, also a biopolitical connotation within the term people which is 'the total state of the sovereign and integrated citizens'.[27] The integrated citizen is the biopolitical subject of the sovereign. The act of subjection is one of representation: citizens integrate themselves by giving notice of themselves as copies of already defined, predictable and controllable given identities. Once people as integrated citizens break away from the closure inherent in their representative identities, they become communities of the singular which pose a threat to biopolitical control.

This is precisely what Agamben sees in the Chinese student protest at Tiananmen square:

'In Tiananmen, the state found itself facing something that could not and did not want to be represented, but that presented itself nonetheless as a community and as a common life.' The threat the state is not willing to come to terms with is precisely the fact that the unrepresentable should exist and form a community without either presuppositions or conditions of belonging (just like Cantor's inconsistent multiplicity). The whatever singularity—this singularity that wants to take possession of belonging itself as well as of its own being-into-language, and that thus declines any identity and any condition of belonging—is the new, nonsubjective, and socially inconsistent protagonist of the coming politics.[28]

25 Agamben, *Means without Ends. Notes on Politics*, p. 66.
26 Agamben, *Means without Ends. Notes on Politics*, p. 31.
27 Ibid.
28 Agamben, *Means without Ends. Notes on Politics*, p. 89.

Within a psychoanalytical context, Agamben's 'nonsubjective, and socially inconsistent protagonist' would be the father who refuses to assume the socially ordained role model of fatherhood. Žižek has argued that there is an inevitable gap between the term father and its presumed representatives in the social world: '"the real father" is a miserable individual obliged to sustain the burden of the Name of the Father, never adequate to his symbolic mandate, and so forth'.[29] This sense of inevitability derives from the prevalence of a mimetic model that continues to shape not only our approach to literature but also our understanding of psychoanalysis, politics and social welfare. Why do we need to be adequate? In other words why do we need to live up to the representative standard of which we are obligated to become a copy and yet are forever condemned to fail, to do so?

Similar to de Man, Žižek seems to be preoccupied with the gap between sign and signified or, as he put it, the 'level of material signs that resist meaning and establishes connections not grounded in narrative symbolic structures: they just relate in a kind of presymbolic cross-resonance'.[30] Following his mentor, the Hegelian psychoanalyst Lacan, Žižek calls the level of material signs, sinthom. The sinthom is a thing that cannot be pinned down. Via this refusal of definition, the sinthom establishes a disjuncture between language and the symbolic order. As we shall see in a discussion of Celan's poem about the madness of Hölderlin, it paradoxically speaks language's non-language: the nonsignifying gibberish of Celan's Pallaksh.

In Žižek's work, the sinthom marks a break with a tradition of flat mimesis, because it does not bemoan the split between sign and signified but celebrates this gap as singularity, as 'a tic' that gives 'body to a cipher of enjoyment'.[31] A striking literary embodiment of the sinthom is the father, Dave Altschuler, in E L Doctorow's novel *World's Fair*. He is a nonsubjective protagonist because he not only fails but, more importantly, does not even attempt to live up to his representative role as subject called "father". In a way he does not leave the level of birth. His mother describes him as 'Full of surprises, from the day he was born'.[32] As such he embodies 'the courage to test the unknown'.[33] The consequences of this courage are disruptive and disappoint social expectations.

29 Žižek, *Enjoy Your Symptom! Jacques Lacan in Hollywood In and Out*, Second Edition with a new Preface by the author (London: Routledge, 2008), p. 7.

30 Žižek, *Enjoy Your Symptom!*, p. 226.

31 Žižek, *Enjoy Your Symptom!*, p. 227.

32 Doctorow, *World's Fair*, (London, Picador, 1985), p. 34.

33 Doctorow, *World's Fair*, p. 15.

Dave Altschuler is deaf to the voice of the symbolic order that demands subjectivization. He refuses to live up to the social role of the father and instead lives at the level of the material sign that cherishes the birth of the new: 'He liked to gamble, take risks; he liked what was new and different.'[34] His risk taking causes the bankruptcy of his business and turns his eldest son Donald into the bread winner of his family. Clearly here is a radical instance of failure to live up to the role of fatherhood. Dave Althuser's "romanticism"[35] seems to preclude any wish to attempt to engage the subject's identification with the name "father".

Romanticism refuses to turn hierarchical and nominative orders operative; it is as much indefinable as it is radically impractical. In Doctorow's *World's Fair* Dave Altschuler's "romanticism" disrupts the social practice of fatherhood. This seems to be romanticism's "madness": its disruptive force which is a form of violence and thus may strike us as "dangerous" and as "mad". The violence in question here is, however, a weak or bloodless one—what Walter Benjamin has called 'divine violence'—it is the disturbing action of refusing to act, of refusing to act as father, functionary, manager, or figure of authority. The dangerous aspect of Dave Altschuler's romanticism is thus the paradoxical violence of not acting out the script as established by the social order.

This is also Altschuler's left wing identity: he does not live up to the role that is representative of him as father or business man. His romantic refusal to perform representative roles is his revolutionary act. In his quiet way he thus enacts precisely through his inaction the revolutionary upheaval whose absence Žižek bemoans in past realizations of social revolutions that have not lived up to their potential: 'If one means by violence a radical upheaval of the basic social relations, then, crazy and tasteless as it may sound, the problem with historical monsters who slaughtered millions was that they were not violent enough. Sometimes doing nothing is the most violent thing to do.'[36] Žižek's provocative appraisal of doing nothing is pertinent to a discussion of Altschuler's combination of romanticism and a left-wing political outlook.

The doing nothing in question here is not so much the gesture of resignation and withdrawal but the creative energy that is set free by the paradoxical clash between action and inaction. His inaction is the act of refusal. This act of refusal negates the status quo and is as such violent, while not shedding blood.

---

34 Doctorow, *World's Fair*, p. 131.

35 Doctorow, *World's Fair*, p. 175.

36 Žižek, *Violence: Six Sideways Reflections*, (New York: Picador, 2008), p. 217.

This juxtaposition of violence and non-violence is at work in artistic creations where and when they unplug us from our socially normative roles and thus prepare the mental space for new beginnings. Such unplugging or, in other words, such cessation of the representative framework that governs our reality as well as our dreams is art's romantic as well as revolutionary legacy and potential. The dreams and the fantasy world of romanticism—which are of course a cliché—are relevant here because our 'emancipatory struggle begins with the ruthless work of self-censorship and auto-critique—not of reality but of one's own dreams'.[37] This concern with the potential of dreams seems to be old fashioned or stereotypically romantic. Here, however, it works for the inclusion of those who have been excluded.

This cohabitation of the old and the potential is encoded into Dave Altschuler's name which literally means "old schooled": he is someone who attended the old school of romanticism but is thoroughly contemporary in his support for democracy and his fascination with technology (media technology and so forth). The old and the new here disrupt the hierarchical structures that govern contemporary society.

His younger son Edgar attempts to describe this disruptive force as: 'my father's leftist politics, his impulsiveness, his impracticability, his romanticism'.[38] Crucial in Edgar's depiction of his father are not the specific categories as such but the force of the unpredictable which is beyond definition. His elder son Donald who as adolescent assumes the traditional economic function of the father by earning a living for the Altschuler family paradoxically calls romanticism the non-describable:

'But he was never satisfied to be what he had chosen to be. Do you know what I mean? You could not define him by what he did'. There was no security in him of definition. You never imagine his finding one thing to do and making a success of it and not try anything else. I don't think he ever found what it was that would make him say. 'This is me, Dave Altschuler, and I am forty-eight years old and I live at such and such an address and I do such and such for a living and I am satisfied with my life and work.' You couldn't pin him down.[39]

This elusion of definition is romanticism's transgression of flat mimesis. It is its non-violence, or in Benjamin's terms, its divine violence. This is not

37 Žižek, *Living in the End Times*, (London: Verso, 2010), p. 401.

38 Doctorow, *World's Fair*, p. 175.

39 Doctorow, *World's Fair*, p. 211.

say that Dave Altschuler is a romantic or neo-romantic poet. He is a lower middle class business man and yet crucially this categorization with the normal sociological repertoire eludes doing justice to his character, even though Doctorow's novel locates him within this social stratification (lower middle class and so on). The point of *World's Fair* is to question this classification of people, to turn them into what Agamben calls non-sub-jects. This nonviolent-violent transformation is part of Dave Altschuler's "romanticism". Here clearly a term used to describe a literary period or way of writing reaches out into a larger social and political sphere where it proves to be a liberating and disruptive force that does not foreclose but opens up a horizon of the non-predictable and non-definable.

The failure of full and adequate representation lays the ground for the free space of the non-predictable and non-definable. The usage of language in terms of simple categorization gives rise to the illusion of both adequate definition and the consequent predictability of what has been thus defined. We have seen how de Man mourns the failure of complete representation in romantic poetry. We might read Doctorow's *World's Fair* as a literary critique of de Man's critical misgivings. His novel celebrates the failure of representation as a force that drives literature's disruption of the status quo: we cannot pin-down the romantic and paradoxical non-father, father Dave Altschuler. Sociological categories apply but yet are inadequate. Altschuler is a subjective non-subject: one who refuses the subject roles of father and middle class businessman. In this way Doctorow's *World's Fair* revolves around the non-definable sinthom of one of its main characters. The term romantic emerges as the name for what is an unnameable object of fascination or desire. It is a name for the non-name "sinthom".

5.4 Žižek, de Man, and Spinoza's Cartesian break with Descartes

Žižek's philosophical focus, however, is that of de Man's: both are con-cerned with the failure of adequate representation or mimesis and as post-structuralists both locate this failure within language itself. Žižek quotes the neo-romantic poet Stefan George's—whom he confuses with Georg Trakl— verse '*So lern ich traurig den Verzicht: kein Ding sei wo das Wort gebricht*' (So sadly I learned renunciation: Where the word breaks up no thing can be).'[40] Žižek cites this quote from Heidegger's *Unterwegs zur Sprache*. He proposes in his reading a quite non-Heideggerian twist that analyzes poetic language not so much as representation and origin of history but rather as the lack of historical adequacy.

---

40 Žižek, *Enjoy Your Symptom!*, p. 193.

Žižek reads the renunciation of George's verse not in terms of language as the precondition of all representative existence. Instead language is the renunciation itself; it is its own lack, because it lacks what it proclaims to represent: 'And where, precisely, is *Verzicht*, renunciation, here? In the fact that the Thing remains forever unrepresentable: the *je ne sais quoi* which makes all the difference between the sublime and the ordinary can never be represented, every object is split into an ordinary ontic entity and the sublime X.'[41] What Žižek calls the 'sublime' or indefinable could be another word for the term "romanticism" in Doctorow's *World's Fair* except for that here it describes not an elevated sphere but the very "ordinary" world of the lower middle class businessman Altschuler. The point of the novel is precisely to question the division of the world into sublimity and ordinariness. This questioning of aestheticism's hierarchical divide is in fact part of its modern romanticism.

Žižek's focus is of course not romanticism or, for that matter, modern literature but what he sees as the proto-psychoanalytical insight of Descartes and German Idealism. He perceives in the latter the truth of the former. Kant's universalism is not the opposite of romantic subjectivism but rather its hidden truth. Žižek is preoccupied with the Kantian noumenal, the so called Thing in itself which is unattainable. Our limit to see outside reality as it is in itself empowers our sense of human autonomy, which Žižek associates with Descartes's *cogito*.

The forever elusive Thing in itself precludes a sense of the universal, for if we cannot reach an adequate understanding of how things truly are, how can we then ever attain a sense of the universal? As Žižek puts it: 'Yet as soon as the Thing in itself is posited as unattainable, *every universality* is *potentially suspended*, it implies a point of exception at which its validity, its hold, is canceled, or, to put it in the language of contemporary physics, a point of singularity—this "singularity" is ultimately the *Kantian subject himself*, namely the empty subject of the transcendental apperception'.[42] The empty subject in question attains not an accurate account of how the world works—the Thing in itself—but instead reaches moral autonomy by doing away with any attachments to things.

Emptied out, the subject can now be filled by ethical attitudes that are completely liberated from the inclination towards the goods of this world.[43] These ethical attitudes may turn out to be rather harmful to our thingy existence as embodied beings (as Žižek has recently put it

---

41 Žižek, *Enjoy Your Symptom!*, p. 194
42 Žižek, *Enjoy Your Symptom!*, p. 209.
43 For a detailed discussion of the darker side of Kantian moral autonomy see Mack, *German Idealism and the Jew*, pp. 23–41.

apropos the Kantian ethical capitalist: 'a capitalist who dedicates himself unconditionally to the capitalist drive is effectively ready to put every-thing, including the survival of humanity, at stake, not for any 'patho-logical' gain or goal, but simply for the sake of the reproduction of the system as an end-in-itself—*fiat profitus pereat mundus* might be his mot-to'[44]) and it is this potential harmfulness that turns Kant into a subjective rather than universal moral philosopher: 'The crack in the universality finds its clearest expression in the hypothesis of 'radical evil,' i.e. in the paradoxical possibility envisaged by Kant (later taken over and further elaborated by Schelling), of evilness qua ethical attitude, of our being evil on account of the principle, not because we succumbed to 'pathological' impulses.'[45] The 'pathological' refers of course to our attachment to things. An attachment to things is pathological because it is epistemo-logically futile: we will never be able to understand the outside "univer-sal" world in itself (the Thing in itself).

Here we reach the point where it becomes apparent that Žižek's intrigu-ing plea for the German Idealist subject as yet another version of the Cartesian *cogito* shares with de Man's approach towards the study of romanticism, a certain preoccupation with the failure of representation to yield an accurate account of what things represented truthfully are. The *cogito* is a synonym for the Kantian empty subject (or, in other words, Žižek's 'substanceless subject' that we have discussed in the preceding chapter): both are subjects that have been emptied out, that have been "freed" from all concrete or thingy content. This willing subjectivication of the subject to the state of an empty vessel, which can be filled by whatever ethical or not so ethical prin-ciples, coincides with the failure of adequate representation.

We realize that we are at the mercy of a voluntarist God who can mis-lead us about our world—what Žižek calls 'the Cartesian *malin genie*'[46]—or, in Kant's case, we face up to limits of our capacities to represent things as they truly are (as the Thing in itself) and as result of this lugubrious realization we withdraw into ourselves. Descartes's *cogito* and the Kantian moral subject are therefore consubstantial with 'the post-trau-matic subject: to get an idea of the *cogito* at its purest, its 'degree zero,' one need only come face to face with an autistic 'monster'.[47] Does the failure of adequate representation—the preoccupation of literary, political, theological, medical and philosophical discussions from Descartes,

---

44 Žižek, *Living in the End Times*, p. 335.
45 Žižek, *Enjoy Your Symptom!*, p. 209.
46 Žižek, *Living in the End Times*, p. 314.
47 Ibid.

Spinoza, Kant via Heidegger to de Man and Žižek—necessarily give rise to the creation of monsters?

In contrast to much of the traditional philosophical discussion Žižek sees in this monstrosity, the core of our universal humanity, one that is premised on the contingent ground of empty subjectivity: 'the very idea of cultural pluralism relies on the Cartesian experience of the empty sub-stanceless subjectivity—it is only against the background of this experience that every determinate form of substantial unity can appear as something ultimately contingent.'[48] Does our failure to represent substance as the Thing in itself leave us no choice but to withdraw from substance, from the world of things?

There is an alternative to this withdrawal into the *cogito* within the Spinozist tradition of a critique of flat mimesis. Spinoza is a true Cartesian in the Žižekean sense, when he takes issue with our fallacious represen-tation of the world as image of ourselves. Yet this critique does not pre-clude engagement with universals. It preconditions, however, this engagement along the lines of epistemological, theological, philosophi-cal and cultural humility. We cannot help but narrate fictions about our world. The crucial point is to be cognizant of the fictional nature of our mimesis. This does of course not mean that everything represented is a fiction but it should alert us to the imaginative texture of our reality, which is a contingent one—contingency here, however, emerges not from the *cogito* but from a critique of teleology as fiction of the with-drawn and substanceles self. Spinoza warns us not to take words and images at face value and, most importantly, not take them literally. Spinoza is the opposite of a purist or perfectionist. He has done away with highly elevated notions such as perfection or purity, precisely because they are fictions that do an injustice to the muddled human and quite thingy condition of contingency and mortality. Here contingency is not enclosed within the subject but rather mediates between the subjec-tive and the substantive (see the discussion in the previous chapter).

Rather than advocate withdrawal into the *cogito*, Spinoza argues for a sense of interdependence; interdependence between extended things (bodies) and minds, between particular and universal, between the pres-ervation of the self and that of others (*conatus*). We engage with the world not by turning into empty subjects that live according to their own auton-omy or teleology, but by creating ever new forms of life. This creation of the new is certainly part of the imaginative texture of our contingent human condition. The point is to differentiate not so much between adequacy and inadequacy but between preservation and cessation,

---

48 Žižek, *Enjoy Your Symptom!*, p. 212.

between the sustainable and the non-sustainable, between a copy of the old and the old as the creation of the new. A post-Spinozist or romantic understanding of autonomy is premised on the critique of the copy as non-sustainable as well as monolithic fiction that precludes the blessing of more life; of more life not only in terms of birth but also, and more importantly, as the more life which is aging. As has been discussed in Chapter 2, Spinoza is the first philosopher to attend to narrative and fiction as the core of his ethical and political critique.

This book presents a plea for an appreciation and novel understanding of art not so much as entertainment or fictional distraction from the problems we face, but as key to problem solving due to its life renewing and thus life preserving impetus. The arts and the humanities here enact what Žižek has recently called a 'dynamized Spinozism' which denotes not the Kantian substanceless subject but 'the same substance (Life)' which 'maintains itself through its metamorphosis'.[49] Creativity in the arts, sciences and the humanities enables such life renewing and life maintaining metamorphoses. If we copy what representations of age tell us we are, we foreclose the new beginning that accompanies life's ever renewed self-preservation.

Rather than imitate and copy what exists, poetry initiates a new beginning. It gives birth to new forms of life that preserve existing ones not via retracing their contours but through holding out the alluring appeal of transformation— a transformation that repairs in an act of creativity. Here literature does not copy philosophy as interpretative science (i.e. hermeneutics and phenomenology). Instead of being subordinated to philosophy, literature and philosophy are here on equal terms: they have become truly indistinguishable.

5.5 Hölderlin, Benjamin, and the Poetry of New Beginnings

Hölderlin enacts the coexistence of the poetic and the philosophical in a sphere—whether this takes place in prose or in verse—where both have abandoned claims to sovereignty. So it is not surprising that his work attracts the attention of literary thinkers such as Benjamin, Heidegger and Paul de Man. The state in between philosophy and literature may strike some readers as unstable and there is certainly a destabilizing in the sense of opaque quality to his writing. Paul de Man has described as "riddle" this rather puzzling nature of Hölderlin's oeuvre. According to de Man Hölderlin's riddle calls into question our established sense of what it means to be human or beyond the human. Humanity turns rather open-ended and fluid in his work. One could say that according to

---

49 Žižek, *Living in the End Times*, p. 307.

Hölderlin, humanity poses an enigma and thus calls for endless new beginnings. De Man turns this enigma into a challenge for literary scholarship: 'How the more-than-human point of view throughout the poetry is to be interpreted will remain the burden of Hölderlin criticism for many years to come.'[50] In his reading of Hölderlin, de Man focuses on a famous phrase: 'an enigma is that which is of pure origin'. *Ein Rätsel ist Reinentsrungenes* is notoriously difficult to translate and indeed de Man focuses on this difficulty and takes issue with Michael Hamburger's approach.

De Man argues that Hamburger's translation shifts the emphasis away from Hölderlin's concern of language to one of persons and personifications. In this way Hamburger says not riddle but mystery rendering the phrase 'mystery those of pure origin' and de Man is quick to fault Hamburger for having left linguistic confinements: 'He [i.e. Mr Hamburger] makes it seem as if Hölderlin was asserting the existence of a transcendental experience that lies beyond the reach of language, when the entire drift of the poem moves into the opposite direction.'[51] Whether Hölderlin's impersonal phrase by implication includes or excludes the possibility of personal experience is an open question. What is evident, however, is that it questions the purported self-containment of things or persons.

The presupposition that anything or anyone could have been born from a pure and independent source is incomprehensible to the point of being enigmatic. Far from asserting the riddle as one of language only, as de Man argues, Hölderlin's famous phrase has an extra-linguistic set of concerns, undermining notions of self-containment or purity. Purity therefore does not emerge as a question of interpretation and thus representation—in other words the ambience of de Man's concern with language—but as being itself put into question: it is enigmatic to the point of being questionable. Being questionable does not mean invalid.

Hölderlin's phrase does not dispute the fact that we appear to be originating from a pure or radically independent origin. This origin would then be our difference that constitutes our individuality. As soon as we are born we are each endowed with a set of differentials that distinguish us from each other, even from those who are our parents and other members of our immediate family. Yet despite the unique nature of birth, of origination, what makes possible the fact of being born is our communality. This tension between the private and the public, between difference and communality characterizes Hölderlin's riddle. It is as such

---

50 De Man 'The Riddle of Hölderlin, de Man, *Critical Writings 1958–1978*, edited and introduced by Lindsay Waters, (Minneapolis: University of Minnesota Press, 1989), pp. 198–213 (p. 202).

51 De Man 'The Riddle of Hölderlin, de Man, *Critical Writings 1958–1978*, p. 210.

one of social interruption and not one concerned with the representational problem only; one that revolves around the sign's failure to coincide with the signified. Birth or origin interrupts in the sense of posing a difference to that from which it originates, out of which it is born. The enigma is that of poetry itself, being situated at the interface between the already there— the subject matter of representation—and the new that interrupts what it emerges from. Here we witness novelty, as the birth of an independent cosmos from the loins of the old, already established one.

5.6 Celan, the Void and the Aftermath of the Nazi Genocide

> It was madness, of course. George Orwell, *Nineteen-Eighty-Four*

Mimesis thus reaches beyond itself. The twentieth century poet and Holocaust survivor Paul Celan sees a contemporary relevance in Hölderlin's romantic legacy that centres on mimesis as a break with itself. The enigma of birth performs such interruptions of the new out of but also paradoxically with the old. As we shall see, part of Celan's fascination with Hölderlin is the loss of communality that can result from such a break. The loss here is one of social isolation and withdrawal from, rather than transforming interaction with the old, with the society as we know it.

This disjuncture proffers new ways of life but it can also result in seclusion and social exclusion. Rather than celebrating such loss of communality as a feat of genius, Hölderlin bemoans such loss as society's disengagement with both age and birth, as not exclusively the suffering of the romantic poet but as the illness of society at large. Celan cites Hölderlin's phrase about the putatively dual aspect of new beginnings— as the enigma of that which appears to be of pure origin—in his poem about the romantic poet entitled 'Tübingen, January'. In this poem, Celan— subjected himself to a variety of psychiatric treatments in postwar France—focuses on the mad Hölderlin who has fallen silent (aside from writing technically refined verse about nature under the assumed name Scardanelli). The mad Hölderlin of Celan's poem has been given refuge by the owner of the Tübingen tower. It is worth citing Celan's poem in full because it commingles a vague sense of madness with the creative force that disrupts our sense of mimesis:

> Eyes talked into
> blindness.
> their—"enigma is
> the purely
> originated"—,their

memory of
Hölderlin towers afloat, circled
by whirring gulls.

Visits of drowned joiners to
these
submerging words:
Should,
should a man,
should a man come into this world, today,
with
the shining beard of the
patriarchs: he could,
if he spoke of this
time, he
could
only babble and babble
over, over
againagain.

'Pallaksh. Pallaksh.'[52]

Hamburger appears to respond to part of de Man's criticism by rendering the impersonal construction of Hölderlin's phrase 'an enigma is the purely originated', as quoted by Celan in 'Tübingen, January'. Celan, however, does not share de Man's involvement with language and its mimetic achievements and failures. On the contrary 'Tübingen, January'—in striking intensity—profiles Hölderlin's madness as a condition of and for modernity, while appraising his poetry as a refusal of mimesis.

Strikingly, the poem opens with a persuasion towards blindness: the opposite of Abrams's mimetic mirror. An evocation not of a reality mirrored, but of one turned upside down follows the citation 'An enigma is the purely originated'. As the last strophe indicates, the poem refuses to evoke Abrams's lamp that illuminates and represents the inner life of the poet. Rather than being a representation of the mad poet, madness emerges as condition of our 'world, today.' The eyes that have been persuaded (*über-redete*) in Celan's original German version into blindness talk of the tower, where Hölderlin spent the last years of his life, not in the singular but in the plural. Celan's recreated Hölderlin towers are transplanted from their elevated position in the sky and submerged into

52 Celan, *Poems. A Bilingual Edition* Selected and introduced by Michael Hamburger, (New York: Persea Books, 1980), p. 145.

a state of water. The poem does not represent so much as re-arrange, re-configure reality. To be more precise, it gives birth to a new reality not seen by the eyes of the sighted but by the non-mimetic words of the blind and the mad.

Crucially, the process of submerging finds its culmination in the question of representation. How to represent our humanity in an inhumane world? The question is related to issues of mimesis, because if we copy what we have become we may state our present condition but not our human potential. Celan shies away from the simple talk of flat mimesis. He coins the notion of talk beyond talk, a *über-reden*, a language beyond language, a representation beyond representation, a seeing that does not operate like a mirror and is not illuminated by a lamp but is submerged in the murkiness and fluidity of water.

Water's fluidity opens the poem's blind sight to the open nature of humanity. This openness has dangerous aspects because it may turn into something that is prone to fall prey to violence and the exertion of limitless power. Have we lost our humanity, whatever this might be? Celan's poem implicitly raises this question within the context of Hölderlin's seclusion and exclusion from society in the tower of Tübingen. It is a question that relates to the disappearance of the gods that Hölderlin's poetry attempts to come to terms with. Following Hölderlin, Nietzsche's Zarathustra fears that the death of God may give birth to a void, where we might mourn the loss of what we took to be humanity. As Andrew Benjamin notes, 'both Nietzsche and Hölderlin— though in different ways—can be read as actively involved with a philosophical or poetic engagement with loss'.[53] Celan's sense of loss is profoundly shaped by the historical coordinates of the Shoah. Clearly there are personal dimensions to this loss and many of his poems mourn or refer in some way or another to the death of his mother after her deportation from Czernowitz to the Ukraine: there 'his mother had been shot as unfit for work'. [54] The Nazi genocide marks a break within the continuity of history, not least because of the pseudo-creator like assumption that shapes its phenomenology: one that divides humanity into those who essentially belong to life (Aryans) and those who should be regarded as having never even been born in the first place (Jews, Gypsies, homosexuals and those suffering from a physical or mental disability).

53 Andrew Benjamin, *Philosophy's Literature*, (Manchester: Clinamen Press, 2001), p. 153.
54 For a detailed discussion of Celan's historical precision and his witnessing of the Shoah see John Felstiner's *Paul Celan: Poet, Survivor, Jew*, (New Haven: Yale University Press, 1995), p. 17.

In this way Nazism radicalizes the pseudo-theology that has already been part of eighteenth- and nineteenth-century anti-Semitism.[55] The Nazi authorities certainly presumed to play the role of a power which has traditionally been the prerogative of a transcendent force. In her own formulation of the death sentence meted out to Adolf Eichmann, Hannah Arendt refers to the assumption of a quasi-God like role by the Nazi perpetrators:

'And just as you supported and carried out a policy of not wanting to share the earth with the Jewish people and the people of a number of other nations—as though you and your superiors had any right to determine who should and who should not inhabit the world—we find that no one, that is, no member of the human race, can be expected to want to share the earth with you. This is the reason, and the only reason, you must hang.'[56]

Arendt finds Eichmann and his fellow perpetrators guilty of playing God. Playing God may sound nonchalant and almost innocuous but it clearly is not. On the contrary, it is linked to the monstrous violence that goes hand and in hand with the conflation of a given particular human society with the presumed omnipotence and omniscience of God. This conflation is the target of Spinoza's critique of anthropomorphic conceptions of God.[57]

Spinoza's critique helped weaken the supernatural aura of traditional conceptions of God, albeit this may not have fully been Spinoza's intention. Hölderlin and Nietzsche wrote what they wrote within a post-Spinozist context of a lost transcendent and therefore lost revealed cosmos. This immanent world may give rise to individual and social flourishing—a truly democratic and non-hierarchical society for which Spinoza has sought to lay the foundations in his *Ethics* and which many romantic poets like Wordsworth, Coleridge, Shelley and indeed Hölderlin saw initially emerging in the French Revolution. Yet it may also give rise to a void where a pseudo-divine notion of omniscience and omnipotence

---

55 On the pseudo-theology of anti-Semitism see Mack's *German Idealism and the Jew: the Inner Anti-Semitism of Philosophy and German Jewish Responses*, (Chicago: University of Chicago Press, 2003). See also J Kameron Carter's *Race: A Theological Account*, (Oxford: Oxford University Press, 2008).

56 Arendt, *Eichmann in Jerusalem: A Report on the Banality of Evil*, (London: Penguin, 1991), p. 279.

57 For a detailed discussion of this point, see Mack's *Spinoza and the Specters of Modernity*.

could return within immanence itself and most horridly in the Nazi conception of a master race.

Clearly Celan sees Nazism not as continuation of the democratic hopes and aspiration of post-Spinozist romanticism, but as horrifying annihilation of any previous attempt to establish the social, economic and political conditions that are conducive to human flourishing. Like Arendt, Celan is deeply cognisant of the interruption that marks the Nazi genocide. This interruption, however, continues elements of various traditions (theology, medicince etc.) which it of course thoroughly corrupts. Neither for Arendt nor for Celan, there is an easy return to traditional conceptions of God and the good society. The Shoah precludes and obstructs journeys that may lead to a homecoming. Rather than returning home, post-Holocaust writing and thought, participates in a post-Spinozist romantic break with the established notions of a world with which we have become familiar. Rather than representing the world of the sighted, the eyes of Celan's poetic voice have turned blind, depicting not a stable but fluid, topsy-turvy world. They relate to neither the mirror nor to the lamp of traditional mimesis but they break away from such representational strategies and submerge into the drowned words of the late taciturn Hölderlin.

The silence of the late Hölderlin brings us to a broader, more theoretical discussion of the issue of madness. One substantial part of Hölderlin's reputation was his mental illness. It is difficult to discuss insanity in literary as well as philosophical discussions because it seems to outdo both philosophy and literature. It seems to confound notions of mastery and formal control and it denotes the opposite of philosophy's assumed claim to rationality.

The discussion that has been proffered within this chapter may help us explore the problematic nature that characterizes endeavours to define or 'measure' madness. Literature can heighten our awareness of the fluidity that characterizes a rigid opposition between the 'mad' and the 'healthy'. The poetry of the eighteenth century poet Hölderlin questions some elements of such rigid distinction. As Foucault has shown, the eighteenth century was preoccupied with the demarcation and the expulsion of what society may come to define as 'mad'.[58] The closing paragraphs of this chapter read Hölderlin's poetry within the context of expulsion from a given society's conceptions of what constitutes norms and standards. The focus of this reading is not so much a poem by Hölderlin but a continuation of our discussion of Celan's 'Tübingen, January'.

What is crucial here is the correlation between Hölderlin's status as a 'mad' poet and the vision of an inclusive society whose loss and absence

---

58 See Foucault's *Madness and Civilization: A History of Insanity in the Age of Reason*, translated by Richard Howard, (New York: Vintage Books, 1988).

his poetry dramatizes. The philosopher W. Benjamin focuses on this sense of loss and absence when he first develops his philosophy of literature in an encounter with Hölderlin's poetry. Benjamin casts Hölderlin's poetry, in particular, and creativity, in general, into a non-normative, non-foundational mode—the detachment of which traverses the trajectory that separates the 'mad' from standards of societal norms. Benjamin insists on poetry as a sphere that cannot be confused with ideology and other forms of political appropriation and yet he equally insists on the social value of such political uselessness. It is this sensitivity to a detached sphere that touches upon the core of our humanity which can easily be confused with the 'mad': Hölderlin's poetry dramatizes absence, loss and pain as the ineradicable constitution of our humanity. He thus includes what a narrow conception of society and politics banishes and attempts to eradicate.

The last strophe of Celan's 'Tübingen, January' profiles the presence of such post-Spinozist or, in other words, romantic sense of inclusion within a post-Holocaust modernity and post-modernity. It falteringly inaugurates a wished for break away from the dislocation of tradition marked by the Shoah. The birth of the truly human here does not exclude the past but rather includes—in a Benjaminian sense of redemption—the tradition from the distortive and inhumane uses to which it has been put. The *Ein Mensch* of Celan's German original is a Yiddish phrase denoting someone who is almost angelic in their support of others. The anticipation of this angelic interruption of the horrid interruptions which have distorted humanity is not a break with the past but rather its redemption in a non-distorted shape: the *Ein Mensch* is endowed with the Biblical 'shining beard of the/patriarchs'. The formal verse break between the 'the' and the 'patriarch' inaugurates a substantial break, one that moves away from the norms and sense of linguistics to the madness of the nonsensical, non-linguistic. It breaks with representational sense and turns to the non-representational babble of words that have no meaning: Pallaksh. Pallaksh.

The nonsense at the close of Celan's poem about Hölderlin evokes the title 'Imbeclity' (*Blödigkeit*) of a poem by Hölderlin, which Benjamin subjects to philosophical analysis in his early essay. Here Hölderlin describes poetry's break as a step into (*tritt nur/Baar ins Leben und sorge nicht*) the new life of a non-hierarchical, non-exclusive society where 'our father, the God of heaven, is open to everyone and grants the thinking day to rich and poor'.[59] The title of Hölderlin's poem anticipates this

---

59 'Jedem offen, so ist ja/ Unser Vater, des Himmel's Gott,/ Der den denkenden Tag Armen und Reichen gönnt' Hölderlin, *Sämtliche Ausgabe. Band 5. Oden II*, edited by D. E. Sattler, (Frankfurt a. M.: Roter Stern Verlag, 1984), pp. 321–22.

break in terms of mental illness, of mental deficiency, in short, in terms of 'imbecility'. Celan also evokes imbecility as the birth of human angelic-like flourishing through the pronunciation of nonsense at the end of 'Tübingen, January'. Reflecting on Hölderlin's poetry, Benjamin reads this sense of imbecility as poetry's philosophical break with social practices that preclude the well being of both individuals and their social contexts. The following chapter will take further the arguments about literature, politics, philosophy and medicine that have been developed in this chapter. We will see how Benjamin develops his idiosyncratic notion of communism on the basis of his reading of literature. Benjamin's break with a mimetic tradition contrasts with Heidegger's subordination of poetry to the forces of history. According to Benjamin art disrupts historical continuity, whereas for Heidegger arts represent and interpret political events. In the latter, literature is subordinated to politics while in the former literature constitutes politics' interaction with reality by changing the way we think.

6 The Birth of Politics out of Literature

To develop and expand the earlier discussion on romanticism's literary, philosophical and medical significance, this chapter first shows how initially Benjamin casts poetry into a transcendental mode of potential interruption that swerves away from current harmful practices and prepares the way for human flourishing. It then analyzes how Benjamin's understanding of the reparative work within art differs from Heidegger's notion of truth as historical origin. According to Benjamin technology's, quasi-medical therapy consists in a disturbance of history's continuity. By breaking the link between the work of art and the aura of its tradition, mechanical reproduction helps give birth to the new cosmos of poetry whose liberating potential Benjamin celebrates in his early essay on Hölderlin.

6.1 Benjamin's Poetics of Kantian Transcendental Philosophy

As has been discussed in the previous chapter, Benjamin fuses philosophy with literature. This fusion helps engender his distinct kind of literary thought that remains aloof—hence his high-flown style of writing—while at same time laying claim to the life changing potential within such serious approach towards literature. In philosophical terms, Benjamin takes poetry so seriously that he develops in his discussion of two of Hölderlin's poems a novel version of Kantian transcendental philosophy.

Throughout his intellectual itinerary, Benjamin's writing and thought was deeply shaped by Kant.[1] One of Kant's most enduring influences on him was the notion of the transcendental. Influence here is not a passive reception of what has been received but the work of creative transformation. In this way, Benjamin, in the later years, coined his own version of Kantianism that despaired of itself when he developed his version of a transcendental messianism. Transcendental messianism establishes the foundations of a break or rupture with the violent state of emergency

---

1 See Mack's *German Idealism and the Jew: the inner Anti-Semitism of Philosophy and German Jewish Responses*, (Chicago: University of Chicago Press, 2003), pp. 155–67.

that paradoxically characterizes the 'normal' path of history and politics to which we have become accustomed.[2]

Part of the central argument of this chapter is the attempt to show how Benjamin, earlier on, cast poetry (the 1914-15essay on two versions of a poem by Hölderlin) in a transcendental mode of potential interruption that swerves away from current harmful practices and prepares the way for human flourishing. In Kant's system, the transcendental delineates both the possibilities and the limits of human knowledge and experience. Introducing his version of the Copernican revolution, Kant declares the thing-in-itself or the noumenon as unreachable and ungraspable by human intellection. Crucially, this noumenal sphere denotes the world that precedes Kant's revolutionary instalment and enthronement of human autonomy: transcendental inquiry establishes the impossible attainment of knowledge about extra-human essences (God, the supernatural, the non-human sphere of nature) but in doing so it opens up vistas of a new space where humanity can construct its autonomy unencumbered by traditional concerns about theological issues. As Robert Pippin has clearly shown, Kant's Copernican revolution inaugurated 'bourgeois' philosophy which became 'central to the self-understanding and legitimation of the bourgeois form of life: the free, rational, independent, reflective, self-determining subject'.[3] Benjamin was deeply attracted to the promise of freedom held out by Kant's political philosophy (and he was of course deeply aware of his own bourgeois family background).

The adolescent Benjamin became acquainted with Kant via the neo-Kantian thought of the German Jewish philosopher and classicist Hermann Cohen. Cohen accentuated the formal aspect of Kant's philosophy that is encapsulated in the term transcendental. The term transcendental denotes a logical procedure via which thought gains its independence from empirical conditions and constrains. As Pippin has put it, Kant 'could do justice to the inseparable intuitive content of concepts and preserve a notion of a priori knowledge by appeal to the claim that there were *pure* forms of intuition, and so there could be a way, independent of actual experience, to specify sufficiently something of the experiential non-conceptual content of any pure concept, and could do

---

2   For a detailed discussion of this point see Mack, *German Idealism and the Jew*, pp. 155–167.

3   Pippin, *The Persistence of Subjectivity: On the Kantian Aftermath*, (Cambridge: University of Chicago Press, 2005), p. 5. For a discussion of the secularized Christian understanding of bourgeois liberty in Kant's moral and political philosophy see Mack, *German Idealism and the Jew*, pp. 23–41.

so a priori'.[4] In a sense, Cohen turned the Kantian transcendental into the foundations of all logical and scientific investigations. Cohen, however, liberated the logical from purely formal connotations:

'To Cohen, logic was the queen of the sciences, but he was not satisfied with pure formalism. Philosophy does not end in logic, but logic must clarify the conditions of all cultural activity, from morality to art'. Logic is indispensible in the understanding of human culture as an integral whole. Logic discovers the laws of form and function—laws which are themselves the mainspring of culture in its three main divisions: science, morality, and art. Therefore, Cohen's theory of knowledge is the core of his humanism because the conditions for producing general human culture are found in logic.[5]

Cohen's logical procedure that outlines the conditions of human culture is precisely denoted by the Kantian notion of the transcendental. The transcendental proposes *a priori* forms of knowing that constitute the foundations of Cohen's logic of science, art and morality. In his essay 'On two poems by Friedrich Hölderlin' Benjamin invokes the Kantian attempt to install knowledge that is independent of, or, a priori to encounters in the empirical world. He does so by citing the following quote by the romantic poet Novalis: 'Every work of art has in and of itself an a priori ideal, a necessity for being in the world.'[6] The pithy sentence evokes a strong sense of aesthetic autonomy. It endows art with a force or necessity that Kant would only have allowed for morality or a moral philosophy of politics and history. The work of art has its own or autonomous necessity (or teleology) but crucially its force-field is not disconnected from, but is a 'being in the world'. As we shall see, Benjamin's thought oscillates in this tension between the work's autonomy or break from the world as it is and the social or political repercussions that such quasi-messianic interruption may engender.

Benjamin composed his essay on Hölderlin at a time that proved to be important for his intellectual development: at the beginning of World War I. The intellectual and socio-political enthusiasm for the war shocked him. He was in particular dismayed about the pro-war writing of his former intellectual mentor Hermann Cohen. Cohen's nationalist sympathies disillusioned the early Benjamin about the social and political significance of

---

4   Pippin, *The Persistence of Subjectivity*, p. 51.

5   Thomas E. Willey, *Back to Kant. The Revival of Kantianism in German Social and Historical Thought 1860–1914*, (Detroit: Wayne State University Press, 1978), p. 109.

6   Benjamin, *Collected Writings. Vol 1*, p. 19.

neo-Kantianism. Cohen was of course one of the most renowned neo-Kantians and he was, in the eyes of the early Benjamin, a war-monger.[7] This coincidence of a highly moralistic and political approach toward a logical (neo-Kantian) transcendental analysis of culture and the politico-ethical espousal of World War I made not just neo-Kantianism the suspect but cast doubt upon the subordination of art to extra aesthetic concerns such as morality or politics. The primacy of the political and the moral could all to easily fall prey to moral and political justifications for exclusionary and violent forms of social interaction as most brutally practiced in warfare.[8] Yet Benjamin's disillusionment with Cohen, in particular, and neo-Kantianism, in general, did not evince his wholesale abandonment of the formal sophistication of Kant's philosophy. As has been intimated in the discussion above, Benjamin transferred the logical grasp of the notion 'transcendental' from its applied sphere of morality and politics to a seemingly cryptic discussion about the value of poetry. Here he stresses the transcendental conditions of the poem. These conditions seem to be set by the logical parameters of Cohen's neo-Kantian thought. They establish the poem as an *a priori* entity, that is to say, as a work of construction that is independent of empirical experience. The poem is truly autonomous. It is conditioned by nothing else but itself.

The work of art is unconditioned to the extent that it is disconnected from the life of its author. Benjamin emphasizes that there is a break between the poem and the poet. So great is the work's independent being that it bears no resemblance whatsoever to the life of either the poet or even the life depicted within it. Benjamin's term the poeticed [*das Gedichtete*] connotes the truth of the poem as something that is unconditioned, *a priori*. The notion the 'poeticied' articulates the condition of the poem as an independent condition of itself, or, in other words, a condition

---

7   Jacques Derrida describes the significance of Cohen defence of World War I as follows: 'It is because he [i.e. Cohen] represents, in a manner so remarkably worked out, a certain type of militant patriotism in the Jewish-German community, it is also because to this end he mobilizes the Kantian reference, indeed the socialist, national, and neo-Kantian reference, that he seemed to me to deserve a special attention, a strategically motivated attention in our context.' Derrida, 'Interpretations at War: Kant, the Jew, German,' *New Literary History*, 22 (Winter, 1991): 39–95 (48). For the Buber/Cohen controversy about World War I see Paul Mendes-Flohr and Jehuda Reinharz (eds), *The Jew in the Modern World*, (Oxford: Oxford University Press, 1995). pp. 571–577.

8   As John McCole has put it, 'The rhetoric of German Idealism, he [i.e. Benjamin] discovered, lent itself all to easily to the sophistry of the 'ideas of 1914'.'McCole, *Walter Benjamin and the Antinomnies of Tradition*, (Ithaca: Cornell University Press, 1993), p. 56.

of its own making without a history, without even a poet, or people to which the poet may happen to belong. As such a radical autonomous, independent being, the poem proves capable to determine a novel form of life: 'In the poetized, life determines itself through the poem, the task through the solution. The underlying basis is not the individual life-mood of the artist but rather a life-context determined by art.'[9] The poem establishes an entirely new space. It creates a new form of life.

Within the work of art we witness both the creation of different modes of living and the emergence of life that establishes a difference to our current one. The mature Benjamin will characterize this space as the messianic interruption of the sudden now (*Jetztzeit*) that breaks with the violence and exploitation which constitutes historical continuity. As a break with the violent practices that sadly characterize history's continuity, Benjamin's messianism is, as Derrida has pointed out, a bloodless one.[10] Andrew Benjamin has shown that it needs to be differentiated from quasi-totalitarian forms of messianism—as criticized by Walter Benjamin's friend and intellectual interlocutor Gerschom Scholem in his research on the false messiah Sahbbatai Zevi—that aim 'at a restoration of a totality that has become apart'.[11] Rather than projecting finality and the restoration of a lost totality (lost during a fall into sin and corruption), Benjamin's messianic interruption 'is to be squared with the continual renewal of life—the continuity of the "*nach*", the "always new" (*immer new*)—especially since it is buttressed by the effective presence of the "*ad infinitum*"'.[12] The redemption at issue here does not put an end to history or to sublunary life as we know it. Instead it repairs life so that it can truly flourish and continue in a novel mode that sustains not only the present but also re-awakens what has been destroyed in the past. My reading of the early essay on Hölderlin contributes to a better understanding of redemption and reparation as a break with history that takes place within history. Benjamin's transcendental messianism centres on such a break: it delineates the conditions that make possible the disruption of a way life that has caused harm and exploitation within the past and the present.

The reparative work in question here is not smooth. It is riddled with contradictions and unease. Human flourishing here emerges not as a

9 Benjamin, *Collected Writings. Vol 1*, p. 20.

10 See Derrida's 'Force of Law. The Mystical Foundations of Authority,' translated by Mary Quaintance, in Drucilla Cornell, Michel Rosenfelf, David Gray Carlson (eds), *Deconstruction and the Possibility of Justice*, (London: Routledge, 1992), pp. 3–67.

11 Andrew Benjamin, *Present Hope: Philosophy, Architecture, Judaism*, (London: Routledge, 1997), p. 42.

12 Andrew Benjamin, *Present Hope*, p. 43.

continuity of what has been but as a disquieting interruption that breaks with established forms of social interaction. As we shall see, Benjamin is fascinated by the madness of the romantic poet Hölderlin. He sees in Hölderlin's mental illness the seeds of human flourishing precisely because of a 'mad' detachment from the violence perpetrated under the status quo. As Samuel Weber has recently put it, 'What appears to fascinate Benjamin above all is the risk of madness'.[13] Weber here discusses a loss of the established sense; a break with the nomenclature that identifies things in current forms of meaning.

Benjamin's reparative work does not renew life by confirming accepted structures but by disrupting these structures. His understanding of what makes us flourish is not acquiescent but profoundly disquieting. It is this uneasiness that makes it intriguing. Benjamin's notion of messianic interruption is sustained by the tension between the secular and the sacred, the theological and the political, the distant and the impassioned, the extraordinary and the ordinary. Could it be that this oscillation of seemingly irreconcilable oppositions radicalizes Benjamin's earlier attempt to create a space of art that is so radically independent of established ways of life that it could prove capable to create so far inconceivable ones? Benjamin's defence of art's autonomy would then appear to constitute a reparative space where human flourishing could take place.

This space needs to be novel so that it is not liable to fall prey to old ways of thinking that are part of the continuum of history. History's continuity perpetuates the wars and feats of exploitation from which Benjamin later on attempts to sever his intervention when he celebrates the reparative and redemptive now of messianic interruption. To the dismay of Benjamin in his earlier years, Cohen's enthusiasm for World War I indicates the close affiliation between historical continuity within thought (Neo-Kantianism) and the continuity of socio-political history. Turning Carl Schmitt's political theology on its head, Benjamin would later characterize this continuity as the permanent state of violent exception.[14] There is, however, in Benjamin's work a sustained 'continual' concern to break with a continuity of destruction and exploitation. Benjamin in his earlier years focuses on art as novel space where such reparative interruption could take place. Benjamin in the later years thinks art,

---

13 Weber, *Benjamin-abilities*, (Cambridge, Mass.: Harvard University Press, 2008), p. 74.

14 For a detailed discussion of this point see Mack's 'Transcendentaler Messianismus und die Katastrophe der Entscheidung: Anmerkungen zu Carl Schmitts und Walter Benjamins Eschatologie' in Stephan Loos and Holger Zaborowski (eds), *Leben, Tod und Entscheidung. Studien zur Geistesgeschichte der Weimarer Republik*, (Berlin: Duncker & Humblot, 2003), pp. 155–166.

technology and the revolutionary potential of communism together: communism politicizes the new cosmos created by art.

6.2 Art's Interconnected Universe

The discussion above could give rise to two sets of possible doubt. First, a critical reader may point out the incongruence between the subject matter of Hölderlin's poetry and Benjamin's thought about the transcendental truth of the poem as the poeticed. As has often been noted, Hölderlin's poetry is not detached but closely involved with empirical events and places. His powers of description are stunningly realistic. His poetry often seems to have the almost uncanny power to evoke geographies visited by the poet (such as Bourdeaux and the south of France). Not to mention the bemoaning of loss and absence as the mantra (as it were) of Hölderlin's poetry. In both versions of the same poem, which is the subject matter of Benjamin's essay, the importance of the people looms large: in one the poets are characterized as 'of the people'—'We, the poets of the people, gladly among the living' ('The Poet's Courage')—and in the second the poets are 'the tongue of the people' ('Timidity'). How does this close involvement square with Benjamin's Kantian emphasis on transcendental conditioning and, associated with it, the *a priori* as independence from existent empirical reality? Second, a critical reader may ask in what ways Benjamin's concern with the transcendental conditions of poetry as the a priori of its self-enclosed making can contribute to any reparative work that may enable novel forms of well being. Is not human flourishing a rather straightforward affair that is closely grounded in the empirical social sciences and the practices of medicine?

Let me first address the first set of concerns. The question of Hölderlin's literalism as opposed to Benjamin's insistence on poetry's independence from any form of literal or empirical conditioning is in fact related to doubts about how art can in any way support societal forms of well being. The scepticism about Benjamin's doing justice to Hölderlin's realistic powers of description replicate the structure of the second set of concerns. They centre on the discrepancy between the suffering that characterizes the current state of affairs within empirical life and art's break with the status quo of empiricism.

Benjamin addresses the first set of concerns himself when he asks why Hölderlin seems to connect the life of the poets to that of the people:

'Why doesn't the poet celebrate—and with a higher right—the *odi profanum*? This question may, indeed must be asked wherever the living have not yet founded any sort of spiritual order'.—In the most surprising way, the poet reaches with both hands into the alien world orders, grabs at people and God to raise within him his own courage—the courage of poets.[15]

Benjamin maintains that we are obliged to ask why the poems under discussion do not celebrate a disdain for the profane and the popular, in short, the people. This question must be asked because under current conditions the life of the profane is radically severed from any spiritual order: the living or the people 'have not yet founded any sort of spiritual order'. Benjamin goes on to say that the poet enacts the foundation of such a spiritual order of the people within the self-enclosed sphere of the poems. The autonomy of art allows for such a foundation. The foundation itself is non-dualist (and in this way non-Kantian because it bridges the gulf between the realms of nature and freedom). The substance of the poeticed names this foundation as the reconciliation or fusion between the order of perception and intellection.

The poetized as the law of identity establishes 'a perceptual-intellectual order, the new cosmos of the poet'.[16] The spiritual is part of the intellectual sphere and the perceptual is the perception of empirical life as it is. These two spheres cannot be reconciled in the conflictual state of the present. Only the free space of art allows for such reparative reconciliation between spiritual/intellectual meaning and empirical/perceptual life, between the Kantian realms of freedom and nature. Crucially Benjamin's politics is marked by this tension between the profane and the spiritual, between historical materialism and theology, between the competing influences of Bert Brecht and Gershom Scholem. His notion of messianism would allow for a coexistence of these tensions where the oppositions in question are no longer oppositional but complementary. The Benjamin of the early years sees such reparative work of infinite completion (rather than competition) taking place in Hölderlin's poetry. Here the poet gives birth to 'the new cosmos' where humanity flourishes within a fused intellectual-perceptual order. Within this novel order the profane (the people) ceases to be simply profane.

It is important to emphasize how strongly Benjamin maintains that 'the new cosmos of the poet' has nothing to do with our empirical one. The myth of the poem bears no resemblance to the Hellenic myth (which, according to Benjamin, is part of humanity's state of corruption) and the people featured in the poem are radically others from either current or past forms of human community:

---

15 Benjamin, *Collected Writings, Vol 1*, p. 23.
16 Benjamin, *Collected Writings, Vol 1*, p. 24.

'Is this life still that of Hellenism? That is as little the case here as that the life of any pure work of art could be that of a people; and as little the case, too, that what we find in the poetized might be the life of an individual and nothing else'. This life is shaped in the forms of Greek myth, but—this is crucial—not in them alone; the Greek element is sublated in the last version and balanced against another element that without express justification was called the Oriental.[17]

Clearly, Benjamin's vocabulary is Kantian. Significantly, he transfers Kant's purity of reason to that of art. Nevertheless there is a stark dualism separating 'any pure art' from the profanity of the people that replicates the Kantian divide between pure reason and the pathology of our (natural) inclinations. Benjamin extends the incompatibility between the purity of poetry and the empirical life of a people to the discrepancy between Hellenic myth and what he calls the Oriental.

In his letters and in his essays on tragedy, Hölderlin confronts the Greek with its apparent opposite, the Oriental. Benjamin is quite close to Hölderlin's thought when he elaborates about the radical interconnection achieved via art. In a letter of 28 September 1803 to the publisher Friedrich Wilmans, Hölderlin characterizes the distinctiveness of his Sophocles translations as follows: 'Greek art is foreign to us because of the national convenience and bias it has always relied on, and I hope to present it to the public in a more lively manner than usual by bringing out further the Oriental element it denied and correcting its artistic bias wherever it occurs.'[18] Hölderlin translates Greek texts against their grain. He foregrounds that which is ostensibly repudiated in them.

The Oriental is what the Greeks defined as the opposite of their civilization, namely, as barbarian (*barbaroi*). In a later letter of 2 April 1804 to Wilmans, Hölderlin argues that his translations brings about what Freud would later call the return of the repressed. The Oriental is what the Greeks deny themselves. This denial is a repression of what is part of their being. Hölderlin's 'eccentric enthusiasm' reveals the unacknowledged presence and over-determination of the repressed: 'I am certain', he writes to Wilmans, 'I have written in the direction of eccentric enthusiasm and thus reached Greek simplicity; I hope to continue to stick to this principle, even if that means exposing what was forbidden to the

---

17 Benjamin, *Collected Writings. Vol 1*, p. 35.
18 Hölderlin, *Essays and Letters*, edited and translated with an introduction by Jeremy Adler and Charlie Louth, (London: Penguin, 2009), p. 215.

original poet, precisely by going in the direction of eccentric enthusiasm'.[19] What Hölderlin describes here as 'eccentric enthusiasm' compares well with Benjamin's notion of interruption: being eccentric, it pushes an entity to break with its homogenous self-image and in doing so persuades it to find a multiple identity in what is perceived to be other than itself. By evoking the Oriental within the confines of Hellenic myth, Benjamin emphasizes that the people of the two Hölderlin poems under discussion are not that of a homogenous group. Rather they are a multitude of difference. They are Greek and what the Greek saw as their other: the Oriental.

Despite the stark dualist opposition between a people and 'pure art' Benjamin does not establish a dualism between social issues and aesthetics. The divide between the life of poetry and that of society in its present and past forms serves to reinforce the necessity of a "new cosmos" established by "pure art". It is the birth of this 'new cosmos' that offers an alternative space where humanity can truly flourish unencumbered by the harmful practices under the status quo. The Oriental not only disturbs the purported homogeneity of "a people" (the Greeks) but, according to Benjamin, it also denotes the reparative force to which such disturbance of established forms of exclusion and suffering may give rise. By unravelling the assumed homogeneity of Hellenic myth, the Oriental finds connections rather than oppositions. It pushes the Greek to its eccentric opposite (the Oriental) and connects the two.

What is crucial here is that the contemplation of art accomplishes this connective work. Here it becomes apparent that poetry in all its purity benefits society at large: 'The contemplation of the poetized, however, leads not to myth but rather—in the greatest creations—only to mythic connections, which in the work of art are shaped into unique, unmythological, unmythic forms that cannot be better understood by us.'[20] The poetized is the truth of poetry which resides in what Benjamin calls the law of identity. The law of identity determines each isolated part of the work of art and in doing so frees it from isolation. It establishes a new cosmos of infinite connections. It renders myth 'unmythic'; frees it from its homogeneity and exclusive location within one people and one culture. While the law of identity appears to be a purely aesthetic term, it has clear impact on societal issues precisely by dint of its radical independence from various political pressures that would force it to reach

---

19 Hölderlin, *Essays and Letters*, p. 220.
20 Ibid.

compromises with practices of opposition and exclusion characteristic of society's status quo:

> This law of identity states that all unities in the poem already appear in intensive interpenetration; that the elements are never purely graspable; that, rather, one can grasp only the structure of relations, whereby the identity of each individual being is a function of an infinite chain of series in which all essences in the poetized are revealed as the unity of what are in principle infinite functions. No element can ever be singled out, void of relation, from the intensity of the world order, which is fundamentally felt. With respect to all individual structures—to the inner form of the verses and images—this law will prove to be fulfilled, so as to bring about, finally, at the heart of all poetic connections, the identity of the perceptual and the intellectual forms among and with another—the spatiotemporal interpenetration of all configurations in a spiritual quintessence, the poetized that is identical with life.[21]

I have cited this rather long and dense quotation because it questions a complete disconnection between poetry and life. Benjamin does not advocate an escape into autonomous art which leaves behind worldly or societal concerns. Indeed his usage of the term "world order" reinforces a conception of poetry that lies at the heart of society. At the end of this important quotation the poetized, or the truth of poetry, indeed coincides with life: 'the poetized that is identical with life'. By establishing an infinite number of interconnections which renders each being free from isolation, poetry's law of identity becomes identical with life itself. What emerges as truth here is how the radical duality between pure art and society in its established form illuminates the distance that separates the destruction perpetrated under the status quo from life's non-exclusive breadth and depth. Poetry's law of identity describes life's infinite, integrated and interconnected diversity of difference which, under the current state of affairs, can only find its abode within art.

Art gives birth to a new cosmos in which life is truly flourishing because it is determined by what Benjamin calls the poetized or the law of identity, which precludes exclusion and homogeneity. The poet's death at the end of the poem accentuates the difference between art and the destructive life of current societal formations. The poet as depicted in Hölderlin's poetry has to die in order to live the limitless interconnection of the world: 'The poet does not have to fear death; he is a hero because

---

21 Benjamin, *Collected Writings, Vol 1*, p. 25.

he lives at the centre of all relations.'[22] The courage of the poet is the courage to let go of societal conventions that stand in the way of poetry's infinite connectivity: 'All known relations are united in death, which is the poet's world.'[23] There is an underlying anxiety of death in the two versions of the Hölderlin poem as discussed by Benjamin. The 'courage' and the 'timidity' of the two titles name a certain relationship to danger and death which Benjamin denotes as heroic. This is not a military heroism. Rather it is a poetic one that flouts societal norms and standards and thus courts danger if not death. In contrast to the heroism of the soldier, the heroism of the poet does not obey orders and conventions but instead overturns what society expects of its members. The courage in question here is the courage to resist biopolitics: It is the individual's refusal to subject his body and soul to the regulations of the body politic.

This refusal has often been dismissed as madness. Hölderlin himself was of course diagnosed as mentally ill.[24] The theme of madness looms large in Hölderlin's literary work (in particular, in his drama *The Death of Empedolces*) as well as in his essays and letters. In the two versions of the poem discussed by Benjamin, madness is not named as such. It is rather depicted as immense vulnerability: as the poet's openness to the intrusion of danger and death. The poet's (mad) heroism consists in the abandonment of any *cordon sanitaire* that could protect the self against harm and impending mortality. The courage or madness of the poet is consubstantial with a loss of immune system that defends the self against the outside world. The same immune system can of course fall prey to

---

22 Benjamin, *Collected Writings*, Vol 1, p. 34.

23 Ibid.

24 There has been some controversy as to whether Hölderlin was really mad or pretended to be so. For a discussion of Hölderlin's pretence to be mentally ill in order to avoid being charged with revolutionary politics see Pierre Bertaux's *Hölderlin*, (Frankfurt: Suhrkam, 1981). Recently Manfred Frank has made clear that Hölderlin did not pretend to be mad. Frank draws on historical documents showing that Hölderlin assumed revolutionary fellow conspirator Sinclair was actually quite conservative during this time of his life and that Sinclair was accused of subversion by those who envied his highly successful career. Hölderlin's fear was therefore not based on any factual grounds. Frank offers a convincing account of Hölderlin's genuine state of mental illness: "When his new 'caregiver,' the psychiatrist Anstalt took him in, Hölderlin turned into a frenzy and cried: 'I don't want to be Jacobinian, away with all Jacobinians. I can walk before the eyes of my merciful *Kurfüsrsten* with a clear conscience!' On August 3, 1801, Sinclair had asked Hölderlin's mother to have her son picked up—with a gruffness and coolness, the meaning of which remains a puzzle for researchers." Frank, *The Philosophical Foundations of Early German Romanticism*, trans. By Elizabeth Millán-Zaibert, (Albany, NY: State University of New York Press, 2004), p. 131.

autoimmunity. The courageous/mad poet has realized that the apparent exclusivity of opposites (such as between the self and the outside) are in truth relational rather exclusive. Hence there is no longer any need for self-defence (such as enacted by the immune system).[25]

This radical openness of the poet to the world calls into doubt the Kantian transcendental *a priori* that serves to ensure independence from the contingency and moral hazards that sometimes shape empirical conditions. Kantian autonomy immunizes self and society, protecting it from the dreaded pathologies of embodied existence. How can we reconcile the duality Benjamin establishes between pure art and the destruction, perpetrated under the status quo with his argument for a radically non-dualistic radically interconnected world? Benjamin has a reason not to forsake a neo-Kantian idealism of some sorts. This is so because he needs to find a strategy by which he can establish a realm of freedom. This realm of freedom is precisely the new cosmos created by poetry. The dualism between the destruction perpetrated under the status quo and the birth of new life under the aegis of art is necessary in order to enable within this new life the reign of non-duality, or, in other words, of the infinitely relational. Benjamin in his earlier works refers to Kant's transcendental idealism in order to theorize art as free space where life can truly flourish. He constructs a divide between art and the destructive life that determines the current state of affairs only to dissolve it within the new cosmos of the poem itself. Within this new cosmos there is no longer any dualism 'for the ultimate law of this world is precisely connection'.[26]

Strikingly, Benjamin's move from a dualism that separates art from the status quo, to the abandonment of all duality within the new cosmos of the poem, retraces Hölderlin's own itinerary from the Kantian *a priori* to a Spinozist conception of an interconnected universe governed by palingenesis (as encountered in his study of Herder).[27] As Hölderlin writes in a letter of 24 December 1798 to his friend Isaac von Sinclair:

'Everything is interconnected, and suffers as soon as it is active, including the purest thought a human being can have'. And properly

---

25 For a discussion of this point see Mack's 'Between Elias Canetti and Jacques Derrida: Satire and the Role of Fortifications in the Work of W. G. Sebald' in Gerhard Fischer (ed.), *W. G. Sebald Schreiben ex patria/Expatriate Writing*, (Amsterdam: Rodopi, 2009), pp. 233–256.

26 Benjamin, *Collected Writings. Vol 1*, p. 32.

27 See David Constantine's *Hölderlin*, (Oxford: Clarendon Press, 1988), pp. 166-68 and Mack's *Spinoza and the Specters of Modernity*, pp. 65–84.

speaking of an *a priori* philosophy, entirely independent of all experience is just as much nonsense as a positive revelation where the revealer does the whole thing and he to whom revelation is made is not even allowed to move in order to receive it, because otherwise he would have contributed something of his own.[28]

Diverging from Spinoza's rational universe of holistic determinism (where suffering has a rather diminutive dimension), Hölderlin's Spinozist vision of an interdependent cosmos acknowledges the presence of pathologies. Indeed the relational back and forth motion between the diverse elements of this interconnected world cannot but cause disquiet. The unease in question here is, however, not destructive but one that promotes rather than hinders growth and flourishing. This is why —within this context of a mutually receptive or open interconnectedness—Hölderlin discusses revelation as collaborative work achieved by both creator and creation. We become detached from established forms of life when we are exposed to the unpredictable forces of an interconnected universe. One result of such exposure is madness.

Until roughly the onset of modernity, and Hölderlin's long eighteenth century, in particular, madness had a touch of the divine about it. It was often associated with inspiration and the mad were seen to be communicating with supernatural powers: as Foucault has put it, 'until the Renaissance, the sensibility to madness was linked to the presence of imaginary transcendences'.[29] Foucault locates the denigration of madness as mental illness around the time at which Hölderlin was diagnosed as incurably ill: '*the constitution of madness as mental illness', at the end of the eighteenth century, affords evidence of a broken dialogue, posits the separation as already effected, and thrusts into oblivion all those stammered, imperfect words without fixed syntax in which the exchange between madness and reason was made. The language of psychiatry, which is a monologue of reason* about *madness, has been established on the basis of this silence.*[30]

Hölderlin had to endure this process of marginalization and silencing at the end of the eighteenth century.

After his long journey on foot from Germany via the Alps to the south of France and back, Hölderlin's status as an outsider was reinforced. His dishevelled exterior was certainly no longer acceptable

---

28 Hölderlin, *Essays and Letters*, p. 117.

29 Foucault, *Madness and Civilization: A History of Insanity in the Age of Reason*, translated by Richard Howard, (New York: Random House, 1965), p. 58.

30 Foucault, *Madness and Civilization*, p. x–xi.

within bourgeois society. He was to many of his old friends a subject of exclusion. In a famous letter to Casimir Ulrich Böhlendorff of November 1802, Hölderlin celebrates his madness or his detachment from the exclusionary practices of society as the life of interconnection with nature, the divine and the people of Bordeaux: 'The violent element, the fire of the sky, and the quiet of the people, their life in the open and their straightforwardness and contentment, stirred me continually, and as one says of heroes I can probably say of myself: that Apollo has struck me.'[31] The description of the sun as 'violent element', as 'fire of the sky' anticipates the paintings of Van Gogh. Hölderlin undergoes a certain detachment from the status quo: he has become receptive to the non-human (the sun and Apollo). The people in question are not homogenous and hence closed off from the elements and the rest of humanity. Instead they live the life of interconnection; they live 'in the open'. The poet radicalizes this openness by being touched not only by the elements but by god himself: the moving phrase 'Apollo has struck me' conveys both certain distance to societal structure and the vision of a true life within the open of an interconnected universe. A radically porous relation to the world comes at the price of detachment from the status quo.

According to the earlier works of Benjamin, a dualism between pure art and the status quo offers purchase on such a relational life of non-duality within the new cosmos created by poetry. Everything depends on the priority of the poem. As shall be discussed in the following section, Heidegger prioritizes history and people-hood. He even reads Hölderlin's people of Bordeaux in terms of exemplifying German essence. By contrast, Benjamin 'turns the people into a sensuous-intellectual function of the poetic life'.[32] I have discussed some quotations from Hölderlin's letters in order to highlight the way in which Benjamin's philosophical and rather abstract discussion is nevertheless faithful to Hölderlin's conception of an interconnected universe created by poetry. The isolation of the poet within a society based on various forms of hierarchy, exploitation and exclusion is a theme that runs throughout Hölderlin's poetic cosmos: the famous quote from the elegy *Bread and Wine* 'and why poets in mean times (*und wozu Dichter in dürfiger Zeit*)' emphasize the gulf that separates the poem from its place within contemporary society.[33]

---

31 Hölderlin, *Essays and Letters*, p. 213.

32 Benjamin, *Collected Writings. Vol 1*, p. 29.

33 Hölderlin, *Sämtliche Werke. Kritische Textausgabe. Vol6: Elegien und Epigramme*, edited by D. E. Sattler, (Frankfurt a. M.: Verlag Roter Stern, 1979), p. 109.

6.3 Heidegger or Poetry as a Function of History/Politics and Art as Basis for Politics in Benjamin

Benjamin's claim, however, that Hölderlin turns the people into a function of his poetry may strike some readers as odd. As we have seen, Hölderlin calls the poets 'tongues of the people'. According to Benjamin, the people concerned here are not socially existent but rather a substantial part of the new cosmos created within the mental space of the poem. There the people can truly be the people of a non-exploitative and inclusive society. The new cosmos of the poem offers a stark contrast to the one prevalent now. It is this contrast that has the potential to further reparative work towards non-exclusive well being within the present and the future. Such work would help restore bygone lives that have been damaged by past practices of exploitation. As we have seen, Benjamin, building upon Hölderlin's notion of an eccentric enthusiasm, renders a given identity as strange, as non-coinciding with itself. In this way Hellenism recognizes itself in what it apprehends as its opposite: the Oriental. The people whom Hölderlin's poetry celebrates are those who have traversed an eccentric itinerary from homogeneity to the law of an inter-connected identity that characterizes the life of the new cosmos as engendered by poetry.

It is in the discussion of a complex relationship between poetry and the people that Benjamin's philosophical approach towards literature differs from that of Heidegger's. As Timothy Clark has shown, Heidegger's philosophy attempts to bring about 'art's death'.[34] The death of art has of course been a concern of Hegel's dialectic. Indeed Heidegger's attempted death of art is quite Hegelian. It is not so much Heidegger's new idea as his radicalization of Hegel's sublation of art within politics and secular history. According to Pippin, Hegel's conception of modernity is marked by both the proto-Heideggerian death of art and the privatization of religion:

> A great subordination of the roles of art and religion in modern life (they both have become essentially 'things of the past') and defense of what Hegel himself calls the "prosaic" character of modern bourgeois life, the unheroic life of nuclear families, civil society, market economies, and representational democracy. Modernity is our unavoidable philosophical fate, and its fate is, at least in essentials, the rational realization of freedom.[35]

---

34 Clark, *Martin Heidegger*, (London: Routledge, 2002), p. 64.
35 Pippin, *The Persistence of Subjectivity*, p. 136.

In contrast to Hegel, however, Heidegger's writing about modernity is quite ambiguous. On one hand, he realizes that it is 'our unavoidable philosophical fate' (unavoidable nihilism as modernity's inner logic as he discusses in his writings on Nietzsche) and, on the other, his philosophy questions the anthropocentrism that he finds most markedly announced at the beginning of modern rational thought, in the work of Descartes. From *Being and Time* (1927) onwards Heidegger takes issue with the human-centred wilfulness of modernity. In contrast to ancient thought, modern Cartesian philosophy does not allow a place for the unconcealed. Modernity seems to be pre-occupied with calculation: 'In modern metaphysics, the sphere of the invisible is defined as the realm of the presence of calculated objects. Descartes describes this as consciousness of the *ego cogito*.'[36] As a form of protest against the modern predominance of the calculating moment, Heidegger increasingly turns his philosophical attention to the truth disclosed in poetry. Here he finds being beyond the all too certain illusion proffered by the clarity of numbers.

This aversion to calculation and, associated with it, human wilfulness has aroused the interest of contemporary eco-criticism. Clark describes Heidegger as a godfather of contemporary ecological consciousness:

> 'The attack on the deeply anthropocentric assumptions of Western thought and religion gives his work an ethical force'. It is chastening to human pride in a way comparable to the ethics of the 'deep ecology' movement. Against the traditional metaphysical drive towards a timeless perspective, a view from nowhere, Heidegger's thinking is based on an acceptance of human finitude.[37]

Heidegger's critique of the will and of anthropocentricism (both narrow down truth to a question of the calculable or, in other words, Cartesian certainty) informs his interest in Hölderlin's poetry. Heidegger's depiction of technology as *Gestell* (enframing) attempts to shed a light on the distortion of modern anthropocentric representations of the world. As we have seen in the above discussion of Benjamin's early essay, Hölderlin's work is permeated by a vision of an interconnected universe where the reductive logic of calculation is only a tiny part (as in the opening of *Bread and Wine* where the bourgeois sphere of 'gain and loss'

---

36 Heidegger, 'What are poets for?' in Heidegger, *Poetry, Language, Thought*, translations and introduction by Albert Hofstadter, (New York: HarperCollins, 1971), p. 125.

37 Clark, *Martin Heidegger*, p. 37.

characterizes the present which excludes the openness of poetry) of a larger, infinite cosmos that cannot be abridged as a simple equation.[38]

While Heidegger criticizes the modern reduction of truth to a question of anthropocentric and utilitarian calculation (as an enframing, as a *Gestell*), he nevertheless upholds a conception of art as a representation of being. Art discloses truth. Benjamin does not dispute this. The truth which Heidegger discovers in poetry differs, however, from that which characterizes Benjamin's understanding of the reparative/messianic-natal rather than representational/mimetic actuality of the work of art. As we have seen in the discussion above, Benjamin theorizes poetry as a key to human flourishing precisely because it is detached and removed from harmful and exploitative practices that shape our current condition of existence. The poets are the tongues of a people not to be reduced to the homogeneity and exclusiveness that attaches to the historical and political connotations of the word *Volk* (this is of course especially pertinent to the time during which Benjamin composed his essay—the beginning of World War I).

While Benjamin denies that Hölderlin's poetry has any relation to the historical and political existence of a people, art 'for Heidegger takes place as a potentially disclosive event within the horizon formed by the word of a specific historical people (*Volk*).'[39] As disclosure of the specificity of a historical people, Heidegger's notion of the truth of art engages a reductionism of sorts, one that does not reduce what it discusses to a question of numbers, but to a matter of history and ideology. By turning poetry into a condition of itself, Benjamin attempts to avoid the exclusions that characterize the reduction of art to historical or ideological truth.

Heidegger's opposition between earth and world prepares for his reduction of poetry to a disclosure of historical and political truth. Here anthropocentricism enters Heidegger's thought via the backdoor. He does not acknowledge his anthropocentric stance but it clearly emerges when he contrasts the non-disclosure of the earth with the openness, the lightening, the *aletheia* or undisclosedness of the world that characterizes

---

38 Manfred Frank has clearly differentiated Hölderlin's (and that of Novalis and Friedrich Schlegel) from the dualism of a divide between nature and the realm of freedom in the work of Descartes, Kant, and Fichte. According to Frank, Hölderlin 'develops a conception of the essence of unity as a structure articulated through that which is not only incompatible with Descartes' and Kant's—but also Fichte's—dualistic intuitions, that, despite its inconspicuous appearance, marks a turning point in modern thought'.Frank, *The Philosophical Foundations of Early German Romanticism*, p. 117.

39 Clark, *Martin Heidegger*, p. 65.

humanity. The world discloses itself as the truth of our historical being: 'Wherever those decisions of our history that relate our very being are made, are taken up and abandoned by us, go unrecognized, and are redis-covered by new inquiry, there the world worlds. A stone is worldless.'[40] The contrast between the natural world of the stone and that of the real world as founded by human history is certainly open to the charge of anthropocentricism. Heidegger nevertheless hedges his truth claims by saying that the being of this historical world can never reach the level of certainty as that practiced in modern calculations: 'The *world worlds*, and is more fully in being than the tangible and perceptible realm in which we believe ourselves to be at home.'[41] The truth of the human world is contin-gent. Heidegger has clearly abandoned a belief in humanitiy's willed con-struction of history. History happens and cannot be planned. Humanity's existence is thrown. Any construction of a plan or meaning within this thrown state of being (*Geworfenheit*) is subject to death and finitude.[42]

The absence of any constructive element in Heidegger's notion of history may hold out the promise of an open-ended and non-exclusive conception of humanity.[43] It becomes highly problematic, however, when

---

40 Heidegger, 'The Origin of the Work of Art,' in Heidegger, *Poetry, Language, Thought*, p. 43.

41 Ibid.

42 Intriguingly, Pippin reads Heidegger's famous being towards death as the admittance of human failure establishing and maintaining a sense of meaning. This admittance makes Heidegger diverge from Kantian and Hegelian idealism: 'Again, Kantian transcendental conditions cannot "fail." That is the whole point of their necessity. The Heideggerian elements of practical sense making can ultimately fail or even be permanently forgotten. That is the whole point of saying that care is shot through with *Nichtigkeit* and is the null basis of nullity.' Pippin, *The Persistence of Subjectivity*, p. 75.

43 For a fascinating reading of the liberating potential within Heidegger's thought see John McCumber, *Metaphysics and Oppression: Heidegger's Challenge to Western Philosophy*, (Bloomington: Indiana University Press, 1999). Heidegger later revised his opposition between earth and world has starkly presented in his essay of 1936 'The Origin of the Work of Art'. Jeff Malpas has recently read Heidegger's phi-losophy of the fourfold in terms of an open-minded and non-exclusive sense of cosmic interconnectedness: 'The elements are thereby counterposed stand to one another, not in a relation of 'strife' or opposition (which is how the relation be-tween earth and world is presented in the 'The Origin of the Work of Art'), but rather in terms of their belonging to one another within the belonging together of the fourfold. This is an important point of difference since it picks up on a charac-terisitic feature of the way Heidegger understands the Event as indeed a gathering of that which differs only in, and through, a prior belonging-together.' Malpas, *Heidegger's Topology: Being, Place, World*, (Cambridge, Mass.: Massachusetts Insti-tute of Technology, 2006), p. 232.

Heidegger espouses the historically and politically contingent as the disclosure of truth. He explicitly does so in the early thirties. Then Heidegger idealizes the, to be ascertained temporality and contingency: in his Freiburg seminar *Logic as the Question of the essence of Language* of the summer of 1934 Heidegger speaks 'of our membership in the people' and concomitantly 'our submission to contingent temporality'.[44] The contingent turns absolute when it discloses a specifically human truth of a specific history of a people. He denies this disclosure of truth to the realm of nature (a quasi-Kantian divide between human and natural history emerges here). In a racist move Heidegger equates the inhabitants of Africa whom he calls 'negroes' ('Kaffern') with the animalistic realm of apes and birds:

> 'Nature too—the organic and inorganic—has a history'. But how do we come to say that the negroes (*Kaffern*) are without history? They have after all a history like the apes and the birds. Or do the earth, the plants, and the animals perhaps not have a history after all? Admittedly, it seems incontrovertible that what passes away automatically belongs to a past; but not everything needs to enter history, which passes away and thus belongs to the past. What about the turning of a propeller? This may turn on a daily basis— but essentially (*eigentlich*) nothing happens. If the airplane, however, transports the *Führer* from Munich to Mussolini in Venice, then history takes place.[45]

Here we witness one of Heidegger's first formulations of the contrast between the properly historical world of a people and the time-bound but history-less realm of nature.

History seems to be premised on the successes and failures of specific Western nations. That Heidegger denies non-Western people 'humanity' and that he thus questions whether they are a people is of course racist: it literally divides us into either the animalistic or the properly 'human'. In later work, Heidegger abandons his racist conceptualization of history but the distinction between the merely natural and the properly human to some (and perhaps defensible) extent remains intact. This distinction calls into doubt Heidegger's credential as non-exploitative deep ecologist.

---

44 Heidegger, *Gesamtausgabe II. Abteilung: Vorlesungen 1919–1944. Band 38. Logik als this Frage nach dem Wesen der Sprache*, (ed.) By Günter Seubold, (Frankfurt a. M.: Klostermann, 1998), p. 58.

45 Heidegger, *Gesamtausgabe II. Abteilung: Vorlesungen 1919-1944. Band 38. Logik als this Frage nach dem Wesen der Sprache*, p. 85.

The critique of technology is already part of his appraisal of the truth of legitimately human history, for the airplane that transports Hitler is itself as insignificant as the history-less time of nature.

Heidegger takes issue with technology as something that is not essentially human but quasi natural: neither the technological achievement of an airplane's propeller nor a stone characterize humanity but the history making trip of the Führer to another fascist leader (Mussolini) does so. What Heidegger seems to be saying is that the modern concentration on the technological is not pertinent to the distinctive historical truth that distinguishes the human from the non-human sphere. In 'The Origin of the Work of Art' Heidegger establishes a threefold connection between history, people-hood and world that constitutes humanity and separates it from the merely natural realm of the earth: 'The world is the self-disclosing openness of the broad paths of the simple and essential decisions in the destiny of an historical people.'[46] As Jeff Malpas has pointed out, after World War II Heidegger significantly includes the earth into the more inclusive account of the fourfold (which embraces men, world, earth and gods).[47] Heidegger developed, however, his philosophy of poetry during the thirties and early forties. Here his conception of art originates in a stark divide that separates history and humanity (world) from the merely natural with which he seems to associate non-Western people (earth). History seems to endow Occidental people with a specific task or telos and thus makes them (for Heidegger) truly human: 'History is the transporting of a people into its appointed task as entrance into that people's endowment.'[48] Without history a people seems to cease being a people; then it is dis- or non-endowed.

The thrown state of our existence implies that we cannot find a task that is intrinsic to us. Instead we have to construct one. History is the work of such contingent construction that is always subject to failure. According to Heidegger, art constructs and reveals the historical task of a people:

'Art is historical, and as historical it is the creative preserving of truth in the work'. Art happens as poetry. Poetry is founding in the triple sense of bestowing, grounding, and beginning. Art as founding is essentially historical. This means not only that art has a history in the external sense that in the course of time it, too, appears along with many other things, and in the process changes

---

46 Heidegger, *Poetry, Language, Thought*, p. 47.

47 See Malpas, *Heidegger's Topology*, p. 232.

48 Heidegger, *Poetry, Language, Thought*, p. 74.

and passes away and offers changing aspects for historiology. Art is history in the essential sense that it grounds history.[49]

Here Heidegger spends some time elaborating art's specific significance for history. It is not only subject to historical changes but it also determines these changes. This means that there would not be any history without art. Art establishes or founds history. Art responds to the contingent or arbitrarily thrown state of our existence by the autonomous foundation of a task which might succeed or fail in transcending arbitrariness. Truth is the success or failure of such a foundation.

Art responds to the arbitrary throw that is our existence by a leap into history as a people's autonomous self-construction within poetry. According to Heidegger, a people and its history originates within and is maintained by the art of poetry: 'To originate something by a leap, to bring something into being, from out of the source of its nature in a founding leap—this is what the word origin (German *Ursprung*, literally, primal meaning leap) means.'[50] The origin of the work of art thus is the leap as denoted within the primal meaning of the German word '*Ursprung*' (origin). It is a leap from the arbitrarily thrown into the art of history and politics: 'The origin of the work of art—that is, the origin of both the creators and the preservers, which is to say of people's historical existence, is art.'[51] Here Heidegger conflates art with the people. Art and the people establish and preserve human history and thus reveal and maintain truth. Art is the truth of a people's historical existence 'because art is by its nature an origin: a distinctive way in which truth comes into being, that it becomes historical'.[52] Heidegger conceptualizes truth, paradoxically, as the risk and contingency implicit within historical foundations. These foundations reveal humanity's truth because they attempt to overcome the quasi-natural condition of our existence which—as purely natural—is comparable to that of the stone: thrown somewhere and while lying there still subject to further dislodgements.

In his lectures on *Hölderlin's Hymn 'The Isther'* Heidegger implicity contrasts the fluid and highly unstable situation of being thrown with the etymological meaning of the German word for writing poetry (*dichten*): '"To poetize", *dichten*—in Latin *dictare*—means to write down, to fore-tell something to be written down. To tell something that, prior to this, has not yet been told. A properly unique beginning thus lies in

49 Heidegger, *Poetry, Language, Thought*, p. 75.
50 Ibid.
51 Ibid.
52 Ibid.

whatever is said poetically.'[53] Here Heidegger interprets poetry in a way similar to Benjamin's own: as a new cosmos or as a properly unique beginning. The new beginning in question here is, however, different from Benjamin's radically novel cosmos that cannot be compared— let alone equated with—a people or an historical formation.

Both Heidegger and Benjamin depict poetry as a form of birth. Their respective understanding of birth differs, however. As has been discussed in the previous section, Benjamin indentifies the origin of well being in a mental rather than physical space: in the transcendentally conditioned *a priori* existence of the poem where everything that bears resemblance to the status quo (the people) is merely a function of this radically new cosmos of what he calls the poeticed. Heidegger, in contrast to Benjamin, makes poetry a function of the people and of its history. According to Heidegger, Hölderlin's poetry serves the function to establish and to reveal the history of the German people. Heidegger reads Hölderlin's fascination with rivers like the Danube or the Rhine as an attempt towards establishing 'symbolic images' of German essence and life.[54] In his discussion of Hölderlin's poem 'Remembrance' ('Andenken'), Heidegger equates the essence of poetry (what he calls "das *Dichterische*") with the foundation of national and historical identity: the poet 'creates the poeticed ("das *Dichterische*") on which dwells as on its ground historical humanity (das geschichtliche Menschentum)'.[55] In a further metaphysical move, Heidegger equates the recalling of a marriage ceremony in the south of France with the birth of German identity: 'the marriage ceremony is the hidden birthday of history, that is to say, the history here of the German people.'[56] Clearly Heidegger de-individualizes the reality of Hölderlin's poem.[57] The birthday in question here remembers the birth of homogenous species' existence—that of the German people. It is a birthday of biopolitics.

Benjamin as well as Heidegger conceives of poetry in terms of new beginnings, of a birth that establishes something new. By turning the poem into a function of history, politics, and national identity, Heidegger, however, aligns the poetic with the biopolitical. The birth in question is

---

53 Heidegger, *Hölderlin's Hymn 'The Isther'*, translated by William McNeil and Julia Davis, (Bloomington, In.: Indiana University Press, 1996), p. 9.

54 Heidegger, *Hölderlin's Hymn 'The Isther'*, p. 18.

55 Heidegger, *Erläuterungen zu Hölderlins Dichtung*, edited by Friedrich-Wilhelm von Hermann (Frankfurt: Klostermann, 1944), p. 106.

56 Heidegger, *Erläuterungen zu Hölderlins Dichtung*, p. 107.

57 For a discussion of how Heidegger readings do not do justice to the poetry he discusses see Veronique Fot's *Heidegger and the Poets. Poiesis/Sophia/Techne*, (New Jersey: Humanities Press, 1995).

that of a species (German people) and not that of diverse human flourishing. As T. W. Adorno, and more recently, Lacaue-Labarthe, has clearly shown, in his attempt to cast the poem as the function of historical and national identity, Heidegger distorts—all protestations to the contrary—the literal, physical and often erotic description of Hölderlin's poetry.[58] He thus reads Hölderlin's expression of gratitude to German women as a trigger for the remembrance of the erotic allure of Bordeaux's "brown women" as the divine essence of Germanness. Nothing could be further away from what Hölderlin is actually saying in the following lines: 'Thank the German women! They have preserved the friendly spirit of the gods' images for us.'[59] The gods in question are the 'brown women' (mentioned in the preceding lines of the poem) of Bordeaux of which the German women are a remembrance. Heidegger, however, turns this memory of erotic quasi-divine attraction into the quasi-theological celebration of an anthropocentric conception of the divine as the German people.

In Heidegger's account, poetry is not an independent entity but one that serves political and historical interests. As his misreading of the erotic aspects of Hölderlin's poetry has shown, Heidegger leaps from the poetic to the historically and politically grounded notions of authority and hierarchy (i.e. women as images of the quasi-divine status of the German people). One could say that Heidegger has endowed Hölderlin's poetry with the pseudo-theological aura of historical and political truth claims.[60] In the wake of Nazism's rise to power Benjamin defines and critiques what he calls aura in his famous essay 'The Work of Art in the Age of Mechanical Reproduction'.

As Alys Eve Weinbaum has recently shown aura plays a political role. It pretends to transmit a community's authentic history and identity— exactly that which Heidegger discovers as poetry's revelation of truth:

> 'Aura is initially associated with "historical testimony,'" "author-
> ity," and "authenticity." However, after first introducing the con-
> cept […], Benjamin continually returns to, augments, and reworks
> it so that aura eventually becomes associated not only with these
> attributes but also with its pretense of their presence, with their
> spectral effect. In other words, while aura initially names that

---

58 See Lacoue-Labarthe, *Heidegger and the Politics of Poetry*, pp. 40–43.

59 Quoted from Lacoue-Labarthe's, *Heidegger and the Politics of Poetry*, p. 41.

60 For a detailed discussion of the notion "pseudo-theology" see Mack's *German Idealism and the Jew*. For both a critique and further development of the term see J Kameron' Carter's *Race: A Theological Account*, (Oxford: Oxford University Press, 2008).

which "withers" or "decays," it later comes to name that which is artificially produced to replace or fill-in where a loss of "authority" or "authenticity" is identified or felt.[61]

Initially Benjamin describes aura as art's cultic value. As Weinbaum has clearly shown, cultic value can be produced technologically. Technology is capable of presenting the illusion of a modern form of aura, as occurs in fascist and other totalitarian forms of propaganda.

Significantly Benjamin defines cult not in terms of religious creeds but as the confirmation of established notions of authority, hierarchy, identity and authenticity. Aura presents a quasi-religious or 'cultic' sense of continuity: it attempts to make authentic a people's history and identity— precisely what Heidegger sees as being revealed by the truth of art. Aura is 'the authenticity of a given object as the quintessence of that which has been its tradition from its point of origin covering its material duration as well as its historical testimony.'[62] According to Benjamin technology's as well as poetry's reparative potential consists in a disruption of history's continuity.

By breaking the link between the work of art and the aura of its tradition and history, mechanical reproduction helps give birth to the new cosmos of the poem whose liberating potential Benjamin celebrates in his early essay on Hölderlin. As we have seen in the first part of this chapter, Benjamin earlier on sees the poem as a mental space where humanity can truly flourish precisely because it offers a space unconstrained by the violence and the practices of exclusion that characterize the status quo. The status quo is of course part of our traditional sense of history and politics. The new cosmos created by poetry interrupts this continuity of misery comparable to the way in which mechanical reproduction has the potential to break with traditional forms of production and perception of social reality.

Benjamin's 'Work of Art in the Age of Mechanical Reproduction' closes with a famous contrast between fascism and communism. His understanding of communism is highly idiosyncratic, because it turns art into the substance and centre of the communist revolution. It is quite astonishing that we encounter Benjamin's earlier uncompromising stance on art as a condition of its own making in his conceptualization of communism. This is so because Benjamin in the thirties turns art into the

---

61 Weinbaum, 'Racial Aura: Walter Benjamin and the Work of Art in a Biotechnological Age' in *Literature and Medicine Vol.* 26 (Spring 2007): pp. 207-239 (217).

62 Benjamin, *Gesammelte Schriften. Vol I/2 Abhandlungen*, edited by Rolf Tiedemann and Hermann Schweppenhäuser, (Frankfurt: Suhrkamp, 1974), p. 477.

heart of a communist revolution that has the potential to disrupt history as the continued and continual state of exploitation and exclusion. According to Benjamin in the later years 'fascism focuses on the aesthetization of politics (*Ästhetizierung der Politik*)' and 'communism responds with the politicisation of art (*Politisierung der Kunst*).'[63] Benjamin's claim that fascism aestheticizes politics can easily be backed up with historical evidence: the Nazis indeed used modern technology in order to endow their politics with aura. His understanding of communism is, however, highly idiosyncratic. Was art indeed at the heart of communism and the ground on which it was built? This question has to be left in the open. As we have seen, Benjamin attempts to revolutionize our conception of art. What is revolutionary about his revision of art is that he emphasizes its natal and not, as has traditionally been done, its mimetic capacities. Heidegger's bio-political interpretation of poetry as ground, revelation and representation of a people's history still clings to a conception of the aesthetic as mimetic. In a sense Heidegger's work on Hölderlin's poetry (of the thirties and forties) exemplifies what Benjamin criticizes as the subordination of art to the ideological commandments of existing politics. Benjamin is concerned with art's societal and political benefit but in ways different to that of Heidegger. Rather than subordinating art to historical forces (of politics and economics), he makes us see its intrinsic revolutionary potential. Art emerges as the force behinds new beginnings that disrupt the violence and the exclusions that are part of history's continuity. Art creates a non-exclusive mental space that has the potential to shape novel political fields where society promotes non-exclusive well being. In the following chapter we will see you how literature's inclusive mental state can assist in changing the way we think about age and aging.

---

63 Benjamin, *Gesammelte Schriften. Vol I/II Abhandlungen*, p. 508.

7   Rethinking Birth and Aging: A Conclusion

This chapter concludes our discussion about aging and birth by making the two terms complementary to each other (rather than exclusive of each other). Romanticism—the subject matter of the two preceding chapters—has a significant role to play in undermining the traditional opposition between youth and age. Lord Henry in Wilde's *Dorian Gray* elaborates as follows:

> 'It is marvellously romantic'. What a blessing it is that there is one art left that is not imitative! Don't stop. I want music to-night. It seems to me that you are the young Apollo, and that I am Marsyas listening to you. I have sorrows, Dorian, of my own, that even you know nothing of. The tragedy of old age is not that one is old, but that one is young.[1]

With these words Lord Henry (in the closing pages of Oscar Wilde's *The Picture of Dorian Gray*) appraises the quasi-redemptive nature of art while complaining about the aching that goes with aging. Lord Henry appreciates a certain type of artistic practice; a form of art which he calls 'romantic'. What distinguishes romanticism in this context is its non-mimetic, non-representational character. It is, as Lord Henry puts it, 'not imitative'. He goes on to reflect upon his own visible fate as bodying forth age and he associates aging with suffering and youth with success and health. In this way, he compares himself with Marsyas while Dorian Gray figures as Apollo. In Greek mythology, Apollo rips off the skin of Marsyas and in this way metes out his punishment for the presumption to question his artistic superiority (Marsyas has done so by asking for a singing competition between himself and the god of poetry).

Romantic art, in Lord Henry's understanding of the term, has a restorative function because it does not imitate or reinforce what we have become used to. Indeed it questions the truth of received wisdom,

---

1   Wilde, *The Complete Works of Oscar Wilde: Stories, Plays, Poems, Essays*, With an introduction by Vyvan Holland, (London: Collins, 1992), p. 162.

representation and myth. This is exactly what Lord Henry does at the end of the quote when he interrogates the assumed dichotomy between the suffering Marsyas and the ever youthful god Apollo. Visible signs of suffering and manifestations of aging have become interchangeable notions in the society that Lord Henry implicitly criticises in the closing sentence of the quote: 'The tragedy of old age is not that one is old, but that one is young.' The tragedy is one of representation. The suffering here derives from a gap between the social stereotype and the emotions, experiences as well as actions of those who are stereotyped by their society—and are seen to display the typical characteristics of a given stereotype. This tragedy of representation is still prevalent today and as Sander L. Gilman has shown not only in popular culture but also in the educated and presumably well-informed field of medical practice. According to Gilman, 'in contemporary America' physicians associate beauty with health, whereas ugliness and bodily signs of aging raise the immediate suspicion of dissolution, decay, in short, disease:

> 'Thus in contemporary America there is an assumption among physicians that the diseased and the beautiful cannot be encapsulated in one and the same category'. Young physicians often see beautiful patients as exemplary or "good" patients, patients who will follow doctor's orders and therefore will regain health. The aged or poor patient, on the other hand, is seen, even by the trained physician, as one who is a "bad" patient, a patient who will probably "make trouble" and whose health will not improve.[2]

One could argue that Wilde's *Dorian Gray* is the most striking and powerful text that potently subjects to ironic treatment such simplistic, stereotypical but nevertheless still prevailing dichotomy between health, youth and beauty as opposed to illness, aging and ugliness. It tells the story of a wish that turns real: Dorian Gray's portrait mutates into a depositary of signs of aging while his actual appearance remains forever young.

There are of course many ironies here. For one the painter of the portrait, Basil Hallward, reiterates his conviction that the portrait is mimetic not of the sitter but of the artist's true inward life: 'it is rather the painter who, on the coloured canvas, reveals himself. The reason I will not exhibit this picture is that I am afraid that I have shown in it the secret of my own soul.'[3] Here Basil Hallward articulates the traditional lamp-like type of

---

2   Gilman, *Disease and Representation: Images of Illness from Madness to AIDS*, (Ithaca, NY: Cornell University Press, 1988), p. 4.

3   Wilde, *The Complete Works of Oscar Wilde*, p. 21.

mimesis which Abrams in *The Mirror and the Lamp* has singled out as a core form of mimesis prevalent in romanticism (see Chapter 5). His fear of exhibiting his painting is thus a fear of psychic exhibitionism. It is a fear fuelled by public norms and perceptions as he makes clear when he criticizes the neo-romantic notion of a work of art as illuminating—shedding like a lamp light on the—soul of the artist: 'We live in an age when men treat art as if it were meant to be a form of autobiography', Hallward complains.[4] While the artist fears his portrait to be a lamp giving access to the inner reaches of his own, rather than the sitter's character, the painting seems to resemble another classic metaphor of traditional mimesis. It appears to be a mirror imaging not the inward regions of the artist's psyche; rather it reflects outward and in a mirror-like fashion represents the otherwise not to be seen personality of the sitter Dorian Gray. This at least is Dorian's wish:

> 'This portrait would be to him the most magical of mirrors'. As it had revealed to him his own body, so it would reveal to him his own soul. And when winter came upon it, he would still be standing where spring trembles on the verge of summer. When the blood crept from its face, and left behind a pallid mask of chalk with laden eyes, he would keep the glamour of boyhood. Not one blossom of his loveliness would ever fade. Not one pulse of his life would ever weaken. Like the gods of the Greeks he would be strong, and fleet, and joyous. What did it matter what happened to the coloured image on the canvas? He would be safe. That was everything.[5]

The work of art literally transforms into a medical device. As such it is socially useful in quite a straightforward manner that chimes with stereotypes of health and illness. It absorbs the aging process to which Dorian Gray would otherwise be bound and in doing so it would ensure his health, flourishing and well-being. His portrait is Dorian's wonder doctor of sorts. Dorian Gray's wish that turns into reality conforms to the ideals and norms of his as well as our society, as described by Sander Gilman in his assessment of contemporary American medical practice. It is also in conformity with the aesthetic ideals of classicism and neo-classicism at least in its vulgar form: the strength and beauty of the Greek gods are proof of their perfect health.

---

4   Wilde, *The Complete Works of Oscar Wilde*, p. 25.
5   Wilde, *The Complete Works of Oscar Wilde*, p. 88.

By turning into a depository for the aging process, his picture frees Dorian Gray from not only illness but also the stigma of ugliness and immorality (bad). At this point, irony again makes an appearance. It disrupts the connection between what is said and the standard or normative meaning of the said. As we have seen via a brief discussion of Gilman's analysis of medical and other societal perceptions and representations of illness, society associates youth, beauty and wealth with health. Wilde's *The Picture of Dorian Gray* refuses to conform to such standardized representations. The story narrates how Dorian's artificial or quasi medical liberation from signs of aging does not ensure his health, flourishing, ethical growth and longevity but, on the contrary, how it leads to his indifference, cruelty and murderous activity. Rather than making him "safe" as he proclaims in the quote above, his eternal youth causes his destruction.

Irony is the trope that characterizes the rhetoric of *The Picture of Dorian Gray*. The rhetorical embraces the ethical and a critique of social practices and expectations. A case in point is what society expects from medicine and what medical practitioners expect from their patients. Both expectations meet in their quasi soteriological idealization of beauty. It is only via a non-exclusively historicist approach to Oscar Wilde's writing and thought that we can do justice to the complexity and ongoing socio-political relevance of *The Picture of Dorian Gray*. As Richard Ellman has shown Wilde was not a straightforward follower of fin de siècle aestheticism. From the composition of the *The Picture of Dorian Gray* onwards Wilde turned aestheticism into a problem to be tested rather that into a creed to be followed or dogma to be obeyed: 'Without surrendering the contempt for morality, or for nature, that had alarmed and annoyed his critics, Wilde now allowed for 'a higher ethics' in which artistic freedom and full expression of personality were possible, along with a curious brand of individualistic sympathy or narcissistic socialism.'[6] Wilde questions morality from an ethical perspective. Morality denotes society's perception of what it means to be healthy. As we have seen there is a prevailing societal tendency to associate health with the appearance of youth as well as beauty and illness with the sign of aging, decay and dissolution.

What Ellmann calls 'higher ethics' is indeed the ethics of literature in its confrontation with accepted creeds—with society's moral standards which might be operative and actual, but nonetheless a distortion of and injustice to the infinite diversity of our humanity. Literature critiques the fiction that governs some elements of what is taken for granted within

---

6   Ellmann, *Oscar Wilde*, (London: Penguin, 1987), p. 288.

society at large. What is taken for granted may sometimes go under the name of morality. By critiquing the untruth or fiction of some aspects of this morality Wilde engages what I would call an ethics of resilience; an ethics that alerts us to the changing nature of our embodied existence and helps us to adapt to change.

Strikingly one of the main themes of Wilde's narrative is Dorian Gray's fear of change. Aestheticism emerges as the opposite of literature's ethics of resilience. While literature persuades us to cope with change, aestheticism attempts to safeguard against transformation and upheaval. It is time to revisit and to revise the purported contradiction between Wilde's assumed celebration of aestheticism in his essays and his critique of it, in *The Picture of Dorian Gray*. Ellmann, amongst others, has described this paradox as follows: 'If *Dorian Gray* presented aestheticism in an almost negative way, his essays, "The Critic as Artist" and "The Soul of Man under Socialism," gave it affirmation.'[7] It is important, however, to distinguish between the aesthetic and aestheticism. The aesthetic denotes both the work of art and the study of the senses (touch, smell, sight and so forth).[8] Aestheticism is something else; it is an ideology or morality that idealizes beauty. This idealization of beauty in terms of health and goodness also characterizes large parts of our normative horizon.[9] Representations of age and illness serve to classify disease as a type of dissolution which comes to represent the opposite of moral worth.

The appearance of decay and disease becomes transformed into categories that demote it as bad and ugly. Continuity thus pervades representations of madness and, other illnesses, from the pre-modern, via the modern to the postmodern: 'The tradition of representing madness in the form of various icons, whether physiognomy or body type, gesture or dress, points toward the need of society to identify the mad absolutely.'[10] Visual representation is the moot point, as Sander Gilman has shown: 'Thus the strength of the visual stereotype is its immediacy. One does not

---

7   Ellmann, *Oscar Wilde*, p. 307. Ellmann, however, goes on to point out that the view of art articulated in Wilde's essay is compatible with the discussion of *The Picture of Dorian Gray* presented in this chapter: 'Arts is a disrupting force. Like criticism, it prevents mere repetition; people must not live each other's lives over and over again.' Ellmann, *Oscar Wilde*, p. 310.

8   For a discussion of this topic see Mack's 'Literature between Medicine and Religion: Herder's Aesthetics of Touch and the Emerging Field of Medical Humanities,' in *Neophilologus* (94, 2010): pp. 541–555.

9   For a detailed discussion of this point see Michael J. Sandel's , *The Case Against Perfection: Ethics in an Age of Genetic Engineering*, (Cambridge, MA: Harvard University Press, 2007).

10 Gilman, *Disease and Representation*, p. 48.

even have to wait for the insane to speak. The mad are instantaneously recognizable.'[11] *Mutatis mutandis* the representation of decay and aging serves to bring to the fore the dissolution of moral norms. Here the exclusion of illness and aging as well as the concomitant idealization of beauty and health (the ideology of aestheticism) goes hand in hand with moral conformity and societal conventionalism.

The Picture of Dorian Gray in fact highlights the surprising coincidence of the presumed opposites: the accepted social creeds of societal morality and the assumed eccentric fictions propounded by aestheticism. How so? Dorian's narcissistic obsession with his youthful beauty is, as the following quote demonstrates, a concern with guarding against any suspicion of sin and other violations of society's moral code: 'He had uttered a mad wish that he himself might remain young, and the portrait grow old; that his own beauty might be untarnished, and the face on the canvas bear the burden of his passions and his sins; that the painted image might be seared with the lines of suffering and thought, and that he might keep all the delicate bloom and loveliness of his then just conscious boyhood.'[12] Dorian's aestheticism is not narrowly narcissistic and it is certainly not idiosyncratic or individualistic. On the contrary it is highly social, trying to ensure social approval and societal respectability. Art turns quite utilitarian. It serves as a secret hiding place for visible signs of what is frowned upon in society: age, aging, ugliness, sins and the passions.

The irony is that rather than being actually at odds with aestheticism, morality in order to perfect itself depends upon artificial devices that produce the effects and the appearance of perfection (beauty and youth as moral embodiments of innocence). *Within this moral idealization of beauty and youth, sin becomes synonymous with age and change.* Society does not allow for signs of aging and stigmatizes them as proof of not only bodily but also moral decay and dissolution. For Dorian aestheticism offers a means of representation that conforms to social expectations of what a moral person looks like.

Wilde's ethical indictment of his and—against the background of Gilman's discussion of contemporary medical practice—our society is that it requires us to veil our organic itinerary from birth via youth to age. We have to turn our lives into fictions in order to live up to the moral ideas prevalent in our society. Dorian Gray becomes a work of art, while, ironically, his portrait embodies his true or real self. In a feast of irony art and life change places—this is the derangement which is Dorion's 'mad

---

11 Ibid.
12 Wilde, *The Complete Works of Oscar Wilde*, p. 78.

wish' that turns real. The character Dorian is not what he seems to be (having become a work of art) and his portrait is no longer what we are accustomed to perceive as work of art (having morphed into the life blood of the sitter). The portrait has become something more than a form of representation: it has turned into an agent, shaping reality (in a sense consuming or eating its path into reality). In this way, the work of art is responsible for the mayhem that unfolds with the course of narration: 'It was the portrait that had done everything.'[13] The transformation of the work of art into a life force has an uncanny equivalent in the change it undergoes. It not only mirrors but actually instantiates a process of aging and decay; a process that is missing in the real Dorian who has assumed the beauty and changelessness of art.

The fate of Dorian's lover, the actor Sibyl Vane, illustrates the exact opposite. Dorian does not love her as such but her art. Sibyl is a living work of art, because as a brilliant actress she turns into the roles she is performing. When Lord Henry asks Dorian: 'When is she Sibyl Vane', the reply is an immediate 'Never'.[14] When Sibyl deteriorates in her acting on account of her love for the flesh and blood Dorian, the latter rejects her. There is another ironic dimension to Sibyl's love for what she takes to be real life but it is an irony unbeknown to her: the 'real' Dorian is artificial whereas his hidden portrait has turned into a space where reality does its work on the true appearance of Mr Gray.

Sibyl Vane's mistake is that she has fallen prey to a conception of the aesthetic as 'flat mimesis'; as copy of the real rather than as an agent of change that transforms our sense of reality. Calling Dorian 'Prince of Life', she expounds a purely representational notion of art, exclaiming: 'You had brought me something higher, something of which all art is but a reflection.' To which Dorian crudely and cruelly replies 'You have killed my love'.[15] Later on, discovering the changed portrait of himself in the attic of his mansion, Dorian realizes the cruelty he has inflicted on Sibyl that will in Ophelia (*Hamlet*) or Gretchen (*Faust*) like fashion lead to her suicide. It is tempting to read this recognition scene as exemplifying the effects of mimesis.

The novel takes issue, however, with conflicting models of mimesis. The portrait is not a mirror of Dorian's soul; on the contrary it embodies rather than represents the changes his facial expressions would organically be subjected to, were it not for the split that turns the flesh and blood Mr Gray into a work of art and his portrait into the instantiation of

13 Wilde, *The Complete Works of Oscar Wilde*, p. 165.
14 Wilde, *The Complete Works of Oscar Wilde*, p. 53.
15 Wilde, *The Complete Works of Oscar Wilde*, p. 75.

organic aging and decay. The novel also disqualifies the lamp-like conception of mimesis according to which a work of art sheds light upon the psyche of the artist. As has been intimated above, the painter of the portrait, Basil Hallward, puts forward this view. Rather than being mimetic of Dorian's life like appearance, like a lamp, so Basil maintains, the portrait illuminates the depth of his own true inner self.

Basil Hallward says as much when he recalls his resolution to keep the picture hidden in a private place where none but himself can have access to it: 'I felt, Dorian,' Basil reveals, 'that I had put too much of myself into it. Then it was that I resolved never to allow the picture to be exhibited. You were a little annoyed; but then you did not realise all that it meant to me'.[16] Dorian is all too glad to oblige but not for the reasons given by the painter. He hints at a rather different explanation for the need for secrecy when he forbids the painter to see his portrait again. Basil Hallward's lamp-like concept of art as representation of the individuality of the painter finds its critical counterpoint in the preface of the novel which states 'To reveal art and conceal the artist is art's aim'.[17] Dorian points to the disturbing impact of art on life—rather than vice versa of life on art as upheld in the mimetic approach to the aesthetic— when he refuses to sit for a portrait ever again: 'I can't explain it to you, Basil, but I must never sit to you again. There is something fatal about a portrait. It has a life of its own.'[18] Here Dorian establishes the radical independence of the portrait from what appears to be real. The irony is of course that what appears to be real is far from being so. There is not so much a copy-mirror-original relationship here—be that as a mirror of the external world of appearance or as a lamp illuminating the depth of the inward sphere—but an ironic reversal of life and art: art has truly become the truth of life and Dorian's real existence has turned into a fiction or mask. Seeing his true life in the picture, Dorian becomes aware of his artificiality. The life of the portrait awakens his conscience: 'It had made him conscious how unjust, how cruel he had been to Sibyl Vane.'[19] This state of consciousness does not last long though. His wish that he will never embody an aging and decaying or ill appearance while alive has turned into reality.

Dorian's desire for the picture to become a mimetic copy of his self by which he could morally orient himself is, however, unrealistic. This is so because his portrait is more than a representation. It has indeed a life of

16 Wilde, *The Complete Works of Oscar Wilde*, p. 94.
17 Wilde, *The Complete Works of Oscar Wilde*, p. 17.
18 Wilde, *The Complete Works of Oscar Wilde*, p. 95.
19 Wilde, *The Complete Works of Oscar Wilde*, p. 81

its own and this life is ironically that of Dorian's embodiment—subject to change, aging and decay. Instead of seeing things as they are, he reads the picture as a symbol. Symbols are static (as pictures are) but his portrait is not a picture or symbol; instead it instantiates life with its itinerary from youth to aging. Dorian hopes for transformation as he could reasonably expect from art but his portrait is no longer a work of art. It has turned into life. Strikingly as the embodiment of his self it evokes shame. The picture's life process of aging solicits its removal from the public sphere. It has to be hidden away in the attic:

> 'His unreal and selfish love would yield to some higher influence', would be transformed into some nobler passion, and the portrait that Basil Hallward had painted of him would be a guide to him what holiness is to some, and conscience to others, and the fear of God to us all. There were opiates for remorse, drugs that could lull the moral sense to sleep. But here was a visible symbol of the degradation of sin.[20]

As the narration unfolds, the picture clearly does not transform the inner life of Dorian Gray: when Basil Hallward sees his changed and ever changing creation—the picture that has become embodied and organic—Dorian kills him. Murder does not have an impact on his conscience either. Instead he forces one of his scientific friends (Alan) to erase every trace of his homicide. Here again he does not have to bear the consequences of his actions; he goes scot-free while his buddy Alan Campbell has been stricken by pangs of remorse for his part in covering up the traces of murder and as a result he commits suicide. None of this touches Dorian. What Dorian reads as 'the symbol of the degradation of his sin' is not an image but a living space—a biotope of sorts—that has become the scene of his aging process.

The sight as well as site of aging is synonymous with sin. This equation of aging and the unseemly—the ugly—with immorality represents the social code that pervades both aestheticism and morality. Aestheticism and the moral norms of society exclude what is perceived to be ugly, dissolving and aging. This is why the picture of Dorian Gray that has morphed into the embodiment of the organic, flesh and blood, Dorian Gray has to be banished into the attic, has to be kept from the public view. Dorian's visible, public face, by stroke of reversal, is that of an ageless fiction. Dorian's face is not the real thing but a mask. It is a fiction of youth. As Dorian puts it in his internal dialogue, 'The mask of youth has

---

20 Ibid.

saved him'.[21] The mask of youth hides Dorian's human condition subject as it is to aging.

7.1 The Stereotype of the Jew as Representation of Aging and Decay

Society's model of perfection is, however, that of youth and beauty—characteristics which are associated with innocence and health. Prejudicial moral standards exclude the flesh and blood reality of aging. Dorian Gray's hiding of his aging, decaying and aching process in the attic of his mansion puts into relief the exclusion of agedness in society at large. Jews, Jewish culture and Jewish history play a significant role here, even though they are quite insignificant and almost invisible in Wilde's novel (as Sander Gilman has pointed out they are much more central in Wilde's play *Salome*).[22] Within traditional Christian anti-Semitism the Jews are place holders for corruption and sin—they were accused of killing Christ the saviour. The long-established stereotype of the Jew as embodiment of sin and decay has been translated into secular or modern forms of anti-Semitism.

Dorian Gray constructs the vision of an old Jew when he attempts to sketch the life of his youthful and beautiful lover, the actor Sibyl Vane in the fourth chapter of the novel: 'The old Jew stood grinning in the doorway of the dusty green-room, making elaborate speeches about us both [i.e. Sibyl and Dorian], while we stood looking at each other like children.'[23] Here you have the innocence associated with childhood as well as youth and the elaboration and 'sin' of the aged, personified in the 'old Jew.' Earlier Dorian describes the 'old Jew' in morally and aesthetically loaded terms as a 'hideous Jew': 'A hideous Jew, in the most amazing waistcoat I ever beheld in my life, was standing at the entrance [of the theatre where Sibyl Vane works], smoking a vile cigar. He had greasy ringlets, and an enormous diamond blazed in the centre of a soiled shirt.'[24] This description is filled with aesthetic as well as moral disgust. The Jew represents not only age ('old Jew') but all the stereotypes associated with it: the monstrous (hideous), the ugly and out of place

21 Wilde, *The Complete Works of Oscar Wilde*, p. 151.
22 'Wilde already indicates in the play that Jews are at the special risk for the madness which results from incest, for Jews permit a form of marriage, parodied in Wilde's play, which fascinated the Christian by its perversion.' Gilman, *Disease and Representation*, p. 176.
23 Wilde, *The Complete Works of Oscar Wilde*, p. 53.
24 Wilde, *The Complete Works of Oscar Wilde*, p. 49.

(amazing and enormous) and material as well as moral filth (vile, greasy and soiled). It is as if the Jew were the public appearance of Dorian's organic and therefore aging self which he hides away in his attic.

In stark contrast to Dorian's prejudicial representation of the 'old Jew', Sibyl Vane's mother points out that 'Mr Isaacs has been very good to us, and we owe him money'.[25] The reality thus contradicts the fiction which anti-Semitism and other of forms of discrimination set out to force upon us as truthful representations. The reality of racism is that of a representative standard, a societal code of approval and disapproval. As Hannah Arendt has shown in her analysis of both anti-Semitism and totalitarianism, prejudicial fiction may be appealing and may thus win over large groups of people if not entire societies, due to their neat and coherent appearance: 'Before they seize power and establish a world according to their doctrines, totalitarian movements conjure up a lying world of consistency which is more adequate to the needs of the human mind than reality itself; in which, through sheer imagination, uprooted masses can feel at home and are spared the never-ending shocks which real life and real experiences deal to human beings and their expectations.'[26] Arendt analyzes here the politics that turns reality into a fiction.

The psychology that underlies totalitarian politics is that which prompts Dorian Gray to exchange his organic life for the mask of youth that should safeguard the conformity of his public appearance with the moral and aesthetic codes of his society ruled as they are by norms of beauty and health. In totalitarianism the pressure to conform to these norms is an all-encompassing political necessity. The population which has become totalitarian sees in this beautification (or aestheticization) of politics—as Benjamin has put in his treatise on the 'Work of Art in the Age of Mechanical Reproduction' (see previous chapter) —a device that guards against the chaos of our diverse human condition: 'Before the alternative of facing the anarchic growth and total arbitrariness of decay or bowing down before the most rigid, fantastically fictitious consistency of an ideology, the masses probably will always choose the latter and be ready to pay for it with individual sacrifices—and this not because they are stupid or wicked, but because in the general disaster this escape grants them a minimum of self-respect.'[27] In terms of political appeal, fictions are much more attractive than our organic reality. Fictions of the real tend to rule our politics and this is no more so than in totalitarianism.

---

25 Wilde, *The Complete Works of Oscar Wilde*, p. 57.
26 Arendt, *The Origins of Totalitarianism*, with an introduction by Samanth Power, (New York: Schocken, 2004), pp. 464–65.
27 Arendt, *The Origins of Totalitarianism*, p. 464.

Here the coherence and consistency of a constructed world safeguards against the mess of our embodied existence. The escape from this embodied existence is an escape from birth— 'anarchic growth'—and aging— 'total arbitrariness of decay'.

7.2 Philip Roth or Revisiting Plato and Aristotle on Mimesis

Throughout his writing Philip Roth has performed various versions of society's hostility to the messiness of our organic unpredictability that confounds the seemingly well defined categories of birth, youth and aging. This is one reason why his novels critique the way fictions of predictability, coherence and consistency hold sway over our sense of reality. Here literature takes issue with the fictions we construct in order to make life simple and easy. Roth has spoken of his 'continuing preoccupation with the relationship between the written and the unwritten world'.[28] He explores this relationship in his novels. This means that the novel becomes a ground on which to test the unwritten world's (lets call this 'reality') entanglement and entrapment with the written world of fiction. Roth's Zuckerman novels are a case in point.

Zuckerman is a fictitious writer who, after completing his liberal arts studies at the University of Chicago, provokes the literary and the non-literary world with an obscene novel *Carnovsky*. The public takes the hero of his novel to be its author: 'They had mistaken impersonation for confession and were calling out to a character who lived in a book, Zuckerman tried taking it as praise—he had made real people believe Carnovsky real too—but in the end he was only himself and with his quick, small steps hurried on.'[29] The novels *Zuckerman Unbound* and *Anatomy Lesson* unfold the ways in which fiction consumes reality. The impact of fiction on real life may, from one perspective be flattering to the writer but it can also have deleterious effects. It has a destructive impact when fictions are not the offspring of literature but are the narratives that surround and reinforce social prejudices and political exclusions. This is the case in *Dorian Gray* where the public only tolerates the fictive but actually present mask of Dorian's youthful appearance whereas his real organic face needs to be hidden away in the attic.

From another perspective, the fact that real people can believe fictive characters to be real testifies to literature's social and political potency as well as—potentially at least—its ethical validity. There are parallels

---

28 Roth, *Reading Myself and Others*, (New York: Vintage, 1961), p. xiii.
29 Roth, *Zuckerman Unbound* in Roth, *Zuckerman Bound: A trilogy and Epilogue*, (New York: Vinatage, 1998), p. 140.

between Zuckerman's early literary career and that of Roth. Roth's
Portnoy's Complaint caused some outrage and charges of obscenity.
Portnoy indicts the Jewish and the non-Jewish world but he also indicts
himself as someone who cannot free himself of what he is indignant
about. He is caught up in his vitriolic outbursts, leashing out against
Jews, Gentiles and ultimately himself:

> 'The Jews I despise for their narrow-mindedness', their self-
> righteousness, the incredibly bizarre sense that these cave men
> who are my parents and relatives have somehow gotten of their
> superiority—but when it comes to tawdriness and cheapness, to
> beliefs that would shame a gorilla, you simply cannot top the *goyim*.
> What kind of base and brainless schmucks are these people to
> worship somebody who, number one, never existed, and number
> two, if he did, looking as he does in that picture, was without a
> doubt The Pansy of Palestine.[30]

Portnoy takes issue with the ways various fictions dominate the world.
Be they Jewish or Christian, Hindu or Islamic, various religions and
cultures suffer from the disease of self-inflation and fetishism. Portnoy
singles out Christianity for the way it takes fiction to be reality: the either
non-existent or, if existent, pathetic figure of Christ assumes the role of
a saviour.

This is fetishism in action: something we know to be ordinary is
nevertheless elevated to be extraordinary or redemptive. The irony is
that Portnoy is of course a fiction too. It is a fictitious mouthpiece that
rants about the way the world at large falls prey to fictive beliefs which
happen to form our reality. Portnoy cannot get over the fact that the real
sometimes gets caught into fictive nets of narratives promising redemption and or superiority. His narration, however, delineates his inability to
interact with the outside flesh and blood world. He is self-entangled, as
the Israeli socialist Noami puts it towards the end of the novel, 'like a
baby.[31] His narration only shuts himself further off from his surround-
ings. Hence his manic monologue only breaks of at the very end of the
novel when the psychiatrist interrupts him establishing the start of his
medical undertakings with the punch line: 'So [*said the doctor*]. Now vee
may perhaps begin. Yes?'[32] The ironic tone that pervades the novel from
beginning to end has not prevented the conflation of narrator with

---

30 Roth, *Portnoy's Complaint*, (New York: Vintage, 1969), p. 168.

31 Roth, *Portnoy's Complaint*, p. 264.

32 Roth, *Portnoy's Complaint*, p. 274.

author. Irony establishes distance, because it says one thing but means another. It guards against taking the written at face value. That the leap from the written to the unwritten proves to be quite common illuminates the way in which representations enthral, shape, dominate and sometimes violate our embodied world. By written I meant not only texts but also images, films, in short all past, contemporary and future media of representation.

As part of this conflation of the representational with the material world, some rabbis , educators, critics and politicians accused Roth of depicting the Jewish community in a derogatory way. This accusation goes back to the 'Goodbye, Columbus wars,' as Rabbi Eugene Borowitz has put it.[33] The novella and the short stories gathered together in this collection brought Roth early literary recognition but also provoked charges of 'Jewish self-hatred.' He was invited to a panel discussion about minority literature at Yeshiva University where straight from the start the attention was turned on his troubled relationship with the Jewish community. As Roth put it, 'the only panellist' the moderator 'seemed truly interested in was me'.[34] The moderator's first question was this: 'Mr. Roth would you write the same stories [gathered together in Goodby, Columbus] if you were living in Nazi Germany?'[35] After the grilling at Yeshiva, Roth resolved never to write about Jews again. This resolution should prove to be short-lived:

'But the Yeshiva battle', instead of putting me off Jewish fictional subjects for good, demonstrated as nothing had before the full force of aggressive rage that made the issue of Jewish self-definition and Jewish allegiance so inflammatory. This group whose embrace once had offered so much security was itself fanatically insecure. How could I conclude otherwise when I was told that every word I wrote was a disgrace, potentially endangering every Jew? Fanatical security, fanatical insecurity—nothing in my entire background could exemplify better than that night did, how deeply rooted the Jewish drama was in this duality.[36]

Issues of definition and identity are bound up with forms and contents of representation. The accusation Roth faced after the publication of his first literary works highlight the way literature becomes subsumed by reality.

33 Borowitz, 'Portnoy's Complaint', Dimension (Summer, 1969): p. 48.
34 Roth, The Facts: A Novelist's Autobiography, (New York: Penguin, 1988), p. 127.
35 ibid.
36 Roth, The Facts, pp. 120–130.

His fictions participate in reality. The public treats them as if they were social or political manifestos.

An even more powerful example of the way fiction has fused with politics and religion is of course the fatwa that has been imposed on Salman Rushdie, his publishers and translators after the publication of *The Satanic Verses*. What causes this non-fictional anger when the public comes face to face with some forms of fiction?—In Roth's and, to a larger and more serious extent in Rushdie's, case it is the fictive breaking of taboos and the transgression of norms and standards. Representation plays a salient role here. As we have seen in the discussion above of *Dorian Gray*, the public may be piqued or annoyed by organic processes of aging and decay. Dorian attempts to save appearance by transferring his organism's aging onto the hidden away picture which by then has morphed from the inorganic into the organic. This morphing of the inorganic into the organic gives fiction 'a life of its own' that can be disruptive of social norms and standards. The moment when art has come to have a 'life of its own' it clearly ceases to be mainly representational. It does no longer mirror the world but contributes to the plurality of the world by its unique form and power of animation.

Art comes to have 'a life of its own' when it highlights the artificiality of conventions, norms and stereotypes. It does so through its unruliness which interrupts the ways in which we are accustomed to think about and perceive ourselves and our world. Part of this confrontational force may cause public repulsion and thereby disruption and outrage. Here art has transmuted from the inorganic into the organic. A striking example is of course the picture of Dorian Gray which ceases to be a picture and is Dorian's actual face. Dorian has to hide his picture that has turned organic in order not to be shamed or exposed by the public. *Mutatis mutandis* Roth outrages the Jewish community by writing about Jews in a way that is not representative of their moral values. Instead of representing Jewish moral life, Roth's novels create a sense of disruption and unruliness. Strikingly, this non-representational sense of the unruly is Roth's sense of his Jewish identity, from Hebrew School onwards:

> 'In those after-school hours at the dingy Hebrew School—when I would have given anything to have been outdoors playing ball until suppertime—I sensed underlying everything a turbulence that I didn't at all associate with the airy, orderly, public school where I was a bright American boy from nine to three, a bubbling, energetic unruliness that conflicted head-on with all the exacting ritual laws that I was now asked to obey devoutly'. In the clash

between the anguished solemnity communicated to us by the mysterious bee-buzz of synagogue prayer and the irreverence implicit in the spirit of animated mischievousness that manifested itself almost daily in the little upstairs classroom of the *shul*, I recognized something far more "Jewish" than I ever did in the never-never-land stories of Jewish tents in Jewish deserts inhabited by Jews conspicuously lacking local last names like Ginsky, Nussbaum and Strulowitz.[37]

It is this sense of unruliness that pervades Roth's novels from his early works on adolescent revolt to his more recent literary approach towards aging and decay. As we have seen throughout this book, *literature is a disruptive force that changes the way we think by interrupting our ways of seeing and doing things*. Literature runs counter to our accustomed lives. It is a counterforce. Roth calls it 'counterlife' (the title of one of his Zuckerman novles). 'Counterliving', as Ross Posnock has put it is 'a way of understanding the capacity—indeed propensity—of individuals and history for defying the plausible and predicable'.[38] *It is this defiance of plausibility, coherence and predictability that Arendt appreciates as politics in its democratic form*. Totalitarianism, as has been discussed throughout this book, holds out the illusionary or fictitious promise of predictability, homogenous coherence and permanence (the thousand years Reich and so forth). In *The Counterlife* Nathan Zuckerman reflects on the relationship between literature and politics during a visit to Israel. At its inception Zionism is literary; it is a counterforce, a countermyth:

'Zionism', as I understand it, originated not only in the deep Jewish dream of escaping the danger of insularity and the cruelties of social injustice and persecution but out of a highly conscious desire to be divested of virtually everything that had come to seem, to the Zionists as much as to the Christian Europeans, distinctively Jewish behaviour—to reverse the form of Jewish existence. The construction of a counterlife that is one's own anti-myth was at its very core. It was a species of fabulous utopianism, a manifesto for human transformation as extreme—and, at the outset, as implausible—as any ever conceived.[39]

---

37 Roth, *The Facts*, p. 121.

38 Posnock, *Philip Roth's Truth: The Art of Immaturity*, (Princeton: Princeton University Press, 2006), p. 274.

39 Roth, *The Counterlife*, (New York: Penguin, 1988) p. 151.

Early Zionism attempted to rupture the stereotype of the Jewish male as decadent, feminine, sissy, non-combative, non-sportive and non-productive. It was a counter-force to standard representations of Jews. In a highly non-predictable way the implausible has become a reality with the creation of the state of Israel.

While visiting Israel, Zuckerman, feels ill at ease with the status quo there. He longs for a new counterlife, a new anti-myth within present day Israel. He questions his brother subscription to 'an idea and a commitment that may have been cogent for the people who came up with it, who built a country when they had no hope, no future, and everything was only difficulty for them—an idea that was without doubt, brilliant, ingenious, courageous, and vigorous in its historical time—but that doesn't really look to me to be so very cogent to you [i.e. to Nathan's brother]'.[40] The unruliness of literature allows for change, aging, decay, interruption and upheaval. It accepts the mutations of life as part of our plurality; as substantial constituent of both nature's and humanity's diversity.

The unpredictability of the diverse and seemingly implausible is literature's subject matter. According to Roth this is exactly what characterizes life. Life is the democracy of the non-homogenous and unpredictable; it is the ongoing flow of organisms that diverge, split up and forever renew themselves confounding categories of youth and aging: 'Life *is* and: the accidental and the immutable, the elusive and the graspable, the bizarre and the predictable, the actual and the potential, all the multiplying realities, entangled, overlapping, conjoined—plus the multiplying illusions!'[41] By allowing for contradictions literature not so much imitates but sustains life, giving succour to its exuberance of both growth and decay—two entities that are not separate and we should thus be careful not to oppose them with each other categorically. In providing the blessing of more life, literature brings together what pure monolithic conceptions of morals would dismiss as contradictory. Life is the infinite diversity of the organic and humanity's addition: its creation of multiplying illusions. These illusions are '*the kind of stories that people turn into lives; the kind of lives that people turn stories into*'.[42] Literature thus changes lives but we can also transform our life by turning into a story. The writer is an impersonator and his work is quite impersonal: it does not so much represent real life but transforms it, turning it into stories. This is how the fictive writer Zuckerman describes another fictive writer (his mentor)

---

40 Roth, *The Counterlife*, p. 153.
41 Roth, *The Counterlife*, p. 310.
42 Roth, *The Counterlife*, p. 115.

E I Lonoff: 'Fiction for him [i.e. for Lonoff] was never representation. It was rumination in narrative form. He thought, I'll make this my reality.'[43] The writing of literature is a cognitive activity. It is a form of contemplative action that may change our world by affecting our cognition—by changing the way we think about and see ourselves and our society.

Throughout his Zuckerman novels Roth questions our standard understanding of literature in terms of mimesis. In *Zuckerman Unbound*, the fictive writer takes issue with the notion of tragedy and art, in general, which derives from Aristotle's *Poetics* and which, as we have seen in this book, still determines our approach to the study of the humanities. Zuckerman reflects upon the infinity of transformation rather than representation which is literature: 'Zuckerman the stupendous sublimator spawning Zuckermanias! A book, a piece of fiction bound between two covers, breeding living fiction exempt from all the subjugations of the page, breeding fiction unwritten, unreadable, uncontainable, instead of doing what Aristotle promised from art in Humanities 2 [i.e. the course Zuckerman attended at the University of Chicago] and offering moral perceptions to supply us with the knowledge of good and bad.' [44] The title of the novel *Zuckerman Unbound* refers to a Greek tragedy and tragedy is the subject matter of the book Zuckerman takes issue with: Aristotle's *Poetics*. Aristotle presents a view of literature as mimetic. In *The Poetics* he argues that, via the representational work it does, art has a useful role to play within society at large. First of all, art's usefulness is moral. By representing our world to us, art renders knowledgeable goodness and evil. Zuckerman sums up this Aristotlean view of art as mimetic at the end of the quote.

At the opening of the quote, he implicitly refers to another and this case non-appreciative approach to poetry and the arts. The reference to maniacs evokes Plato's charge according to which art is socially and morally disruptive. Strikingly this disruption manifests itself as illness: as mental illness. In contrast to Aristotle, Plato argues that poetry is highly dangerous (rather than useful) and he makes a strong plea for banning poets from the life of his utopian republic. Plato's banishment of art may at first strike us as unappreciative. The opposite is, however, the case. Following the scholarly findings of the art-historian and classicist Edgar Wind, Agamben has shown that Plato's fear of art derives from his sense of its enormous power over our lives: 'The power of art over the soul seemed to him so great that he thought it could by itself destroy the very foundations of his city; but nonetheless, while he was forced

---

43 Roth, *Exit Ghost*, (London: Jonathan Cape, 2007), pp. 200–201.
44 Roth, *Zuckernman Bound*, pp. 273–274.

to banish it, he did so reluctantly, 'since we ourselves are very conscious of her spell'.[45] Art can potentially destroy Plato's city, because it is uncontainable and disruptive.

Literature and art's disruption may preclude any didactic values that are commonly associated with its social or moral usefulness (representing to us the knowledge of good and bad). It also runs counter to medicine's understanding of poetry as yielding health benefits—helping to alleviate suffering. In *Anatomy Lesson*—the immediate sequel to *Zuckerman Unbound* and a novel that satirizes a potential competition between literature and medicine in terms of social beneficence—Zuckerman clearly sides with Plato and counters Aristotle's arguments about representation, recognition and catharsis as advanced in *The Poetics*.

Trying to recover from nearly fatal injuries incurred during his visit to Chicago—a visit that should pave the way to abandoning his work as a useless albeit disruptive writer and to become a useful medic instead—Zuckerman realizes that reading poetry which represents his dire condition (Donne's 'The Collar') does not alleviate pain: 'He'd got the book down to read 'The Collar', hoping to find something there to help to wear his own. That was commonly believed to be a function of literature: an antidote to suffering through the depiction of our common fate.'[46] This is indeed the standard defence of literature's contribution to medicine. Literature's representational capabilities help patients to reconcile themselves with their fate. They can find themselves in representations of illness and can thus rest assured that they are not alone but share the common condition of our humanity which is one that is prone to physical and mental pathologies.

Aristotle argues that the hero of tragedy is not an exceptionally well or ill endowed person but one who is ordinary who represents everyday man. Tragedy represents the way we reach our human limits and thus dissolve morally, mentally and physically. The knowledge gathering in question here is one of registering who we are supposed to be: limited, mortal creatures and not immortal gods. From Aristotle onwards the traditional mimetic model of literature is closely bound up with the hierarchical, orderly-normative sphere of religion. In Chapter 3 we have seen how in a modern biopolitical context the markets and population control assumes the role of religion as verification of truth, beauty and goodness. Within a religious society, the knowledge of good and bad is that of humanity's limits and their acceptance. What is accepted here is the

---

45 Agamben, *The Man Without Content*, translated by Georgia Albert, (Stanford: Stanford University Press, 1999), p. 4.

46 Roth, *Zuckernman Bound*, p. 298.

inevitability of illness and death. This is who we are: failing creatures who are carriers of mortality and pathology.

Roth's *Anatomy Lesson* warns against a confusion of literature with medicine. Literature's distinction from medicine does, however, not invalidate its restorative potential. This potential is, however, not a calm or didactic one, but that of the unquiet, the mad. In the *Ghost Writer*, the young Zuckerman encounters via his literary idol, the fictive writer E. I Lonoff, Henry James's conception of literature's dark drive. The elderly Lonoff requests to have three sentences from James's story 'The Middle years' 'hanging over his head while beneath them he sat turning his own sentences: "We work in the dark—we give what we have. Our doubt is our passion and our passion is our task. The rest is the madness of art"'.[47] The young Zuckerman is taken aback: 'I would have thought the madness of everything but art. The art was what was sane, no? Or was I something missing?'[48] What Zuckerman is missing here is the disruptive and unsettling force of literature and art. In *Zuckerman Unbound* he has become acquainted with the uncontained and with what made Plato ban the artists from his city.

Literature and art's passion is to be doubtful. Doubt drives the constant revision of artistic work on a formal level. The rest which is the madness of art manifests itself in its craziness, in its disruptive effect on its audience. It makes the audience doubtful of what it has become accustomed to believe to be true, good, beautiful and representative of our human condition. From early on, Roth's novels have focused on sex as being akin to art's disruptive as well as restorative aspects. In his more recent novels Roth couples sex with aging. This combination of the sexual energy with the aging process calls into doubt traditional representation of the elderly. By depicting age within the context of sex, Roth questions the opposition between birth or youth and aging. The hero of *Shabbath's Theatre* is an elderly man who refuses to live up to representations of what it means to be old. He rebels against death and thrives in his sexual as well as obscenely artistic life: 'Oh Shabbath wanted to live! He thrived on this stuff! Why die?'[49] As Frank Kermode has put it apropos *Shabbath's Theatre* 'there is no shortage of erotic fiction; what distinguishes Roth is outrageousness'.[50] Kermode reads this outrageous novel, however, in the traditional framework of representation that has come

---

47 Roth, *The Ghost Writer*, (London: Vintage, 1988), p. 77.
48 Ibid.
49 Roth, *Shabbath's Theatre*, (London: Vintage, 1996), p. 172.
50 Kermode, *Pleasing Myself: From Beowulf to Philip Roth*, (London: Allen Lane The Penguin Press, 2001), p. 256.

down to us from Aristotle's *Poetics*. He focuses on what he sees as the serious, representational and Aristotlean tragedy-like character of the novel:

> 'It seems essential to understand the seriousness of Roth's trans-gressive imaginings'. He is hilariously serious about life and death. In his new book [i.e. *Shabbath's Theatre*] life is represented as anar-chic horniness on the rampage against death and its harbingers, old age and impotence. There is only one possible outcome: life can't win against its enemy; it can at best put on a scandalously good show.[51]

The monolithic scenario with only one possible outcome—death disease and moral failings as a reminder of humanity's limitations—is precisely what the preceding discussion of *How Literature Changes the way we Think* has argued against. It is the Aristotlean, and in the modern era Heideggerian as well as de Manian account of literature's inevitable entanglement in representing what we have become accustomed to see as our life.

There is no denying the facts of death and disease. The flat representa-tion of these facts does, however, a disservice to art's and literature's so far untapped resources that not so much represent what we are but offer alternatives to the *status quo* by showing us our unrealized or unacknowl-edged lives. In this innovative form of representation the arts help us imagine what we could be as well as confront us with what societal norms do not countenance. This non-representational—in the sense of non-normative—show of art is disruptive.

The shows Shabbath put on public display are obscene and call into doubts norms and regulations. This is part of their hilarity. The sexual disruptions of an elderly man are what the art of this novel is: 'There was a kind of art in his providing an illicit adventure not with a boy of their age but with someone three times their age—the very repugnance that his aging body inspired in them had to make their adventure with him feel a little like a crime and thereby give free play to their budding per-versity and to the confused exhilaration that comes of flirting with disgrace.'[52] Sex is no longer simply sex here: it has become a form of art that disrupts our relationship to standard forms of representation which depict aging in terms of pain and therefore a shrinking or closed in world—a limited world that does no longer allow for the uncontainable

---

51 Ibid.
52 Roth, *Shabbath's Theatre*, p. 213.

and excessively expansive urges of libidinal energy. Elaine Scarry has provided the following account of representations of aging, which Roth's *Shabbath's Theatre* counteracts and violates:

> 'As the body breaks down, it becomes increasingly an object of attention', usurping the place of all other objects, so that finally, in the very old and sick people, the world may exist only in a circle of two feet out from themselves; the exclusive content of perception and speech may become what is eaten, the problems of excreting, the progress of pains, the comfort or discomfort of a particular chair or bed. Stravinsky once described aging as: 'the ever-shrinking perimeter of pleasure'. This constantly diminishing world ground is almost given in representations of old age.[53]

Shabbath's Theatre calls the given representations of old age into doubt. Roth's recent novels contend with Scarry's representative description of the aging process's 'exclusive content': a content that is filled with the absence of youth and birth. Literature here renders inclusive what he we have come to thinks and perceive as excluded or exclusive.

This disruption of what we are used to see as representations of old age is partly achieved through the evocation of madness. One housewife Mickey Shabbath tries to seduce accuses him of being a "maniac" and she goes on to substantiate her charge through an account of his inter-generational abnormality: 'You have the body of an old man, the life of an old man, the past of an old man, and the instinctive force of a two-year old.'[54] Shabbath, however, turns the tables on the accuser, calling the moral idea of fidelity madness: 'The *madness*. There is no punishment too extreme for the crazy bastard who came up with the idea of fidelity. To demand of the human flesh, fidelity the cruelty of it, the mockery of it, is simply unspeakable'.[55] Within this context the novel compares its hero with that of another protagonist of aging. *Shabbath's Theatre* in all its profanity evokes the cruelty meted out on King Lear by his two daughters Regan and Gonerill. The novel establishes parallels between Mickey Shabbath, the elderly but virile man whom society mocks and casts out of its halls of residence and the outcast Lear who is "mightily abused."[56] Mickey quotes Lear's 'Pray, do not mock me. I am a very foolish fond,

53 Scarry, *The Body in Pain: The Making and Unmaking of the World*, (Oxford: Oxford University Press, 1985), pp. 32–33.

54 Roth, *Shabbath's Theatre*, p. 335.

55 Roth, *Shabbath's Theatre*, p. 336.

56 Roth, *Shabbath's Theatre*, p. 297.

old man', and elaborates on what it means not to be in 'perfect mind'[57]: 'The mind is the perpetual motion machine. You're not ever free of anything. Your mind's in the hand of *everything*.'[58] The madness of the old Lear turns into the sexual excess of Mickey Shabbath whose craziness is his breaking of the norms associated with aging: his mind will not let go of the world and his world refuses to diminish—it manifests the opposite of a shrinking perimeter of pleasure cited above.

Shabbath Theatre's quotations from *King Lear* are quite significant. As Helen Small has shown, Shakespeare's play counters Aristotle's account of aging: 'At this moment [i.e. Lear soliloquy in 3.4. 28-36] such a reading would say Lear is not—as Aristotle's rhetorical portrait of old men had it—made 'small minded' by age. He is not reduced to chilliness, cowardice, or a desire for 'nothing more exalted or unusual than what will keep him alive'.[59] Even though he may be mad, Lear intelligence is quite active and perceptive (rather than non-functional or 'senile'). He 'is capable of smelling out the bad faith that speaks in injunctions to be patient, when what is intended is that one surrender meekly to injustice. "Being weak, seem so," as Regan says (2.4.190)'.[60] Regan and Gonnerill's physical assault on Lear transmutes into the social as well as psychological cruelty which Roth's novel makes us cognize as a certain moral code which we need to live up to. We have to live up to society's representation of "human purity."[61] This ideology of purity mocks and denies the reality of youth within age by stigmatising the coupling of sex with aging. The outrage of Mickey Shabbath is precisely that he is both erotic and old.

The associations of sex include what it may on occasion result in: procreation or birth. As a sexually driven elderly man, Mickey commingles what society represents as binary opposites. Rather than opposing age and birth/youth with each other, he reconciles them rendering compatible what is supposed incompatible. In doing so he unmasks the representative morality of aging as cruel mockery against which he protests in Lear like fashion: 'That is what it comes down to: caricaturing us, insulting us, abhorring in us what is nothing more than the delightful Dionysian underlayer of life.'[62] As modern Lear Mickey Shabbath vents his anger at the segregation of the procreative and the youthful from what is

---

57 Roth, *Shabbath's Theatre*, p. 296.

58 Roth, *Shabbath's Theatre*, p. 297.

59 Small, *The Long Life*, (Oxford: Oxford University Press, 2007), p. 84.

60 Ibid.

61 Roth, *Shabbath's Theatre*, p. 274.

62 Roth, *Shabbath's Theatre*, p. 237.

represented and considered to be old: '"No, too old for that. Finished with that". He waves his hand almost angrily, "That's *done*. That's *out*. Good-bye girl-friends".'[63] It is as though the aged need to live up to their representations. They need to be old and sexless and non-creative. Otherwise the representative role they must play has to be reinforced via insult and mockery.

The elderly have to find their way into the nomenclatural box where they are cut off from youth or birth: 'All the existence, born, and unborn, possible and impossible, in drawers. But empty drawers looked at long enough can probably drive you mad.'[64] Mickey leaves the representative drawers open and does not fill them with his age. This drives society mad. So mad that Mickey, again a modern version of Lear in this respect, is 'waiting to be murdered'[65] by those who cannot endure what represents to them his madness.

Roth's recent novels from *The Dying Animal*[66] to the *The Humbling* interrupt channels that connect representations of aging to accustomed forms of our thinking about age, youth and birth. In this context we could read his *Everyman* as an attempt to change our perception of what is our common biological itinerary. Literature disrupts the monolithic path of the trajectory traversing birth and death. It highlights within the supposedly shrinking world of aging 'that sharp sense of individuation, of sublime singularity, that marks a fresh sexual encounter or love affair and that is the opposite of the deadening depersonalization of serious illness'.[67] Roth's everyman diverges from what we have come to cognize and recognize as aging, decay and death. The ending of this short novel is striking. Even though, it, as we all do, ends in death, the moment preceding anesthetization [for what proves to be a fatal surgery] is not that of a closing but expanding world: 'He went under feeling far from felled, anything but doomed, eager yet again to be fulfilled, but nonetheless he never woke up.'[68] There is of course no denying: death is our common fate and aging is the life experience of everyman and every woman.

This experience is, however, not restricted to those who we commonly represent as elderly or aged. Aging starts with birth. Literature questions fictions and the fictitious opposition between birth and aging is one of them. The moment before death might indeed be the feeling of the 'eager

---

63 Roth, *Shabbath's Theatre*, p. 395.
64 Ibid.
65 Roth, *Shabbath's Theatre*, p. 450.
66 For a brilliant discussion *The Dying Animal* see Small's *The Long Life*, pp. 227–336.
67 Roth, *Everyman*, (London: Vintage, 2007), p. 134.
68 Roth, *Everyman*, p. 182.

yet to be fulfilled'. It is this disruption and restorative reconfiguration of what we previously thought to be separate and incompatible that is part of literature's interruption of the fictitious prejudices, stigmas, norms and segregations that render not only the world of the aged an ever-shrinking perimeter of pleasure. Literature expands our world, opens it up to what is there but so far has been neglected or marginalized. It counteracts pain not as quasi-medical antidote to suffering we have already incurred but by cogitatively expanding society's sense of our truly open world, freeing it from fictions that diminish it to one where suffering turns out to be—but does not need to be—our common lot. Literature's is thus the truthful—but not empirically real—cosmos where we encounter admonishments of the fulfilled and wide open even in moments that precede oblivion. By allowing for possible worlds of non-diminishing reality in the here and now, literature changes the way we think and that not only about aging, but also about birth and youth. Driven by an idea about mimesis, this book has tried to provide a glimpse of literature's so far untapped cognitive resources which we may need to unplug in a radically changing environment of present and future challenges.

Literature's so far undiscovered resources are not so much representations of traditional ethics as well as politics but the ground on which new forms of the ethical and the political may take shape. In order to emphasize literature's public relevance Martha Nussbaum has invoked the image of the poet-judge. Nussbaum attempts to counter Plato's view of poetry as endangering the public via an appreciation of the emotive significance of ethics: 'But then a lover of literature who wishes to question Plato's banishment of literary artists from the public realm must, in pleading her case, make some defense of the emotions and their contribution to public rationality.'[69] The ethical significance of the emotions describes the evocation of 'sympathetic friendship' and 'empathetic identification'.[70] The emotive as well as ethical value of literature is here closely affiliated with a mimetic model of the arts and the humanities. This book does not take issue with the traditional view of literature in terms of mimesis and empathy. Instead it has delineated a different approach via a discussion of the arts and the humanities as modes of both discovery and change. The traditional view from Aristotle to Heidegger, de Man and Zizek has emphasized knowledge of the past and the present (literature as yielding moral knowledge, historical knowledge, economic knowledge and so forth). The new paradigm

---

69 Nussbaum, *Poetic Justice: The Literary Imagination and Public Life*, (Boston: Beacon Press, 1995), p. 54.
70 Nussbaum, *Poetic Justice*, p. 35.

which has been proposed in this book enables us to see literature in a novel way: as a mode of discovery in which and through which we may be better able to come to terms with contemporary as well as prospective challenges. *How Literature Changes the Way we Think* has brought together aesthetics and ethics in a manner that is new as well as appropriate for an ever more changing and thus future oriented world at the dawn of the twenty first century. We look back to the past to be better prepared for the promises and the anxieties of the future which characterize our age of transformation.

Selected Bibliography

Abrams, M. H., *The Mirror and the Lamp: Romantic Theory and the Critical Tradition.* Oxford: Oxford University Press, 1953.

—'Structure and style in the greater romantic lyric' in *The Correspondent Breeze: Essays on English Romanticism.* New York, pp. 76–108, 1984.

Agamben, G., *Homo Sacer: Sovereign Power and Bare Life*, trans. Daniel Heller-Roazen. Stanford: Stanford University Press, 1998.

—*Means without Ends. Notes on Politics*, trans. Vincenzo Binetti and Cesare Casarino. Minneapolis: University of Minnesota Press, 2000.

—*The Man Without Content*, trans. Georgia Albert. Stanford: Stanford University Press, 1999.

Appiah, K. A., *The Ethics of Identity.* Princeton: Princeton University Press, 2005.

Arendt, H., *The Origins of Totalitarianism*, with a new introduction by Samantha Power. New York: Schocken, 2004.

—*The Human Condition*, second edition; with an introduction by Margaret Canovan. Chicago: University of Chicago Press, 1998.

—*Essays in Understanding 1930–1954: Formation, Exile, and Totalitarianism*, edited with an introduction by Jerome Kohn, New York: Schocken, 1994.

—*Eichmann in Jerusalem: A Report on the Banality of Evil*, London: Penguin, 1991.

Auerbach, E., *Mimesis: The Representation of Reality in Western Literature*, trans. Willard R. T. Princeton, NJ: Princeton University Press, 1953.

Baker, C.,. *The Echoing Green: Romanticism, Modernism, and the Phenomena of Transference Poetry.* Princeton: Princeton University Press, 1984.

Bakhtin, M. M., *The Dialogic Imagination: Four Essays. Edited by Michael Holquist.* Austin: University of Texas Press, 1981.

Banville, J., 'Against the North Wall.' Rev. of *Point Omega*, by Don DeLillo. *New York Review of Books*, 8 April, pp. 40–41, 2010.

Barash, J., *Martin Heidegger and the Problem of Historical Meaning.* New York: Fordham University Press, 2003.

—*Politiques de l'histoire: L'historicisme Comme Promesse et Comme Mythe.* Paris: Presses Universitaire de France, 2004.

Bate, J., *Romantic Ecology: Wordsworth and the Environmental Tradition.* London: Routledge, 1991.

Bayley, J., *The Romantic Survival: A Study in Poetic Evolution.* London: Constable, 1957.

Beer, G., *Open Fields: Science in Culural Encounter*. Oxford: Oxford University Press, 1999.

—*Darwin's Plot: Evolutionary Narrative in Darwin, Eliot and Nineteenth-Century Fiction*. Cambridge: Cambridge University Press, 2009.

Beer, J., *Romantic Influences: Contemporary–Victorian–Modern*. Basingstoke: Macmillan, 1993.

—*Post-Romantic Consciousness: Dickens to Plath*. Basingstoke: Palgrave-Macmillan, 2003.

Benjamin, A., *Style and Time: Essays on the Politics of Appearance*. Evanston, Illinois: Northwestern University Press, 2006.

—*Philosophy's Literature*. Manchester: Clinamen Press, 2001.

—*Present Hope: Philosophy, Architecture, Judaism*. London: Routledge, 1997.

Benjamin, W., *Collected Writings. Vol 1*. Marcus Bullock and Michael W. Jennings (eds). Cambridge MA.: Belknap, 1996.

—*The Arcades Project*, trans. Howard Eiland and Kevin McLaughlin. Cambridge, Mass.: The Belknap Press of Harvard University Press, 1999.

Berman, R., *The Great Gatsby and Modern Times*. Urbana and Chicago: Illinois University Press, 1996.

Bhabha, H. K., *The Location of Culture*. London: Routledge, 1994.

Blanchot, M., 'Everyday Speech', *Yale French Studies* 73, pp. 12–20, 1987.

Bloom, H., *Yeats*. New York: Oxford University Press, 1970.

—*The Anxiety of Influence: A Theory of Poetry. 1973*. London: Oxford University Press, 1975.

Bornstein, G., *Yeats and Shelley*. Chicago: University of Chicago Press, 1970.

—*Transformations of Romanticism in Yeats, Eliot, and Stevens*. Chicago: University of Chicago Press, 1976.

—*Poetry and Repression: Revisionism from Blake to Stevens*. New Haven: Yale University Press, 1980.

Botting, F., *Gothic Romanced: Consumption, Gender and Technology in Contemporary Fictions*. London: Routledge, 2008.

Bowie, A., *From Romanticism to Critical Theory: The Philosophy of German Literary Theory*. London: Routledge, 1997.

Bruccoli, M. J., *The Composition of 'Tender is the Night': A Study of the Manuscripts*. Pittsburgh: Pittsburgh University Press, 1963.

Bryer, J. R., Alan, M., and Ruth, P., (ed.). *F. Scott Fitzgerald: New Perspectives*. Athens, GA: University of Georgia Press, 2000.

Bukatman, S., *Terminal Identity: The Virtual Subject in Postmodern Science Fiction*. Durham, NC: Duke University Press, 1993.

Butler, J., *Precarious Life: The Powers of Mourning and Violence*. London: Verso, 2004.

Carlson, T. A., *The Indiscrete Image: Infinitude and Creation of the Human*. Chicago: University of Chicago Press, 2008.

Cavell, S., *In Quest of the Ordinary: Lines of Skepticism and Romanticism*. Chicago: University of Chicago Press, 1988.

Celan, P., *Poems. A Bilingual Edition* Selected and introduced by Michael Hamburger. New York: Persea Books, 1980.

Chavkin, A., (ed.). *English Romanticism and Modern Fiction*. New York: AMS, 1993.

Christensen, J., 'The romantic movement at the end of history', *Critical Inquiry* 20.2, pp. 452–76, 1994.

Clark, T., *Martin Heidegger*. London: Routledge, 2002.

Constantine, D., *Hölderlin*. Oxford: Clarendon Press, 1988.

Conway, D. W., *Nietzsche & Politics*. London: Routledge, 1997.

Currie, M., 'Controlling Time: *Never Let me Go*,' in Sean Matthews and Sebastian Groes's (eds), *Kazuo Ishiguro: Contemporary Critical Perspectives*. London: Continuum, pp. 91–103, 2009.

Damasio, *Looking for Spinoza: Joy, Sorrow, and the Feeling Brain*. London: Harcourt, 2003.

Danto, A. C., *Transfiguration of the Commonplace: A Philosophy of Art*. Cambridge, MA: Harvard University Press, 1981.

Davies, Damian Walford and Richard Maggraf Turley, (eds) *The Monstrous Debt: Modalities of Romantic Influence in Twentieth-Century Literature*. Detroit, MI: Wayne State University Press, 2006.

Dennett, D. C., *Consciousness Explained*. Boston: Little, 1991.

Derrida, J., 'Interpretations at war: Kant, the Jew, German,' *New Literary History*, (22), pp. 39–95 (Winter, 1991).

—'Force of law. The mystical foundations of authority,' trans Mary Quaintance, in Drucilla Cornell, Michel Rosenfelf, David Gray Carlson (eds), *Deconstruction and the Possibility of Justice*. London: Routledge, 1992,

Dickstein, M., *A Mirror in the Roadway: Literature and the Real World*. Princeton, NJ: Princeton University Press, 2005.

Dillon, S., *The Palimpsest: Literature, Criticism, Theory*. London: Continuum, 2007.

Disch, L. J., *Hannah Arendt and the Limits of Philosophy*. Ithaca, NY: Cornell University Press, 1994.

Doctorow, E. L., *World's Fair*. London, Picador, 1985.

Donoghue, D., *Yeats*. Fontana Modern Masters. London: Fontana, 1971.

Dryden, E. A., 'From the piazza to the enchanted isles: Melville's textual rovings', *After Strange Text: The Role of Theory in the Study of Literature*, Gregory S. Jay and David L. Miller (eds). Tuscaloosa, AL: University of Alabama Press, 1984.

Duban, J., (ed.) *Melville and his Narrators*. Special issue of *Texas Studies in Literature and Language* 31, 1989.

Edelman, L., *Transmemberment of Song: Hart Crane's Anatomies of Rhetoric and Desire*. Stanford: Stanford University Press, 1987.

Ellmann, L., *The Nets of Modernism: Henry James, Virginia Woolf, James Joyce and Siegfried Freud*. Cambridge: University of Cambridge Press, 2010.

Ellman, R., *The Identity of Yeats*. (2nd edition). London: Faber, 1964.

Ellmann, *Oscar Wilde*. London: Penguin, 1987.

Esposito, R., *Bios: Bioplitics and Philosophy*, translated and with an introduction by Timothy Campbell. Minneapolis: University of Minnesota Press, 2008.

Felman, S., *Writing and Madness (Literature/ Philosophy/ Psychoanalysis)*, Palo Alto. California: Stanford University Press, 2003.

—(Ed.) *Literature and Psychoanalysis: The Question of Reading: Otherwise*. Baltimore: The Johns Hopkins University Press, 1982.

Felstiner, J., *Paul Celan: Poet, Survivor, Jew*. New Haven: Yale University Press, 1995.

Feuerbach, L, *Das Wesen des Christentums*. Stuttgart: Reclam, 1984.

Foucault, M., *The Birth of Biopolitics: Lectures at the Collège de France 1978–1979*, Michel Snellart (ed.). and trans. Graham Burchell, Basingstoke: Palgrave Macmillan, 2008.

—*The Will to Knowledge: The History of Sexuality: Vol. 1*, trans. Robert Hurley. London: Penguin, 1998.

—*Madness and Civilization: A History of Insanity in the Age of Reason*, trans. Richard Howard. New York: Vintage Books, 1988.

Frank, M., *The Philosophical Foundations of Early German Romanticism*, trans. Elizabeth Millán-Zaibert. Albany, NY: State University of New York Press, 2004.

Fry, P. H., *Wordsworth and the Poetry of What We Are*. New Haven: Yale University Press, 2008.

Gelpi, A., *A Coherent Splendor: The American Poetic Renaissance, 1910–1950*. 1987. Cambridge: Cambridge University Press, 1990.

Ghosh, T. K, (ed.) *The Golden Notebook: A Critical Study*. New Delhi: Prestige, 2006.

Gilman, S. L., *Multiculturalism and the Jews*. London: Routledge, 2006.

—*Disease and Representation: Images of Illness from Madness to AIDS*, Ithaca. NY: Cornell University Press, 1988.

Harris, A., *Romantic Moderns: English Writers, Artists and the Imagination from Virginia Woolf to John Piper*. London: Hudson, 2010.

Heaney, S., *The Redress of Poetry: Oxford Lectures*. London: Faber, 1995.

Hecht, A., *The Hidden Law: The Poetry of W. H. Auden*. Cambridge, MA: Harvard University Press, 1993.

Heidegger, M., *Poetry, Language, Thought*, trans. and intro. by Albert Hofstadter. New York: HarperCollins, 1971.

—*Gesamtausgabe II. Abteilung: Vorlesungen 1919–1944. Band 38. Logik als this Frage nach dem Wesen der Sprache*, Günter Seubold (ed.). Frankfurt a. M.: Klostermann, 1998.

—*Hölderlin's Hymn The Isther*, trans William McNeil and Julia Davis, Bloomington, In.: Indiana University Press, 1996.

—*Erläuterungen zu Hölderlins Dichtung*, Friedrich-Wilhelm von Hermann (ed.). Frankfurt: Klostermann, 1944.

Hölderlin, F., *Sämtliche Ausgabe. Band 5. Oden II*, D. E. Sattler (ed.). Frankfurt a. M.: Roter Stern Verlag, 1984.

—*Essays and Letters*, edited and translated with an introduction by Jeremy Adler and Charlie Louth. London: Penguin, 2009.

Holmes, R., *The Age of Wonder: How the Romantic Generation Discovered the Beauty and Terror of Science*. New York: Pantheon, 2008.

Ishiguro, K., *Never Let Me Go*. London: Faber and Faber, 2005.

Jasper, D., *The Sacred Body*. New York: Continuum, 2009.

Kameron, C. J., *Race: A Theological Account*. Oxford: Oxford University Press, 2008.

Kant, I., *Critique of Judgment*, trans. Werner S. Pluhar and Mary J. Gregor. Indianapolis: Hackett Publishing, 1987.

Kermode, F., *The Romantic Image*. London: Routledge, 1957.

Kureishi, H., *The Buddha of Suburbia*. London: Faber and Faber, 1990.

Lacoue-Labarthe, P., Heidegger and the politics of poetry, trans. and intro. Jeff Fort. Urbana: University of Illinois Press, 2007.

Larmore, C., *The Romantic Legacy*. New York: Columbia University Press, 1996.

Larrissy, E., *Reading Twentieth Century Poetry: The Language of Gender and Objects*. Oxford: Blackwell, 1990.

—(ed.) *Romanticism and Postmodernism*. Cambridge: Cambridge University Press, 1999.

—*Blake and Modern Literature*. Basingstoke: Palgrave-Macmillan, 2006.

Lefebvre, H., *Critique of Everyday Life, Volume 1: Introduction*. 2nd edition. Trans. John Moore. London: Verso, 2008.

Lewis, B., *Kazuo Ishiguro*, Contemporary world writers series. Manchester: Manchester University Press, 2000.

Mack, M., *Spinoza and the Specters of Modernity: The Hidden Enlightenment of Diversity from Spinoza to Freud*. New York: Continuum, 2010.

—*German Idealism and the Jew: The Inner Anti-Semitism of Philosophy and German Jewish Responses*. Chicago: University of Chicago Press, 2003.

—*Anthropology as Memory: Elias Canetti and Franz Baermann Steiner's Responses to the Shoah*. Tübingen: Niemeyer, 2001.

—'The Holocaust and Hannah Arendt's philosophical critique of philosophy: *Eichmann in Jerusalem*,' *New German Critique* pp. 35–60 (Winter 2009).

—'Transzendentaler Messianismus und die Katastrophe der Entscheidung. Anmerkungen zu Carl Schmitts und Walter Benjamins Eschatologie,' Stephan Loos and Holger Zaborowski *Leben, Tod und Entscheidung. Studien zur Geistesgeschichte der Weimarer Republik*. Berlin: Duncker & Humbolt, pp. 155–166, 2003.

—'Between Elias Canetti and Jacques Derrida: Satire and the role of fortifications in the work of W. G. Sebald,' in Gerhard Fischer (ed.) *W. G. Sebald: Schreiben ex patria/ Epatriate Writing*. Amsterdam: Radopi, pp. 234–256, 2009.

—'Hannah Arendt's philosophy of plurality: Thinking and understanding and *Eichmann in Jerusalem*', in Andrew Schaap, Danielle Celermajer and Vrasidas Karalis (eds) *Power, Judgment and Political Evil. In Conversation with Hannah Arendt*, Farnham, Surrey: Ashgate, pp. 13–26, 2010.

—'Modernity as an unfinished project: Benjamin and political romanticism', *Walter Benjamin and the Architecture of Modernity*. Andrew Benjamin and Charles Rice (eds). Melbourne: re.press, 2009.

—'Literature between medicine and religion: Herder's aesthetics of touch and the emerging field of medical humanities,' in *Neophilologus* pp. 541–555 (94, 2010).

Man, Paul de. *Allegories of Reading: Figural Langauge in Rousseau, Nietzsche, Rilke, and Proust*. New Haven; London: Yale University Press, 1979.

—*The Rhetoric of Romanticism*. New York: Columbia University Press, 1984.

Mathewes, C., *Evil and the Augustinian Tradition*. Cambridge: Cambridge University Press, 2001.

Matthews, S., and Groes, S., (eds), *Kazuo Ishiguro: Contemporary Critical Perspectives*, Preface by Haruki Murakami. London: Continuum, 2009.

McCarthy, C., *The Road*. London: Picador, 2007

McCole, *Walter Benjamin and the Antinomnies of Tradition*. Ithaca: Cornell University Press, 1993.

McGann, J., *The Romantic Ideology: A Critical Investigation*. Chicago: University of Chicago Press, 1983.

McKusick, J. C., *Green Writing: Romanticism and Ecology*. New York: St Martin's, 2000.

Meltzer, F., *Hot Property: The Stakes and Claims of Literary Originality*.Chicago: University of Chicago Press, 1994.

Mendes-Flohr, P., and Reinharz, J., (eds), *The Jew in the Modern World*.Oxford: Oxford University Press, 1995.

—*German Jews: A Dual Identity*. New Haven: Yale University Press, 1999.

Miller, G., 'Why loneliness is hazardous to your health' in *Science, Vol. 331* no. 6014 pp. 138–140, 14 January 2011.

Morton, T., *Ecology Without Nature: Rethinking Environmental Aesthetics*. Cambridge: Cambridge University Press, 2010.

Nehamas, A., *Nietzsche: Life as Literature*. Cambridge, Mass.: Harvard University Press, 1985.

Neumann, B., 'National socialist politics of life' in *New German Critique* (85 Winter) pp. 107–130, 2002.

Neveldine, R. B., *Bodies at Risk: Unsafe Limits in Romanticism and Postmodernism*. New York: State University New York Press, 1998.

Nussbaum, M., *Not For Profit: Why Democracy Needs the Humanities*. Princeton: Princeton University Press, 2010.

—*Poetic Justice: The Literary Imagination and Public Life*. Boston: Beacon Press, 1995.

Olschner, L., *Im Abgrund der Zeit: Celans Poetiksplitter*. Göttingen: Vadenhoeck & Ruprecht 2007.

'Olson, L., *Modernism and the Ordinary*. Oxford: Oxford University Press, 2009.

Orwell, G., *Nineteen Eighty-Four*. London: Penguin, 1989.

Pippin, R., *The Persistence of Subjectivity: On the Kantian Aftermath*. Cambridge: Cambridge University Press, 2005.

Posnock, R., *Philip Roth's Truth: The Art of Immaturity*. Princeton: Princeton University Press, 2006.

Rajan, T., *Dark Interpreter: The Discourse of Romanticism*. Ithaca, NY: Cornell University Press, 1980.

—Displacing post-structuralism: Romantic studies after Paul de Man," in *Studies in Romanticism* (24) Winter, pp. 451–474, 1985.

Ricoeur, P., *Memory, History, Forgetting*, trans. Kathleen Blamey and David Pellauer. Chicago: University of Chicago Press, 2004.

—*Onseself as Another*, trans. Kathleen Blamey. Chicago: University of Chicago Press, 1992.

Richardson, A., *British Romanticism and the Science of Mind*. Cambridge Studies in Romanticism (47). Cambridge: Cambridge University Press, 2001.

—'Apostrophe in life and in romantic art: Everyday discourse, overhearing, and poetic address', *Style* 36.3 (2002), pp. 363–85.

Ricks, C., *Allusion to the Poets*. Oxford: Clarendon, 2002.

Roe, N., *Fiery Heart: The First Life of Leigh Hunt*. London: Pimlico, 2005.

—(ed.) *Romanticism: An Oxford Guide*. Oxford: Oxford University Press, 2005.

Ronell, *Avital The Test Drive. With Photographs by Suzanne Doppelt*. Urbana: University of Illinois Press, 2005.

—*Crack Wars: Literature, Addiction Mania*. Urbana: University of Illinois Press, 1993.

—*The Telephone Book: Technology, Schizophrenia, Electronic Speech*. Urbana: University of Illinois Press, 1989 .

Rose, J., *On Not Being Able to Sleep: Psychoanalysis and the Modern World*. London: Verse, 2004.

Rose, N., *The Politics of Life itself: Biomedicine, Power, and Subjectivity in the Twenty-First Century*. Princeton, NJ: Princeton University Press, 2007.

Roth, P., *American Pastoral*. London: Vintage, 1998.

—*Portnoy's Complaint*. New York: Vintage, 1969.

—*Reading Myself and Others*. New York: Vintage, 1961

—*The Facts: A Novelist's Autobiography*. New York: Penguin, 1988.

—*The Counterlife*. New York: Penguin, 1988

—Roth, *Shabbath's Theatre*. London: Vintage, 1996.

—*Zuckerman Unbound* in Roth, *Zuckerman Bound: A trilogy and Epilogue*. New York: Vinatage, 1998.

—*Exit Ghost*. London: Jonathan Cape, 2007.

—Roth, *Everyman*. London: Vintage, 2007.

Rouff, G. W., (ed.) *The Romantics and Us: Essays on Literature and Culture*. New Brunswick, NJ: Rutgers University Press, 1990.

Sandel, M. J., *The Case Against Perfection: Ethics in an Age of Genetic Engineering*. Cambridge, MA: Harvard University Press, 2007.

Sandy, M., "Still the reckless change we mourn': Wordsworth, loss and the circulation of grief', in *Grasmere 2009: Selected Papers from the Wordsworth Summer Conference*. Penrith, pp. 72–83, 2009.

Scarry, E., *The Body in Pain: The Making and Unmaking of the World*. Oxford: Oxford University Press, 1985.

Small, H., *The Long Life*. Oxford: Oxford University Press, 2007.

Smith, R., *Being Human: Historical Knowledge and the Creation of Human Nature*. New York: Columbia University Press, 2007.

Spinoza, *Ethics*, edited and translated by Edwin Curley with an introduction by Stuart Hampshire. London: Penguin, 1996.

Steiner, G., *Real Presences: Is There Anything in What We Say?* London: Faber, 1989.

Steiner, *The Real, Real Thing: The Model in the Mirror of Art*. Chicago: University of Chicago Press, 2004.

—*The Scandal of Pleasure: Art in an Age of Fundamentalism*. Chicago: University of Chicago Press, 1995.

Taylor, C., *Sources of the Self: The Making of Modern Identity*. Cambridge: Cambridge University Press, 1989.

Tucker, R. C., (ed.), *The Marx-Engels Reader*, Second Edition. New York: Norton, 1978.

Vendler, H., *Our Secret Discipline: Yeats and Lyric Form*. Oxford: Oxford University Press, 2007.

Waugh, P., *Practising Postmodernism, Reading Modernism*. London: Arnold, rpt.1992.

Weinbaum, A. E., 'Racial Aura: Walter Benjamin and the work of art in a biotechnological age' in *Literature and Medicine* Vol. 26, pp. 207–239 Spring 2007.

Wilde, O., *The Complete Works of Oscar Wilde: Stories, Plays, Poems, Essays*, With an introduction by Vyvan Holland. London: Collins, 1992.

Willey, T. E., *Back to Kant. The Revival of Kantianism in German Social and Historical Thought 1860-1914*. Detroit: Wayne State University Press, 1978.

Wilkinson, R. and Kate P., *The Spirit Level: Why Equality is Better for Everyone*. London: Penguin, 2010.

Yousef, N., *Isolated Cases: The Anxieties of Autonomy in Enlightenment Philosophy and Romantic Literature*. Ithaca, NY: Cornell University Press, 2004.

Zeki, S., *Splendors and Miseries of the Brain: Love, Creativity, and the Quest for Human Happiness*. London: Blackwell, 2008.

Žižek, S., *Living in the End Times*. London: Verso, 2010.

—*Violence: Six Sideways Reflections*. New York: Picador, 2008.

—'A plea for a return to *Différance* (with a minor *Pro Domo Sua*),' *Critical Inquiry* 32, pp. 226–249, Winter 2006.

—*The Paralax View*, The Massachusetts Institute of Technology Press, 2006.

—*Enjoy your Symptom! Jacques Lacan in Hollywood and Out*, Second Edition with a new preface by the author. London: Routledge, 2001.

Subject Index

DATE DUE
